Unravelling Textiles
A Handbook for the Preservation of Textile Collections

Unravelling Textiles

A Handbook for the Preservation of Textile Collections

Foekje Boersma

with Agnes W. Brokerhof, Saskia van den Berg and Judith Tegelaers

Translated from Dutch.

First published in 2000 as *Op de keper beschouwd: Handboek voor het behoud van textielcollecties* by Stichting Textielcommissie Nederland

First published 2007 by Archetype Publications Ltd.
Archetype Publications Ltd.
6 Fitzroy Square
London W1T 5HJ
www.archetype.co.uk

Tel: 44(207) 380 0800
Fax: 44(207) 380 0500

© Chs 1, 2, 6, 7, 8, 9: Foekje Boersma, Ch. 5: Agnes W. Brokerhof, Ch. 11: Saskia van den Berg and Chs 3, 4: Judith Tegelaers 2007

Front cover: detail of a 16th-century tapestry (photo courtesy ICAT textielrestauratie b.v., collection Castle de Haar, Haarzuilens)

Note: The rights of Foekje Boersma, Agnes W. Brokerhof, Saskia van den Berg and Judith Tegelaers to be identified as the authors of this work have been asserted by them in accordance with the Copyright, Designs and Patents Act 1988.

The authors and the publisher take no responsibility for any harm or damage to collections or health hazards that may be caused by the use or misuse of any information contained herein.

ISBN-10: 1-873132-64-6
IBSN-13: 978-1-873132-64-7

British Library Cataloguing in Publication Data
A catalogue record for this book is available from the British Library.
Printed on acid-free paper
All rights reserved. No part of this publication may be reproduced, stored in a retrieval system, or transmitted, in any form or by any means, electronic, mechanical, photocopying, recording or otherwise, without the prior permission of the publisher.

Aerolam, Ageless, Aplix, Araldite, Aramid, Art Sorb, Cellite Fibre, Cellite Aluminium, Centerfoam, Correx, Courtelle, Crylor, Cupro, Dacron, Dacrylate Acrylic Varnish 103-1, Desi Pak, Dralon, DRI-SIL, Dulux 2030 Y20R, Ebicel, Élan, Enkalon, Etamine, Ethafoam, Eulan, Fibrefill, Filmoplast, FreshPax, Gluton, Gudy-O, Hexlite, Ibicel, Itef, Kapaline, Kubicel, Lascaux, Lexan 9034, LightCheck, Lycra, Marvelseal 360A, Medite ZF, Melinex, Meraklon, Mitten, Modacryl, Moistop, Mowilith, Multifoam, Mylar, NexaLotte, Nextel Suede Coat 3101, Nopafoam, Orlon, Paracide, Paradow, Paraloid, Perlon, Perspex, Plastazote, Plexiglas, Polyethylene, Pro Sorb, Redon, Rhovil, Rilsan, RP System, Scotchguard, Sellotape, Setamul, Stabiltex, Tergal, Terlenka, Terylene, Tetex, Trimite J166, Trimite Terrethane 440, Trevira, Trimite Selabond RJ119, TNT, Touch N Tuff, Tyvek, Vapona, Velcro, Vilene, Vinamul, Zirpro are registered trade names.

Typeset by Kate Williams, Abergavenny
Printed and bound in Italy by Printer Trento srl

Contents

	Preface	xi
	Introduction	xiii
	Acknowledgements	xv
1	**Materials**	**1**
	1.1 Fibres in general (polymers)	1
	1.1.1 Classification	1
	1.1.2 The chemistry and physics of polymers	2
	1.1.3 Cellulose	3
	1.1.4 Proteins	3
	1.2 Vegetable fibres	4
	1.2.1 Flax/linen	4
	1.2.2 Cotton	5
	1.3 Animal fibres	7
	1.3.1 Wool/hair	7
	1.3.2 Silk	8
	1.4 Man-made fibres	10
	1.4.1 Semi-synthetic fibres	10
	1.4.2 Synthetic fibres	11
	1.4.3 Morphology	12
	1.4.4 Other synthetic fibres made from inorganic material	12
	1.5 Textile techniques	12
	1.5.1 Spinning	13
	1.5.2 Weaving	13
	1.5.3 Binding systems	13
	1.5.4 Tapestries	14
	1.5.5 Other techniques	14
	1.5.6 Decorative techniques	14

1.6 Dyeing and printing textiles	16
1.6.1 Natural dyes	16
1.6.2 Synthetic dyes	17
1.7 Textile finishes/after treatments	18

2 Degradation of textiles — 21

2.1 Natural decay of cellulose	21
2.1.1 Oxidation	21
2.1.2 Hydrolysis	22
2.1.3 Cross-linking	22
2.1.4 Influence of environmental circumstances	22
2.2 Natural decay of proteins	23
2.2.1 Photodegradation	23
2.2.2 Hydrolysis	24
2.2.3 Influence of environmental circumstances	24
2.3 Natural decay of other fibre material	24
2.4 Physical-mechanical processes	24
2.4.1 Response to moisture	25
2.4.2 Response to mechanical forces	25
2.4.3 Response to tension	26
2.5 Intrinsic decay	26
2.6 Other factors	27
2.7 Identifying degradation	28

3 The museum environment — 31

3.1 The properties of the environment	32
3.1.1 Temperature	32
3.1.2 Relative humidity	32
3.1.3 Air pollution	35
3.2 Measuring and recording the museum environment	36
3.3 The control of environmental conditions	37
3.3.1 Division into zones	38
3.3.2 Conditioning of the environment	38
3.4 Summary	42
3.5 Appendix	43
3.5.1 Psychrometric chart	43
3.5.2 Materials and their equilibrium moisture content (EMC)	44
3.5.3 The effect of organic materials on the changes in the indoor climate	45

4 Light — 47

4.1 Introduction	47
4.1.1 Electromagnetic spectrum; wavelength	47
4.1.2 Light intensity, luminance and reflection	47
4.1.3 Damage	48

	4.2 Measuring devices	48
	4.2.1 Lux meter	48
	4.2.2 UV meter	49
	4.2.3 Blue wool standard	49
	4.2.4 LightCheck strips	49
	4.3 Visible light	50
	4.3.1 Damage to materials	50
	4.3.2 Light sources	50
	4.3.3 Measures to reduce light levels	51
	4.4 UV radiation	51
	4.4.1 Damage to materials	51
	4.4.2 Light sources	51
	4.4.3 Measures to filter out UV radiation	52
	4.5 Infrared radiation	52
	4.5.1 Damage to materials	52
	4.5.2 Light sources	52
	4.5.3 Measures to eliminate IR radiation	52
	4.6 Light sources	52
	4.6.1 Fibre optics	56
	4.6.2 Energy efficiency	57
	4.7 Presenting a textile collection	57
	4.7.1 Lighting design	57
	4.8 Recent developments	59
5	**Insects and fungi in textile collections**	61
	5.1 Insects	61
	5.1.1 Characteristics	61
	5.1.2 Development	61
	5.1.3 Requirements	62
	5.1.4 Insects in textile collections	62
	5.2 Fungi	67
	5.2.1 Fungi in textile collections	67
	5.2.2 Characteristics and development	67
	5.2.3 Requirements	68
	5.2.4 Damage caused by fungi	68
	5.2.5 Active or not?	68
	5.3 Integrated pest management	69
	5.3.1 The five steps of IPM	69
	5.3.2 Detection	71
	5.4 Disinfestation and disinfection methods	72
	5.4.1 Insects	72
	5.4.2 Fungi	74
	5.4.3 Other methods	76
	5.4.4 Choosing the most appropriate disinfestation method	78

6 Storage — 81

6.1 Storage facilities — 81
- 6.1.1 General guidelines — 81
- 6.1.2 Preventive measures — 82
- 6.1.3 Quarantine — 83

6.2 Storage systems and materials — 83
- 6.2.1 Suitable systems — 83
- 6.2.2 Suitable materials — 85
- 6.2.3 Access to and use of storage facilities — 87
- 6.2.4 Objects in storage — 88
- 6.2.5 Location of collection(s) in museum buildings — 89

6.3 Storage of textiles — 89
- 6.3.1 Large and/or long two-dimensional textiles — 89
- 6.3.2 Small two-dimensional textiles — 91
- 6.3.3 Flat textiles with pile — 93
- 6.3.4 Flat, composite objects — 93
- 6.3.5 Three-dimensional textiles — 93
- 6.3.6 Three-dimensional objects — 96

7 Transportation — 101

7.1 Determining the object's fragility — 101

7.2 Risk analysis of the transportation route — 103
- 7.2.1 Means of external transportation — 104

7.3 Optimising the object and/or route — 105

7.4 Determining the necessary protection and designing the packaging — 105

7.5 Packing the object — 106

7.6 Transporting/couriering — 106

7.7 Unpacking and checking the object — 106

7.8 Evaluate and improve approach — 106

8 Textiles on display — 107

8.1 Temporary exhibitions — 107

8.2 Textiles as part of a (semi-)permanent exhibition — 107

8.3 Textiles in interiors — 108
- 8.3.1 Light — 108
- 8.3.2 Environment — 109
- 8.3.3 Abrasion — 109
- 8.3.4 Replicas — 109
- 8.3.5 Seasonal closure — 110
- 8.3.6 Showcases or open display? — 110
- 8.3.7 Climatic conditions and showcases — 111
- 8.3.8 Light and showcases — 112

8.4 Exhibiting textiles — 112
- 8.4.1 Large and/or long two-dimensional textiles — 112
- 8.4.2 Small two-dimensional textiles — 114
- 8.4.3 Flat textiles with pile — 115

	8.4.4 Flat, composite objects	115
	8.4.5 Three-dimensional textiles	116
	8.4.6 Three-dimensional objects	118
	8.5 Appendix	120
	8.5.1 Materials for making a padded, fabric-covered board	120
	8.5.2 Instructions for making a padded, fabric-covered board	121
9	**Materials for conservation**	**123**
	9.1 Research	123
	9.2 Products	124
	9.2.1 Sheet materials for making supports	124
	9.2.2 Materials used in making supports	125
	9.2.3 Adhesives and tapes	125
	9.2.4 Barrier foils	126
	9.2.5 Packaging material	126
	9.2.6 Personal safety	127
	9.2.7 Fabrics, non-wovens and fabric tapes	127
	9.2.8 Other materials	128
10	**Conservation and restoration**	**131**
	10.1 The history of conservation	131
	10.2 Terminology	133
	10.3 The textile conservator	133
	10.3.1 Ethical code	134
	10.3.2 Contracting out conservation work	134
	10.4 Defining tasks	135
	10.4.1 Mechanical cleaning of textiles	135
	10.4.2 The removal of dust	136
11	**Documentation**	**137**
	11.1 The documentary task: registration and documentation of a museum collection	137
	11.2 Computerisation	137
	11.3 Objects entering the collection	138
	11.3.1 Registration of objects entering a collection	138
	11.4 The sending out of objects	139
	11.5 The acquisition of objects	139
	11.5.1 Describing the object	140
	11.5.2 Location control and the moving of objects	144
	11.5.3 Numbering of textile objects	144
	11.5.4 Condition reports	145
	11.5.5 Photography	146
	11.6 Appendix	149
	11.6.1 Form of entry	149
	11.6.2 Form of return	151

12	**Collection management**	**153**
	12.1 Collection plan	153
	12.2 Maintenance plan	154
	12.2.1 The condition report	155
	12.3 Disaster plan	155
	12.3.1 Textile calamities and first aid	156
	12.3.2 Water damage	156

Glossary	159
Bibliography	161
Index	169

Preface

Judith Tegelaers, Netherlands Textile Committee

Unravelling Textiles: A Handbook for the Preservation of Textile Collections is an initiative of the Netherlands Textile Committee. Founded in 1962, the committee has played an active role in the preservation of textiles in both museum and private collections. It encourages the gathering and exchange of information and knowledge about textiles, with special attention being given to their preservation and conservation. The committee organises conferences and workshops and issues publications. Connections are maintained with other textile-oriented organisations, both in the Netherlands and abroad.

The term 'textile' covers a wide spectrum – from domestic items to objects of a religious, ceremonial or artistic character. Textile objects that survive today can tell us about their history. Articles of clothing that have been patched and mended can inform us about patterns of use of the wearer and traditional methods and materials of manufacture and repair. Little remains today, however, of the everyday clothing of ordinary people. Clothing was traditionally reused until threadbare. For example, a woman's dress may have been altered to fit a child; then used for a lining; and, when that was worn out, used again for the filling of a quilted blanket or as a dust cloth. In the past, people had to be more resourceful and textiles were recycled until they became rags.

Recently, there has been greater awareness of the need for preventive conservation for the safekeeping of cultural heritage, resulting in the demand for more specialised staff. The traditional position of the curator has moved away from preservation towards research on the collection and the preparation of exhibitions. New posts have been specifically created for collection care and preservation, requiring expert knowledge of preventive conservation and an understanding of the degradation processes.

This trend towards appointing professionals with specific knowledge in the preservation of collections is reflected in the team of authors of this book, which includes a textile conservator, a museum consultant, a registrar and a conservation scientist. They represent the interdisciplinary cooperation that forms the basis of the preservation of cultural heritage.

This book sets out to present the basic information necessary for the professional safekeeping of textile collections. It is aimed at curators, owners of textile collections and collection management staff. It should also provide useful information on preventive conservation issues for conservators and students.

First published in the Netherlands as *Op de keper beschouwd. Handboek voor het behoud van textielcollecties*, this English edition has been made possible with the help of two Dutch funds: the Mondriaan Stichting and the Prins Bernhard Cultuurfonds. *Unravelling Textiles: A Handbook for the Preservation of Textile Collections* is a revised version of the original Dutch edition.

Much of the information in this book relates to the temperate maritime climate of northern

Europe, where outdoor temperatures fluctuate between 5 °C and 25 °C, the average temperature is 8 °C with an average relative humidity of 82%. High humidity is common, mainly in spring and autumn, whereas extremely dry conditions can occur during periods of frost in winter. Nevertheless, the general thrust of the book has global relevance.

Introduction

Foekje Boersma

Textiles are remarkable and exist in many forms. They can be made from a wide range of fibres including: cotton, flax, wool, silk, acrylic and polyester. The processes involved in making textiles from these fibres are diverse e.g.: spinning, weaving, braiding, knotting, embroidery, dyeing and printing. It is not surprising that so many different articles are made from textiles: tapestries, clothing, upholstery, flags, samplers, fans and handbags to name but a few. This diversity of materials, methods of production and decoration, together with the vulnerability of textiles, presents a challenge to those concerned with the preservation of textile objects.

Textiles have a significant role in our daily lives: many interiors are furnished with textiles for comfort, decoration and insulation; people wear clothing to protect themselves against the elements, to enhance their appearance and often to reflect a particular status or lifestyle. While a coronation cloak is a status symbol, a traditional dress or punk clothing are forms of group expression. A uniform can indicate a certain grouping or profession. The very familiarity of textiles results in their often being overlooked as part of our cultural heritage.

The Netherlands has a rich textile history and some very important textile collections. During the 17th century – referred to as the 'Golden Age' – textiles were important trade goods and merchandise. In fact, beautiful examples of chintz and *ikats* from the Far East (India and Indonesia) can still be found in Dutch collections. Textile production was of great significance to the country: growing flax, the production of woollen cloth (*laken*) and dyeing were pillars of the economy. In the 20th century these industries, which were by then located mainly in the regions of Twente and North-Brabant, declined as textiles were being produced more cheaply elsewhere in the world.

Throughout the centuries, textiles have played an important role. They are an indispensable source of information for those studying the past as they complement and illustrate our national history. For example, the hat worn by governor Ernst Casimir (in the collection of the Rijksmuseum, Amsterdam), with its round bullet hole surrounded by blood stains, is a silent witness to the violent attempt made on his life. A famous series of Dutch tapestries, now in the collection of the Zeeuws Museum in Middelburg (province of Zeeland), depicting the sea battles between the Protestant Dutch and the Catholic Spaniards in the 16th century is in fact a pictorial record of the conflict. On a smaller scale, a banner made in honour of the Golden Jubilee of a local brass band is equally important as a record of regional culture and history.

Textiles should also be preserved for their technical aspects. The techniques which are used around the world to make and decorate textiles are diverse and often very complex. The knowledge of traditional handicrafts is disappearing as machines take over the production of textiles. Today there are few young people who can knit, crochet or knot, let alone weave or make bobbin lace. Good technical documentation is therefore essential if these skills are not to be lost completely.

Textiles are a medium that have long been used by artists and which should also be preserved for aesthetic reasons. Tapestries have a rich history and there were periods in which they were of greater financial and artistic value than paintings. During the 20th century, artists gave the medium a new impetus with such works as those produced by the Amsterdamse School and the Bauhaus.

In *Unravelling Textiles*, the preventive conservation of textiles is discussed. Since textiles are made from impermanent materials, care is required if they are to be preserved for future generations. Objects and situations differ, and it is therefore impossible to give standard solutions. This book addresses this issue by providing both the theory of textile degradation, climate control, safekeeping and documentation, and practical examples, thereby allowing readers to choose the best solution for their particular situation.

The book is divided into three parts – theory, practice and support. In the first part (chapters 1–5), an overview is given of the most common textile fibres, production processes and decoration techniques. Degradation processes of textiles are discussed and the effects on textiles of the environment – temperature, relative humidity, air pollution and light – are explained further. The second part (chapters 6–9) covers the practical issues of textiles in storage, transit and exhibition, as well as the materials which can safely be used in the vicinity of textiles. The third part of the book (chapters 10–12) considers documentation, conservation and restoration, and collection management.

There are many reasons why textiles form such an important part of our cultural heritage, but we shouldn't forget that first and foremost, textiles can be very beautiful and are often quite simply a delight to behold!

Acknowledgements
Foekje Boersma

This book has been made possible by the enthusiastic cooperation of a great number of people who have spared their valuable time to support and advise me on this publication. This book would not have been completed without the contributions of: Judith Tegelaers (Regional Museum Advisor, Ergoedhuis Zuid-Holland) who wrote chapters 3 and 4; Agnes W. Brokerhof (Senior Conservation Scientist, the Netherlands Institute for Cultural Heritage) the author of Chapter 5 and Saskia van den Berg (curator at Purmerends Museum and lecturer in collection registration and documentation at the Reinwardt Academie in Amsterdam), who explained the documentary task of a museum in Chapter 11. My sincere and deepest gratitude goes to my co-authors for their unconditional support and for sharing their specialist knowledge.

I would like to thank the members of the editing board for their scrupulous editing of the Dutch text: Jaap Mosk (final editor, then editor at the Netherlands Institute for Cultural Heritage); Steve Cok (then Conservation Advisor, Rijksmuseum, Amsterdam); Judith Hofenk de Graaff (then Head of the Conservation Research Department of the Netherlands Institute for Cultural Heritage); and Judith Tegelaers (Regional Museum Advisor, Ergoedhuis Zuid-Holland). The translation into English was greatly helped by the editors: Paul Ryan, Peggy Birch, Teresa Heady and Alexandra Clark.

The content of the Dutch book was supervised by a reference group: Nettie Cassee (Regional Conservation and Care Advisor, then Stichting Museaal en Historisch Perspectief Noord-Holland); Emmy de Groot (then Deputy Head of the Conservation Department at the former Stichting Werkplaats tot Herstel van Antiek Textiel, Haarlem); Linda Hanssen (Head of the Conservation Department, Wereldmuseum, Rotterdam); and Suzan Meijer (head of the textile conservation department, Rijksmuseum, Amsterdam). Their constructive criticism and help in collecting information and images is greatly appreciated.

I am also very grateful to the following museums and/or institutions for allowing me access to their storage facilities and exhibition spaces: Catharijne Convent, Utrecht; the Netherlands Institute for Cultural Heritage, Rijswijk; Koninklijk Leger- en Wapenmuseum, Delft; Museum Jannink, Enschede; Nederlands Leder- en Schoenenmuseum, Waalwijk; Rotterdams Historisch Museum, Rotterdam; Stedelijk Museum, Alkmaar; Stichting Zuiderzeemuseum, Enkhuizen; Wereldmuseum, Rotterdam.

I also owe thanks to the following for their advice, help and support: Jennifer Barnett (Historical Textile Research Consultant); Sieske Binnendijk (Catharijne Convent); Nico Boeijink (then Regional Conservation and Care Advisor, Stichting Museaal & Historisch Perspectief Noord-Holland); Jaap van der Burg (Helicon Conservation Support b.v.); Adriana Buurman-Brunsting; Sjoukje Colenbrander (Textile Historian); Erco Lighting Nederland b.v.; André Groeneveld (Stichting Zuiderzeemuseum); Peter Hallebeek (Netherlands Institute for Cultural Heritage); Elsje

Janssen (Coordinator of Collections Management, Municipal Museums of Antwerp); Sjouk Hoitsma (Rotterdams Historisch Museum); Ton Jütte (Netherlands Institute for Cultural Heritage); Annette Kipp (Netherlands Institute for Cultural Heritage); Margriet Koot; Iris Kost (Helicon Conservation Support b.v.); Trudy Langeveld-van Lith (Textile Conservator); Hester Lensink (Netherlands Institute for Cultural Heritage); René Lugtigheid (then Stichting Werkplaats tot Herstel van Antiek Textiel); Carin van Nes (Netherlands Institute for Cultural Heritage); Nel Oversteegen (Netherlands Institute for Cultural Heritage); Luiz José Pedersoli Jr (then at the Netherlands Institute for Cultural Heritage); Mariska Pool (Koninklijk Leger- en Wapenmuseum, Delft); Frits Regter (Netherlands Textile Committee); Ruben de Reu (De Tiendschuur); Juliette van Seeters (Stedelijk Museum Alkmaar); Inge Specht (Nederlands Leder- en Schoenenmuseum); Tuuk Stam (Catharijne Convent); Loutje den Tex (Textile Conservator); Marijke van de Weerdt (Amsterdams Historisch Museum).

1

Materials

1.1 Fibres in general (polymers)

1.1.1 Classification

Textiles are made from fibres, which can be divided into two main groups depending on their origin: natural or man-made (chemically manufactured). Natural fibres can be subdivided into vegetable (plant), animal, and mineral fibres (Table 1). Vegetable fibres consist mainly of cellulose. They can be further categorised by the manner in which they occur in the plant, namely bast fibres (such as flax, hemp, jute and ramie), seed fibres (cotton and kapok), leaf fibres (manila and sisal) and fruit fibres (coconut). Animal fibres are made of protein and can be divided into hair/wool and silk. Asbestos is an example of a mineral fibre (inorganic).

Man-made fibres can be divided into two subgroups: synthetic and semi-synthetic (Table 2).

Table 1 Schematic overview of the most common natural fibres.

Vegetable fibres				Animal fibres		Mineral fibres
Bast	Seed	Leaf	Fruit	Hair/wool	Silk	Asbestos
Flax	Cotton	Manila	Coconut	Sheep	Bombix mori	
Jute	Kapok	Sisal		Camel	Tussah	
Hemp		Pineapple		Alpaca (domesticated llama)		
Ramie		Banana		Vicuña (wild llama)		
Nettle		Palm		Mohair (Angora goat)		
		Yucca		Angora (Angora rabbit)		

Table 2 Schematic overview of the most common synthetic fibres (based on Timar-Balazsy and Eastop 1998: 4; Bois 1971: 18; Brommer 1990: 101).

Semi-synthetic fibres			Synthetic fibres			
Cellulose	Protein	Other	Polyamide	Polyester	Acrylic	Other
Viscose (rayon)	Casein	Glass	Nylon	Dacron	Orlon	Rhovil (polyvinyl chloride)
Cupro (rayon)	Ardil (peanut)	Rubber	Perlon	Trevira	Redon	Lycra (polyurethane)
Acetate		Metal	Enkalon	Terlenka	Dralon	Meraklon (polypropylene)
Triacetate		Carbon	Rilsan	Tergal	Crylor	Polyethylene
Lyocell			Aramid	Terylene	Courtelle	
Modal					Modacryl	

*Polyethylene and polypropylene are so-called polyolefine fibres

Synthetic fibres are manufactured from chemicals, by building polymer chains from monomers (see section 1.1.2), which may have a natural origin (usually from oil). The chemically prepared material is dissolved or melted and extruded through a spinneret (a cap with minuscule holes). In principle, man-made fibres can be of an infinite length (filament). Semi-synthetic fibres are made from modified natural raw material, which is also extruded through a spinneret.

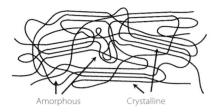

Figure 1 Crystalline and amorphous areas in a polymer.

1.1.2 The chemistry and physics of polymers

All organic fibres are made from polymers. These polymers are made of long molecules which are built from many smaller units, called monomers, joined together as in a string of beads. The size of a polymer molecule can be represented by its mass; however, it is more commonly understood that the degree of polymerisation (DP) indicates the average number of monomers joined together to form a polymer. The higher the DP, the larger the molecular mass of the polymer. Polymers have a complex three-dimensional structure.

The polymer chains in textile fibres are arranged in a relatively orderly way: each fibre type has a characteristic structural arrangement. The straighter and smoother the polymer chains of a fibre type, the better these chains can be ordered (like matches fitting neatly into a box). When the polymer chains are more bulky, for example due to the presence of large side groups, it is much more difficult to create an orderly arrangement. In a polymer there is often a mixture of areas in which the chains are aligned and areas in which the chains are in disorder. The aligned areas are called the 'crystalline areas', the disordered areas 'amorphous' (Fig. 1). Crystalline areas are rigid – the movement between individual polymer chains within the crystalline area is restricted because they are constrained in space. In addition, dipole–dipole interactions (such as hydrogen bonds) and van der Waals forces are present between the chains.

The degree of crystallinity of a fibre, represented as a percentage, strongly affects the mechanical properties (e.g. tensile strength and flexibility) of the fibre: the higher the degree of crystallinity, the stronger and more rigid the fibre.

Amorphous areas have a more open structure that allows more movement and it is in these areas that the fibre absorbs moisture and where reactions with external substances first take place. Chemical reactions, i.e. degradation processes, start in the amorphous areas. Fibres with a low crystallinity will therefore suffer more from exposure to agents of degradation. Unaged cotton has a degree of crystallinity of around 70%, flax up to 90%, silk roughly 60% and wool about 30%. The values for various (semi-)synthetic fibres are: rayon up to 40%, nylon and polyester from 65 to 85% and acrylic around 70%.

The mechanical qualities of fibres are described by a number of standardised properties such as tenacity, tensile strength, elongation at break and elastic modulus. Tenacity indicates the specific stress necessary to break a fibre of a certain diameter (represented in cN/tex, g/denier or g/dtex, g/tex). Tensile strength is the breaking strength of a fibre expressed as a force per unit of cross-sectional area (kg/cm^2). Elongation at break (the elongation of the fibre when it breaks under load) is given as a percentage of the original length of the fibre and is therefore a measure of the stretching properties of a fibre. The elasticity of a fibre is the ability of a material to resume its original form, size or shape after removing the forces that caused its deformation. It is represented by the elastic modulus, or Young's Modulus (E), which can be calculated from the ratio of the stress on the loading plane to strain along the loading direction.

Fibres with a high crystallinity (e.g. flax) are very strong and have a relatively high tenacity. Amorphous fibres such as wool are weaker, but are more elastic – i.e. they have a higher percentage elongation at the breaking point.

Another important property is the temperature at which the polymer changes from a rigid, brittle form to a rubbery, soft and flexible state. This is described as the glass transition temperature (Tg) and is especially relevant to polymers with a low crystallinity, built up mainly by linear chains (such as some of the man-made polymers). The glass transition temperature is different for each polymer. A disordered polymer can therefore appear in three forms: glass-like (at temperatures well below its Tg), rubber-like (at temperatures above its Tg but still below its melting point) or fluid (at temperatures above its softening range) (Fig. 2). Such polymers are thermoplastic and can be found in textile collections as man-made fibres such as acetate, triacetate, acrylic and nylon. Thermoplastic polymers may have been used in the conservation of a textile, e.g. when synthetic adhesives such as Mowilith, Setamul, Vinamul (polyvinyl acetates) and Lascaux and Paraloid (acrylates) were used to attach a support fabric. When a polymer has a Tg of about 20 °C (i.e. room temperature) or lower, it will be rubber-like at room temperature, making it sticky and malleable. During storage or exhibition, these materials can cause problems if the temperature fluctuates, causing the material to constantly change from a glass-like to a rubber-like state and vice versa. In a rubber-like condition, the thermoplastic material will become sticky and there is a danger that it might adhere to dust, packaging, adjacent objects or even to itself.

In contrast to the thermoplastics, thermosets are polymers which will not soften, flow or distort appreciably when subjected to sufficient heat and pressure. When the temperature is raised even higher they will not melt, but eventually will disintegrate. These polymers are always cross-linked, which means that they consist of a three-dimensional network maintained by chemical bonds. Examples are Bakelite (phenol-formaldehyde resins), epoxy resins and some alkyd resins – materials from which some accessories found in textile collections may be made.

1.1.3 Cellulose

Vegetable fibres consist mainly of cellulose, a polymer built up from cellobiose units (Fig. 3). Cellobiose is a disaccharide, i.e. it consists of two glucose units. Glucose, a monosaccharide, exists in nature in a ring structure in two forms: the so-called α-glucose and β-glucose. The difference is in the position of the hydroxyl side group attached to the fourth carbon in the ring. Amylase, a component of starch, is the result of linking only α-glucose units together to form a polymer with a spiral structure. Cellulose contains only β-glucose units linked together forming a linear structure or straight chain. This allows the chains to form a compact structure, strengthened by the formation of many hydrogen bonds between the polymer chains where the crystalline areas dominate. Cellulose has many hydrophilic side groups and can therefore absorb water quickly and hold it in its amorphous areas and at the surface of the crystalline regions.

1.1.4 Proteins

Animal fibres consist of proteins, which are polymers built up from the 21 naturally occurring amino acids, which can be linked together in a different order and compilation to form various

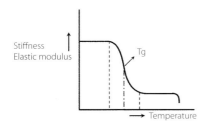

Figure 2 Graphic presentations of the thermoplastic phases.

Table 3 Summary of the most common fibres and their physical data (Timar-Balazsy and Eastop 1998; Gohl and Vilensky 1987; Hollen 1988).

Fibre	Fibre length (mm)	Fibre diameter (μm)	Degree of polymerisation	Crystallinity (%)	Tenacity dry (cN/tex)	Tenacity wet (cN/tex)	Elongation at break (%)	Moisture regain†
Flax	20–60‡	20–80	up to 36,000	90	29.0–33.4	29.0–33.4	1.8–2.0 dry, 2.2 wet	7–12
Cotton	6–65	11–22	11,000	65–80	26.5–44.1	29.0–56.3	3–7 dry, 9.5 wet	7–11
Wool	30–500	15–70	10,000–60,000	25–30	10.5–14.9	6.1–14.0	25–35	13.6–16.3
Silk	infinite	12–30	300–3,000	60–70	24.6–39.6	22.0–35.2	10–25	8.9–11.0
Rayon	infinite	12–22	200–700	35–40	53.0–62.0	44.0–53.0	15–30	10.7–16.0
Acetate	infinite	–	130–225	40	9.7–11.5	5.7–6.6	–	6.5–9.0
Nylon	infinite	14–24	50–80	65–85	40.6–51.2	35.3–45.0	18–25	3.5–5.0
Polyester	infinite	12–25	115–140	65–85	35.3–70.6	35.3–70.6	22–40	0.1–0.8
Acrylic	infinite	15–25	2,000	70–80	35.3–36.2	26.5–33.5	15–45	1.2–2.0

† Expressed as a percentage of the dry weight at 20 °C and 65% relative humidity (RH)
‡ Elementary fibres

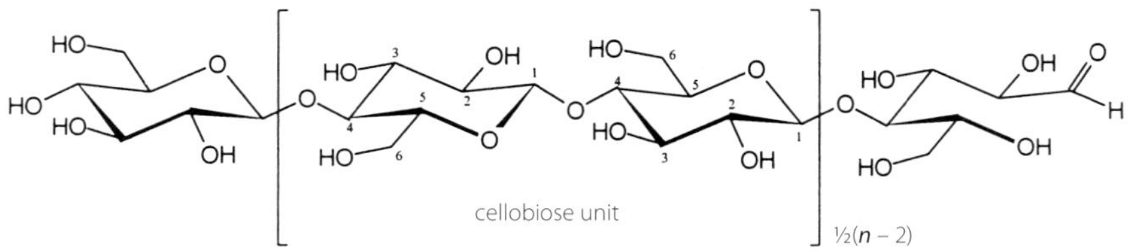

Figure 3 Chemical structure of cellulose with the cellobiose units consisting of two glucose units (with numbered carbon atoms) (n = degrees of polymerisation)(courtesy L.J. Pedersoli jr., Netherlands Institute for Cultural Heritage).

Figure 4 Linking together amino acids by means of peptide bonds (courtesy L.J. Pedersoli jr., Netherlands Institute for Cultural Heritage).

proteins. The chemical bond between two amino acids is called a peptide bond (Fig. 4). The types, percentages and sequence of the amino acids have an enormous influence on the properties of a protein. The primary structure of a protein is determined by the amino acid sequence. When sulphur is present in the protein (as in wool), the primary structure is further defined by the location of disulphide cross-links which are formed between two cysteine units (which contain sulphur), resulting in one cystine unit. The secondary structure refers to spatial arrangements of amino acids that are near one another in the linear sequence. Some of these steric relationships are of a regular kind, giving rise to a periodic structure. The α-helix and β-pleated sheet are elements of secondary structure (Fig. 10).

1.2 Vegetable fibres

1.2.1 Flax/linen

Flax (*Linum usitatissimum*) is a plant from which the bast fibres are used to make textiles. Once the fibres of the flax plant are worked into yarn it can be regarded as linen. Flax grows in temperate to subtropical climates and its use as a raw material for textiles has been known for a very long time. The oldest linen discovered originates from ancient Egypt, where linen bandages were used among others in the ritual embalming of the dead. Originally, flax was grown from the area of the Mediterranean Sea into southern Russia. From the late Middle Ages, linen was an important product in Europe. In northern France and the southern Netherlands (Belgium and Zeeland) the cultivation of flax was of great economic importance. This industry, which generated a lot of wealth, dwindled with the rise of cotton in the late 18th and early 19th century and moved to Ireland and Russia.

Production
Flax is sown in early spring. The plant can reach heights of about 90 to 120 cm in a few months and develops with a single, smooth stem on which only a few side branches are formed to carry the flowers. The plant has small white or blue flowers, which then develop into seed balls. It is harvested when these seed balls begin to ripen and the plant slowly loses its leaves and becomes a yellow-green colour. As the flax fibres are found mainly in the outer layer or bark of the stem, the whole plant is reaped or pulled from the soil so that as much length of fibre material as possible is obtained. The fibres are grouped into bundles held together by a sticky material called pectin. These bundles are of the same length as the stem and are referred to as the 'technical fibres'. These technical fibres are in turn built up from so-called 'elementary fibres', which are also held together by pectin.

The processes necessary to free the technical fibres from the flax stem are complex and extreme. After the flax is reaped, the stems are pulled through a comb, as a result of which the seed balls are pulled off. The linseed in these balls is not thrown away but pressed to obtain linseed oil. The stems are then subjected to a process called 'retting', in order to loosen the technical fibres. This chemical process, similar to rotting, is conducted under the influence of moisture, so that certain fungi and bacteria can dissolve the pectin between the technical fibre bundles. Traditionally this was achieved by leaving the uprooted flax spread out on the fields where the necessary moisture was supplied by rain and dew, or laid in shallow water-filled ditches. This type of retting often took weeks to achieve. Another method was to pack bundles of stems together in a large tank which was then filled with water at around 30 °C; this stimulated the reproduction of the necessary microorganisms – a process lasting three to four days. Today, artificial retting methods are used. Chemicals are added to the warm water of the retting bath to accelerate the dissolution of the pectin (a matter of four to six hours). It is important that the retting process does not continue too long otherwise the pectin between the elementary fibres will dissolve.

After retting, the flax stems are dried and then broken (scutching) to break the woody core of the stem so that the waste falls out. Finally, before the fibres can be spun, flax has to be 'hackled'. This process splits the technical fibre bundles into finer and softer fibre bundles. Hackling is done with combs, either by hand or by machine. The bundles can be spun dry or wet. When spun wet, the coarse threads (rove) are passed through warm water which softens the pectin between the elementary fibres. By stretching these coarse threads while spinning, the elementary fibres slide alongside each other, as a result of which finer and thinner threads can be spun. Dry spun threads, on the other hand, have better moisture regain and feel softer.

Morphology
The colour of flax fibres can vary between light blond and grey blond depending on the climate, the agricultural conditions of the soil and the retting process. The fibres have a shiny surface caused by a thin layer of a protective coating. Under the microscope, at a magnification of 100× or more, the characteristic cross markings of the flax fibre can be seen, often referred to as the nodes (see Fig. 5). These are thought to be fissures in the cell walls. A cross-section of the fibre shows the relatively thick cell walls which add to the firm and tough character of linen.

Chemical and physical properties
Flax, being a vegetable fibre, is mainly composed (65%) of cellulose (see section 1.1.3). Other substances present include hemicellulose (16%), pectin (3%), lignin (2.5%), proteins (3%), wax and fatty substances (1.5%) and minerals (1%) (Lehrgang 1986). Hemicellulose is a collective noun for several different polysaccharides present in the cell wall and in the middle lamella. It is very hygroscopic and swells more in water than cellulose. Pectin is the adhesive that binds together the elementary fibres. Lignin, a woody substance, is found in the middle lamella of fibre bundles and in the cell wall. It is a hydrophobic substance that rapidly turns brown and acid under the influence of light. The degree of polymerisation of cellulose in flax can reach 36,000 and the polymer has a very high crystallinity of 90%: flax is therefore a strong, inextensible fibre, with an increased tenacity when wet. Linen creases easily due to its high crystallinity. It can absorb and release water very quickly compared to other fibres. Linen is also a bad insulator, which is why it is comfortable to wear in warm weather (Table 3).

1.2.2 Cotton

Cotton is a seed fibre from the Gossypium plant family. The two principal types of cotton are *Gossypium herbaceum* from India and *Gossypium hirsutum* from North America. The cotton plant grows in warm and especially humid climates. Cotton was first brought to western Europe from the Arab countries by the Crusaders. The word 'cotton' is derived from the Arabic, *el koton*. In Germany it is still called *Baumwolle* (literally tree wool) – as people thought that the fibre looked like wool and they knew it came from 'trees'.

Cotton has long been used for the manufacture of textiles. In Peru, archaeological cotton fragments were found dating back to 3000 BC. Writings in Sanskrit describing the use of cotton were found in India dating from around 1500 BC (Groeneweg 1987: 7). From the 12th until the 18th/19th century, Europe obtained its cotton mainly from India. As the trade route was long and dangerous, and the manufacture of cotton was labour-intensive, it

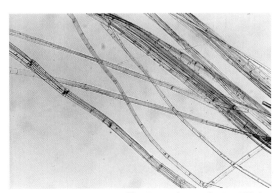

Figure 5 Microscopic view of flax (original magnification 100×).

was considered a luxury product for centuries. In the 19th century, however, large quantities of cotton were imported from North America. Within a century the use of cotton in Western textiles (especially in household fabrics) grew explosively, due to the introduction of mechanical spinning techniques. Currently, cotton is still obtained mainly from the United States, but it is also imported in large quantities from Russia and China. Egypt still produces cotton that is famous for its long fibre.

Production

From the cotton seeds, which are sown in spring, a shrub grows to a height of 1–2 m. The shrub flowers have many small, creamy white flowers that die within a few days leaving the green seed pod or fruit. When the pod is ripe it bursts open and the cotton 'fluff' becomes visible (Fig. 6). The cotton fibres that are attached to the seeds in the fruit have two functions: (1) they regulate the moisture content of the ripening fruit as the seeds grow and (2) they help the distribution of the seeds after the ripe fruit bursts (as the fibres dry in the sun until they become light enough to be carried away by the wind). It is therefore important to pick the cotton at the right time before the fluff is blown away. Cotton, which was traditionally picked by hand, is today more often harvested by machine.

After picking, the cotton is first dried and then the seeds are separated from the fibres by means of a de-seeding machine. Next, the cotton is packed into bales to be transported to a place of manufacture. Upon arrival at its destination, the cotton must first be disentangled before the fibres can be spun. The cotton fluff is combed to remove impurities and short fibre material; the more the fibres are combed, the finer the eventual threads.

Morphology

The cotton fibre varies in length from roughly 6 to 65 mm. The length of the fibres is not only dependent upon the climate and the agricultural conditions, but also on the level of ripeness of the fruit at the time of picking. Cotton is mainly white but there are also Indonesian and South American species that are light brown. The fibre consists of one cell which is built up from a number of layers. The extremely thin outer layer or cuticle is composed of a waxy layer and protects the fibre against chemicals and other degrading agents. The primary cell wall just underneath the cuticle is relatively hard and consists mainly of cellulose (see section 1.1.3), pectin-like materials, proteins and wax. The largest part of the fibre is formed by the secondary cell wall consisting of cellulose. This layer is formed in the second stage of growth when the fibre has reached its length. One layer of cellulose after another is formed in 'day rings' with the purpose of consolidating the cell (Fig. 7). Under the microscope, at a magnification of 100× or more, the characteristic 'turns' in the cotton fibre can be seen; the so-called natural twists (Fig. 8). These twists or convolutions are formed when the cotton fibre dries after the fruit bursts open. The cotton fibre is, in effect, a hollow tube with a relatively large lumen (transportation channel), which collapses during the drying process of the fibre.

Chemical and physical properties

Cotton consists mainly of cellulose (87%) with a small amount of pectin (1.2%), proteins (1.3%), wax and fatty substances (0.6%) and minerals (1.2%) (Lehrgang 1986). The degree of polymerisation of cellulose in cotton is around 11,000 and cotton has a crystallinity of 70% (Timar-Balazsy and Eastop

Figure 6 Cotton plant with burst open pods.

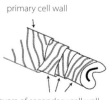

Figure 7 Morphological diagram of the cotton fibre (after Gohl and Vilensky 1983: 43).

Figure 8 Microscopic view of cotton (original magnification 150×).

1998: 11, 20). Cotton is therefore a relatively strong fibre with an increased tenacity when wet. It has an elongation at break of about 3 to 7% for a dry fibre, which increases to 9.5% for a wet fibre. It is a relatively elastic fibre that will return to its old form when tension is released. Cotton can absorb water quickly but releases it fairly slowly, which is why cotton clothing often feels clammy on a hot and humid day (Table 3).

1.3 Animal fibres

1.3.1 Wool/hair

Animal fibres, which originate from the fur of mammals, can be divided into wool and hair. Both kinds can be found in many animals and it is often difficult to tell the difference. Chemically speaking, wool and hair both consist of the protein keratin. When speaking of 'wool', we usually mean the wool of sheep. In ethnographic collections 'wool' can also originate from other animals such as goats and camels. The Spanish merino sheep, a cross between the native Spanish sheep and the sheep cultivated by the Romans, gives a beautiful quality of wool with frizzy, fine fibres (4–12 cm) (Paassen et al. 1977: 25). Due to an embargo on the export of merino sheep, Spain maintained a monopoly within Europe for long time. This embargo was lifted in the 18th century and merino sheep were exported throughout the world. At the end of the 19th century, merino sheep were introduced to Australia, which has since become the most important wool-producing country in the world. The wool from English and Scottish sheep is somewhat coarser with almost smooth, shiny and very long fibres (20–55 cm) (Paassen et al. 1977: 25).

Production
In order to obtain the wool or hair, the animal is often shorn or combed. Sheep are shorn once a year: the wool obtained is called 'fleece wool'. The soft wool from the first shearing is called 'lamb's wool' and 'slipe wool' is the wool obtained from a slaughtered sheep. This lower quality type of wool is scraped off the skin after a chemical pre-treatment. 'Recovered wool' is obtained by shredding old woollen or half-woollen fabrics and by spinning the wool fibres again.

Fleece wool is first sorted to separate the longer and better quality fibres originating from the shoulders and the back from those of lesser quality originating from the belly and the legs. Usually the wool is washed to remove impurities. In the past, wool was often spun unwashed (this still happens in nomadic tribes). As washing also removes some of the wool fats, a lubricant is frequently added to make the spinning process easier.

Mohair, cashmere
Goats' fur is also used for textiles. The best-known fur comes from the angora or camel goat, a species native to Turkey. The hairs, called mohair, can reach a length of 30 cm; they are not very curly, and are shiny and very elastic. Cashmere (or Kashmir) wool originates from the cashmere goat, a species that lives in the area in and around the Himalayas. The fur of these goats is not obtained by shearing, but by combing. These hairs are short, very soft and have a beautiful shine. Cashmere wool, a luxury product, is used among other things in the manufacture of cashmere shawls.

Alpaca, vicuña wool
In the ancient cultures of southern America, wool was mainly obtained from llamas and alpacas, but the wool of the wild vicuña was also harvested. Alpaca wool is shiny brown to black in colour and the hairs have a length of 10 to 20 cm. Vicuña wool is softer and shiny reddish-brown or white.

Camel and rabbit, cow and horse
In North Africa and the Middle East the combed-out hairs of the camel and dromedary have long been used; these are golden brown, about 10 cm long and very fine. The fur of the angora rabbit (originating in the Far East) is also combed out. The hairs are 2 to 8 cm long and are very fine and light. The wool is called angora.

Another example of the use of hair is the application of the hair of horses and cows. The long hair of horses is often used (unspun) in, for example, upholstery stuffing; horsehair can also be used as an inner lining or support in collars. Cow hair is sometimes spun and used in carpet weaving. Both are very resilient and tough.

Morphology
The length and cross-section of wool and hair fibres, as well as their appearance, differs. The diameter varies from 15 to 70 μm and the length from 30 to 500 mm. There are also many similarities, however, which can be seen under a microscope by enlargement of 200× or more. The fibres have an irregular surface with overlapping scales that point towards the tip of the fibre (Fig. 9). In some wool types the medulla (at the core of the hair) is visible. The fibres

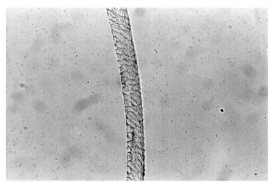

Figure 9 Microscopic view of wool/hair (original magnification 200×).

Table 4 An overview of the most common amino acids in animal fibres (residues/1000 g fibrous protein) (data from course material in chemistry from the Netherlands Training School for Conservators 1987/88; Timar-Balazsy and Eastop 1998: 43).

Amino acid	Wool (merino)	Silk fibroin	Silk sericin
Alanine	100	294	55
Arginine	65	5	29
Aspartic acid	55	13	138
Cysteine	100	2	1
Glutamic acid	110	10	58
Glycine	75	446	127
Histidine	5	1	13
Isoleucine	25	7	6
Leucine	60	5	7
Lysine	20	3	33
Methionine	5	1	1
Phenylalanine	20	6	4
Proline	70	4	6
Serine	95	121	320
Tyrosine	40	52	34
Threonine	60	9	83
Valine	45	22	27

in the wool of rabbits and goats often have more than one medulla.

Chemical and physical properties
The constituent material of wool and hair is a protein called keratin. The α-helix molecules are bundled together in a regular way to give protofibrils, microfibrils and macrofibrils. Each hair is wrapped in a cuticle made up of protein scales. If a hair is heated, particularly with steam, and then pulled, the relatively weak hydrogen bonds in the α-helices are stretched and broken. This allows the molecules to elongate without breaking. As the hair continues to stretch, the helix structure breaks down and is replaced by β-pleated sheet (Fig. 10). This process is reversible.

One of the most important characteristics of wool is that its polymer chains contain the amino acid cysteine, which contains sulphur. Depending upon the type of wool, the amount of cysteine present can vary between 3 and 12%. Disulphide cross-links are formed between the protein chains, forming very strong bonds. The more sulphur there is present in the wool, the stiffer the fibres (see section 1.1.4). The amount of amino acid units in keratin varies between 10,000 and 60,000 and it has a crystallinity of 30% or even less (Timar-Balazsy and Eastop 1998: 11, 48) (Tables 3 and 4).

Wool is an efficient heat insulator (its function in nature) due to the static air which is locked between the scales and between the fibres. It is a very elastic but relatively weak fibre.

Wool can absorb a lot of water – up to 200% of its dry weight. When wool takes up moisture it feels warmer to the touch due to the fact that the bonding of moisture by wool is an exothermic reaction that releases heat. Wool, especially when it is aged, becomes weaker when wet.

Felting
Wool is the only natural fibre material that can be felted. This is due to the unique scale-like structure of the fibres. Felting is done in a warm, alkaline environment in which the fibres swell and the scales open. By mechanically working the fibre mass, the scales hook onto each other. Upon drying the fibres shrink, which fixes the entangled structure.

1.3.2 Silk

Silk is produced by the caterpillars of the Bombycidae family, the best known being the *Bombyx mori*. The word 'silk' is thought to have originated from the Greek word *Seres*, which means the people from Eastern Asia, i.e. the Chinese. It is believed that the cultivation of silk in China dates back to around 3000 BC. For about 2,000 years, China held the monopoly in silk cultivation. Wearing silk was regarded as the privilege of royalty and nobility.

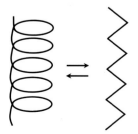

Figure 10 Schematic view of the α and β structure in wool/hair.

The outside world knew very little about it and the penalty for anyone spreading knowledge about the cultivation of the silk caterpillar was death. Legend has it that around 140 BC the first eggs of the silk moth were successfully smuggled out of China by a Chinese princess. She married outside the borders of China and smuggled the eggs out in her hair (Geijer 1982: 108). China then allowed the export of silk products which reached the Western world via the famous Silk Road. Knowledge about the production of silk also travelled to the West along the same route. It is recorded that in AD 522, two monks smuggled the eggs of the moth in a hollow bamboo staff to Byzantium, and by this means knowledge of the cultivation of silk spread to the West; first to southern Europe and from the 16th century also to northern Europe. Wild silk, which can be found all over the world, is produced by the Tussah caterpillars.

Production
Cultivating silk caterpillars is a precarious business. Each female moth lays 400 to 500 eggs and the silkworms are just a few millimetres long when they first hatch. They feed only on the leaves of the mulberry tree and are very sensitive to climatic changes and disease. If everything goes well, the caterpillars grow in five weeks to a length of roughly 8.5 cm, after which they pupate in order to undergo the change into a moth. For that purpose caterpillars make a cocoon of silk thread; a liquid crystalline protein, called fibroin, is extruded by the silkworm through two glands in the mouthparts – thereby producing two threads of fibroin. At the same time, the worm secretes another protein called sericin, an adhesive that binds together the two fibroin threads and probably also encourages the fibroin to crystallise. In the air, a continuous silk thread is thus formed. By describing a figure of eight with their heads, the caterpillars slowly encapsulate themselves, a process that takes roughly four days. Without human intervention, the caterpillar inside the cocoon would metamorphose (change) into a moth, which would eventually chew its way out of the cocoon, rendering the silk useless. Therefore the caterpillars have to be killed before metamorphosis takes place. This is done by subjecting the cocoons to steam or hot air. In order to reclaim the silk as a thread, the cocoons are put into a bath of hot water to dissolve the sericin slightly. The ends of the silk threads are picked from the cocoons with brushes and the cocoons are unrolled. To obtain the individual silk filaments (the pure fibroin), the silk is degummed by means of dissolving the sericin in boiling soapy water. As a result of this process silk loses about 25% of its weight (see section 1.7).

The silk thread spun by the caterpillar is about 3 km long; the beginning and end parts of the thread are not very fine and are used for so-called waste silk (e.g. chappe silk). Just 600 to 900 m can be unrolled at a time. To give an idea of production yield: 40,000 eggs yield 24,000 cocoons, which together give about two kilos of pure silk (Groeneweg 1987: 15; Paassen *et al*. 1977: 33–4).

Wild Tussah caterpillars produce very irregular threads in which the fibroin and sericin are mixed and therefore cannot be separated. The silk thread is irregular, less glossy and somewhat fluffy.

Morphology
The surface of the silk filament is very smooth and reflects light, which accounts for its glossy look (Fig. 11). Silk filaments have a triangular cross-section. Wild silk can be recognised by its slightly thicker thread, with a more irregular surface.

Chemical and physical properties
As previously described silk consists of the protein fibroin (the spinning solution) and sometimes a small amount of sericin (the silk glue). Fibroin is almost completely composed of the amino acids glycine, alanine and serine: simple amino acids with small side groups that can be closely packed together as chains (Table 4). Due to the numerous possibilities of forming hydrogen bonds the fibroin is even stronger. The protein fibroin has a β-sheet structure.

Silk has a very high tenacity due to its three-dimensional structure and high crystallinity. Because of the numerous hydrogen bonds, and

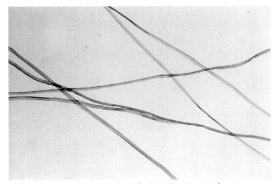

Figure 11 Microscopic image of silk (original magnification 100×).

its compact structure, however, it is not very elastic. When silk is stretched (by more than 2%) the hydrogen bonds break and the polymer chains move alongside each other. In their new position hydrogen bonds are formed, fixing the new form (see Table 3).

1.4 Man-made fibres

Silk has always been greatly valued for its gloss and fineness. Because the product was so precious, attempts were made from the 17th century onwards to reproduce the fibre by means of chemical production methods using a similar principle to that of the silkworm: extruding the spinning liquid through a spinneret with minute holes into the air or a coagulating bath. At an international exhibition in Paris in 1889, clothing made from artificial fibres was exhibited for the first time by the Frenchman, Hilaire de Bernigaud, Count of Chardonnet.

1.4.1 Semi-synthetic fibres

Semi-synthetic fibres are produced by chemically altering a natural product. The natural product is usually dissolved, modified if necessary, and extruded through a spinneret. When the material is dissolved in organic solvents, the spinning liquid is extruded into warm air, so that the solvents evaporate and the fibre solidifies. When the material is dissolved in an aqueous solution, it has to be extruded into a coagulating bath in which the dissolved material hardens. Semi-synthetic fibres such as rayon are produced from cellulose. Animal material can also be used in the production of fibres, e.g. casein gives 'milk wool'. Natural rubber can be modified and even mineral resources have found their way into the production of fibre material, such as metal filaments or glass fibre.

Rayon
A large proportion of the semi-synthetic fibres produced are those made from cellulose, known as rayon. The process of manufacturing has not really changed since its development at the end of the 19th century. Wood or the short fibres of cotton (called linters), are generally used as the source of cellulose. The cellulose is treated chemically so that it dissolves into a viscous liquid, called viscose. The spinning liquid is extruded via the spinneret into warm air or a coagulating bath. The end product is once again pure cellulose. The two basic types of rayon – viscose rayon and copper rayon – are described here. Viscose is manufactured from an aqueous solution of cellulose xanthate which is extruded into an acid bath. To make copper rayon, cellulose is dissolved in a solution of copper sulphate and ammonia and extruded into a coagulating bath of diluted sulphuric acid. Copper rayon has a more beautiful gloss than viscose and is a stronger fibre. Examples of copper rayon are Cupro and Bamberg silk.

Rayon fibres have many of the characteristics of natural cellulose fibres – they crease easily and absorb moisture well – but there are some significant differences. The degree of polymerisation of rayon is considerably lower than that of natural cellulose and the fibres are more amorphous than natural fibres. As a result, this regenerated cellulose suffers more from degradation processes than natural cellulose and under similar conditions it will show signs of degradation (such as loss of strength) more quickly. In contrast to the natural cellulose fibre, the strength of a rayon fibre also decreases when wet (see Table 3).

Modal
Modal fibres are also made by the viscose process but with a higher degree of polymerisation and modified precipitating baths. This leads to fibres with improved properties such as better wear, higher dry and wet strengths and better dimensional stability.

Lyocell
Since 1992, lyocell fibres have been produced using a solvent spinning process. Lyocell fibres, like other cellulosic fibres, are moisture-absorbent and biodegradable. The regenerated cellulose has a relatively high degree of polymerisation and hence the fibres have a dry strength higher than other cellulosic fibres, approaching that of polyester. They also retain 85% of their strength when wet. Lyocell fibres are used mainly for clothing fabrics, especially outerwear, and it has been shown that due to its fibrillating property, non-woven fabrics can be made.

Acetate
Acetate and triacetate are manufactured from cellulose. The end product is an acetic acid ester of cellulose. The basic material is first treated with acetic anhydride, which results in the formation of acetate side groups on the polymer chains of the cellulose. Next the product is dissolved in acetone and this spinning liquid is extruded into the air

where the acetone evaporates and the fibre hardens. The resulting fibre is elastic but not very strong and absorbs only a little moisture. Acetate has a low softening point and can be dissolved in a number of organic solvents such as acetone (see Table 3).

Other semi-synthetic fibres

An important animal semi-synthetic fibre is made from casein (a constituent of milk). In appearance the material is like wool, but it lacks wool's beneficial properties. The fibre is not very strong and is sensitive to water.

Rubber fibres are obtained from the sap (latex) of the rubber tree, *Hevea brasiliensis*. Latex can be extruded through a spinneret or can be rolled into thin sheets from which the threads are cut in strips. The threads are then vulcanised to increase their elasticity. Vulcanisation is a treatment with sulphur under the influence of heat, which causes the polymer chains to cross-link. Rubber threads are sensitive to moisture, air and light and are therefore often wrapped in another fibre material. They are very elastic and have complete recovery. Rubber is therefore used in elastic.

1.4.2 Synthetic fibres

Synthetic fibres form a large part of all our textiles. They are used on their own or mixed with other synthetic or natural fibres. Synthetic fibres are made from polymers that have been manufactured artificially. They can be divided, depending upon the constituent monomers, into: polyamide, polyester, acrylic, polyolefin and polyurethane (spandex) fibres (see Table 2). The spinning solution can be extruded in three different ways: into warm air in which the volatile solvent evaporates (Orlon, Rhovil); into a coagulating bath in which the spinning liquid precipitates; or by extruding the melted spinning liquid into cold air (nylon, Terlenka). Synthetic fibres are often stronger than natural fibres. Usually very light in weight and elastic, they absorb little moisture and are sensitive to high temperatures.

Polyamide

One of the first synthetic fibres to be produced was nylon; a polyamide fibre, which was launched in 1938 in the United States by the DuPont Company. The most well-known is nylon 6,6, synthesised from the starting materials hexamethylene diamine and adipic acid which are linked together by means of amide bonds (identical to proteins). Almost at the same time, the I.G. Farben Company in Germany polymerised caprolactam and created a different form of the polymer, identified as nylon 6.

DuPont began commercial production of nylon in 1939. The first experimental testing used nylon as a sewing thread in parachute manufacture and in women's hosiery. Nylon stockings were shown in February 1939 at the San Francisco World Fair. During the Second World War, nylon replaced Asian silk in parachute fabric. It also found use in tyres, tents, ropes, ponchos and other military supplies, and was even used in the production of a high-grade paper for US currency. After the war, the conversion of nylon production to civilian uses began and when the first small quantities of post-war nylon stockings were advertised, thousands of women lined up at New York department stores to buy them. By the end of the 1940s, it was also being used in carpeting and car upholstery.

Nylon is a very strong fibre with a crystallinity of 65 to 85%. It hardly absorbs any moisture. It is very resilient due to the many hydrogen bonds and crystalline areas which prevent the polymer chains from sliding alongside each other. It is these very properties that allow nylon to resume its former shape when released from stretching (see Table 3).

Another polyamide fibre, Aramid (a contraction of aromatic and polyamide) was developed between 1955 and 1965 in the US. The fibres have high melting points and were useful as high performance fibres for air and space travel.

Polyester

Polyester was first produced in England under the name of Terylene (1940). Chemically speaking, it is a polymer made from ethylene glycol with either terephthalic acid or dimethylterephthalate, which forms ester linkages to become polyethylene terephthalate (PET). It is used in clothing, home furnishings, hoses, power belting, ropes and nets, thread, tyre cord, car upholstery, sails, floppy disk liners and as fibrefill for various products including pillows and furniture. Polyester fibre is very crystalline and therefore very strong. The material is hydrophobic and hardly retains any moisture (see Table 3).

Acrylic

Acrylic and polyolefins are made by addition polymerisation (as opposed to condensation) and, as a result, the degrees of polymerisation are of the order of thousands rather than hundreds for the other synthetic fibre polymers. The first acrylic fibre, Orlon, was produced from 1950 onwards. It is a 100% polyacrylonitrile, a polymer made up from the monomer acrylonitrile. This fibre was also made as a copolymer with 35 to 85% acrylonitrile – the Modacryl fibres. It is used for clothing, home furnishings, simulated fur, wigs and hairpieces, fleece, knit-pile fabric backings, non-wovens and stuffed toys.

Acrylic fibres are 70 to 80% crystalline yet they feel soft; this is due to the lack of strong bonds between the polymer chains, which can therefore slide alongside each other easily. Similar to polyester, the fibres are hydrophobic and absorb very little moisture (see Table 3).

Polyolefins
Two polyolefin polymers are used to make synthetic fibres: polypropylene and polyethylene. Polyethylene was first produced in the UK in 1933 by polymerising ethylene under high pressure to form the low-density polythene. In the 1950s, crystalline polypropylene and high-density polyethylene (HDPE) were invented. Both of these polyolefins are very important in plastic moulding and for making plastic sheeting. Alternatively, they can both be spun into synthetic fibres.

Elastic fibres
Polyurethane fibres are produced by the reaction of glycols and diisocyanates. Usually the reactions form block copolymers containing at least two different chemical structures – one rigid and the other flexible. The flexible segments stretch while the rigid sections act as molecular anchors to allow the material to recover its original shape when the stretching force is removed. Varying the properties of the segments and the ratio of flexible to rigid segments controls the amount of stretch. Elastane yarns, commonly known as Spandex, are characterised by their ability to recover from stretching. These yarns are composed of at least 85% (by mass) of a segmented polyurethane. If stretched to three times their unstretched length, they will revert rapidly to almost their original length when the tension is removed. Although elastane was first synthesised in 1937, it was not marketed as a commercial fibre until 1958.

1.4.3 Morphology

The appearance of a (semi-)synthetic fibre under a microscope depends on the shape and form of the holes in the spinneret. The cross-section can have a variety of shapes, for example, round, triangular or star-shaped. The fibres have a regular thickness and a smooth surface (Fig. 12). Small speckles can sometimes be seen distributed over the entire fibre; this is the delustring agent, which is added to reduce the hard shine of the synthetic fibres.

1.4.4 Other synthetic fibres made from inorganic material

There are many man-made fibres made from inorganic material including glass, carbon, metal and ceramic. Glass is produced by melting glass pellets in an electric furnace at around 1500 °C, after which the melt is passed through small holes in a plate at the base of the furnace. After cooling in air, the fibres can be either wound up or spun centrifugally to form a web.

Glass fibres have high rot resistance, low moisture uptake, are brittle and have low breaking extensions. Glass is used extensively for insulation (glass wool) and also for reinforcing plastics. Other lesser uses include flame-resistant curtains and furnishing fabrics.

Carbon fibres contain at least 90% carbon obtained by thermal carbonisation of organic fibre precursors. They are characterised by having high strength, especially when embedded in a matrix such as an epoxy resin. The main end uses are as reinforcement fibres in composites for the aircraft and aerospace industries and sports goods.

1.5 Textile techniques

A textile is composed of fibres. In order to gain some coherence, the fibres are usually spun into threads

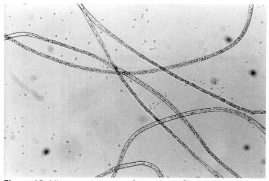

Figure 12 Microscopic image of a synthetic fibre (nylon at an original magnification of 100×).

or yarn, which in turn are used in the manufacture of fabric. There are also other ways in which coherence between the fibres can be obtained. Of the natural fibres, wool fibres can be felted directly into fabric. Modern non-wovens such as Fibrefill and Vilene are made from synthetic fibres. These fibres are joined together by means of a binding agent (an adhesive), melted together (heat-set) or entangled by means of needles (needle punch). The fibres with nearly unlimited lengths such as silk and the (semi-)synthetic filaments do not have to be worked into threads as they can be used in fabrics as untwisted bundles.

1.5.1 Spinning

Most fibres, however, are spun into threads or yarns. Previously this was done by hand using a spindle, but today machines are used. The fibres can be twisted to the right or to the left, causing an S-twist or Z-twist (Fig. 13). These can then be plied together. The direction of the ply is usually contrary to the direction of the twist. The appearance of the yarn is not only influenced by the materials used but also by the tension applied during twisting and plying.

Figure 13 S-twist and Z-twist.

1.5.2 Weaving

There are numerous techniques for making fabric out of yarns. The most common technique is weaving, which uses one or more warp sets mounted on a loom, and one or more weft sets, that are added while weaving. In the fabric, the warp is run parallel in one direction and the weft perpendicular. The wefts turn on either side of the fabric and form the selvedges. There are many weaving techniques, some of which are more than 1,000 years old, and many different types of looms, from primitive and mobile (still used by nomadic tribes) to extremely advanced machines (such as the Jacquard loom).

1.5.3 Binding systems

The warps and wefts can be woven into a fabric in a number of different ways. The different types of weaves can be divided into three main groups, according to the type of binding:

- Plain, linen, calico, tabby or taffeta weave – each weft crosses over and under one warp (Fig. 14).
- Twill weave – in order to make this type of fabric, a more complex loom is needed. Every weft crosses over two or more warps and then under one or more warps. The crossings of warp and weft form a diagonally striped pattern (for example a denim fabric) (Fig. 15).
- Satin weave – to make a satin weave at least five warps and wefts are needed. The warp and weft cross each other at points that do not touch. As a result either the warps or the wefts form floats on the front of the fabric giving it a soft shine (Fig. 16).

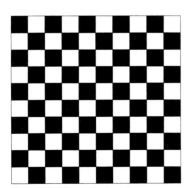

Figure 14 Schematic view of a plain weave.

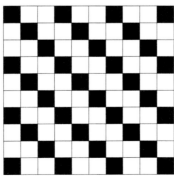

Figure 15 Schematic view of a twill weave.

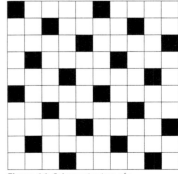

Figure 16 Schematic view of a satin weave.

All other weaving techniques are based upon the above-mentioned three principles. Some examples are:

- Velvet – a warp-pile weave in which the pile is produced by the warp that is raised in loops above the ground weave through the introduction of rods during weaving – the loops thus created may be left as loops or cut to form a pile.
- Lampas – a term used to indicate a figured weave in which the pattern (composed of weft floats bound by a binding warp) is added to a ground weave.
- Damask – a self-patterned weave (with one warp and one weft) in which the pattern is formed by a contrast of binding systems, usually satin.

1.5.4 Tapestries

The weaving of tapestries is based on the plain weave with – its most important feature – the wefts completely covering the warps. The image and fabric are created at the same time. The wefts do not run from selvedge to selvedge, but only cover that part of the warp where their colour is necessary for the design. Tapestries have another characteristic: when a tapestry is displayed, the direction of the warp is horizontal. This is for a practical reason because tapestries were originally made to cover entire walls. The widths of these walls varied considerably and were usually larger than the height of the room. If one considers that on a loom the warp has an infinite length, whereas the weft can only achieve the width of the loom, it becomes apparent that the height of a tapestry is better determined by the wefts, meaning that the width of the tapestry is determined by the length of the warps. Other explanations have also been put forward; in the design of the tapestry there are usually very strong architectural elements or trees and the contours of such design elements are easier to weave when they run horizontally on the loom. Another reason could be that tapestries shrink by roughly 5 cm per m after being removed from the loom as they recover from the tension applied on the warps when mounted on the loom. Such shrinkage would be less noticeable in the width of a tapestry than in the height. Whatever the explanation, the fact remains that tapestries are hung from the wefts, which means that the entire weight of the tapestry (on average 1 kg/m) hangs from the weakest element (Fig. 17).

1.5.5 Other techniques

Tablet weaving is a technique in which the warps run through holes in tablets. By rotating the tablets in relation to each other, patterns are formed. In the manufacture of oriental pile carpets, another technique is found – a combination of weaving on a loom and knotting. Around every two warps on the loom, short pieces of thread are knotted (several different knotting techniques can be used), with the ends pointing to the front to create a pile. Every row of knots is secured by several woven wefts followed by another row of knots, etc. (Fig. 18).

Threads can also be worked into fabric in other ways besides weaving, for example, by knitting and crochet. In these techniques, fabric is created by one endless thread and not, as is the case in weaving, from a system of threads. There are yet more techniques such as knotting (e.g. macramé, tatting, etc.), plaiting (sprang), needle lace and bobbin lace, in which threads are intertwined or knotted with each other. It is important to realise that the method of processing fibres in threads and fabric has a direct influence on the properties of a textile material. Linen damask has different properties from linen bobbin lace even though it is made from the same basic material, and felt has different qualities from knitted woollen fabric. With the application of a certain technique, stiffness (inflexibility), gloss and the insulating properties of a fabric can, among others, be manipulated.

1.5.6 Decorative techniques

Numerous techniques have been developed to embellish fabrics. Embroidery techniques create a pattern on the foundation fabric with needle and thread. A traditional means of practising embroidery techniques is the sampler; in which several different motifs were taught using mainly cross-stitch. Appliqué techniques employ pieces of fabric or other material (glass, beads, shells, stones) fixed to a fabric. In some techniques, threads are pulled together or removed from a fabric to create an open structure.

Metal thread
The application of metal threads, particularly silver and gold, has a long history. Metal threads were directly woven into the fabric or added later in the form of embroidery (Fig. 19). The earliest metal threads were made by cutting thin strips from precious metal sheets or by drawing thin rods of

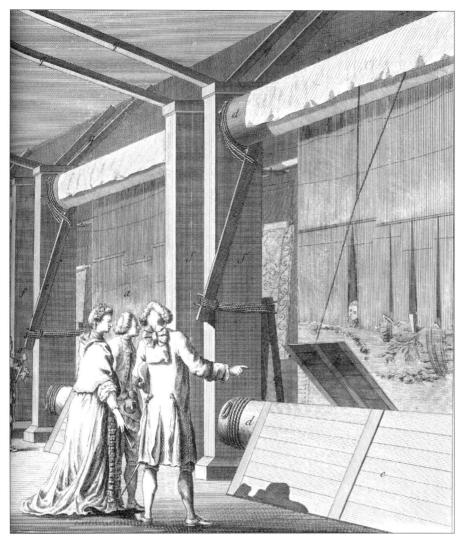

Figure 17 'Haute Lisse' loom (tapestry woven on a loom with the warp tensioned vertically) (Diderot 1959).

Figure 18 The knotting of a carpet on a vertical loom (Turkey) (photo courtesy A. Bruinsma).

pure metal through progressively smaller openings in a wooden or metal plate to form threads. These threads could, if necessary, be twisted in order to create a three-dimensional effect. Often the strips or threads were wrapped around a linen or silk core in order to make the thread stronger and to economise on metal for a given surface area. A cheaper method involved attaching gold or silver leaf to a support of paper, skin, gut or intestinal membrane. The gilded or silver-plated material was then cut into small strips, which were either worked into textiles directly or first wrapped around a textile core. In order to produce even cheaper metal threads, silver-gilt or silver-plated lesser quality metals such as copper were used; these were processed directly into threads or again first attached to a support. A huge variety of metal threads can be found on banners used in appliqué, embroidery and fringes.

In some cases, textile objects may not even be recognised as such, e.g. in the case of painted banners (Fig. 20). The enormous diversity of forms of textiles, the fibres from which they are made and the techniques of manufacture, make the safekeeping and care of textiles a complex undertaking.

1.6 Dyeing and printing textiles

One of the most frequently used decorative techniques is the dyeing of fibres, threads or fabrics. In the dyeing process, several different techniques can be applied to obtain specific effects. Instead of dyeing a piece of fabric as a whole (creating a uniform colour), areas can be tied off (tie-dye, plangi and tritik) or isolated (batik), so that the dye can only penetrate the exposed areas of the fabric (also referred to as resist dyeing). Warps and/or wefts can be dyed before they are woven into a fabric and used to create such designs as checks and stripes. Alternatively they can be tied off and dyed in order to create a pattern, a technique referred to as *ikat* (Fig. 21). Instead of dyeing fabric in a dye-bath, it can be printed using a variety of techniques. Until the end of the 19th century natural dyes were used, prepared from plants, animals and minerals. The first synthetic dyestuff, 'mauve', was discovered by the chemist William Henry Perkin in 1856 and from that time on synthetic dyes have been used progressively more in dyeing textiles.

Figure 19 Detail of embroidery with metal threads (photo courtesy ICAT textielrestauratie b.v.).

Figure 20 Remains of a painted banner (photo courtesy ICAT textielrestauratie b.v.).

1.6.1 Natural dyes

The natural dyes can be divided in three groups.

Vat dyes
These are dyes which are insoluble in water but which can be dissolved in an alkaline solution using a chemical process (reduction). The dissolved, reduced form is colourless and is referred to as the *leuco*-form of the dye. The textile is dipped into a vat containing this *leuco*-form, after which it is exposed to the air (Fig. 22). In the air, the *leuco*-form oxidises back to the original insoluble dye. The bond between these dyes and the textile is not very strong but the precipitated dye is mechanically fixed to the fibres. The obtained colours are relatively lightfast. The best-known example from this group is indigo, derived from plants belonging to the Indigofera

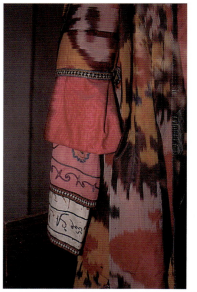

Figure 21 Details of a kaftan made from *ikat* and moiré fabrics (photo courtesy L. Hanssen).

Figure 22 An indigo vat (photo courtesy J.H. Hofenk de Graaff).

family, with the most important being *Indigofera tinctoria* L. from East Asia. Woad (*Isatis tinctoria* L.), which also belongs to the same family, produces the same blue dye and has been used for centuries in Europe. The purple dyes obtained from certain molluscs found in the Mediterranean and on the west coast of southern America were also applied as vat dyes. Purple was the most precious colour of ancient times as enormous numbers of molluscs are necessary to obtain even a small amount of dye. To illustrate this, only Roman emperors were allowed to use the purple colour in their togas.

Mordant dyes

Some natural dyes can only be successfully fixed to textile after an initial preparation of the fibres with mordants. This can be achieved with solutions of metals such as aluminium, tin and iron which bind to the fibre polymers. The mordant is not only used to bind the dyestuff to the fibre, making it more wetfast, but also affects the end colour. Following this process the textile is dipped into a dye-bath and the dye binds itself to the mordant. Examples of natural mordant dyes are:

- Kermes (from the Arabic, *qirmiz*), a crimson dyestuff. The females of the scale insect *Coccus ilicis* (renamed as *Kermes vermilio* (Planchon)), carry a water-soluble red dye called kermes. The colour component is kermesic acid. The insects, which live on oak trees in the Mediterranean region, are dried and crushed in order to obtain the dyestuff.
- Cochineal, used for the production of scarlet, crimson, orange and other tints, and for the preparation of lake and carmine. The scale insect *Dactylopius coccus cacti* (Costa) originates from Central America, where it feeds upon cacti (Fig. 23). The females carry the dye in their body; it is obtained by killing the insects in boiling water or in hot ovens. The colour component is carminic acid, which is related to kermesic acid. The dye was introduced into Europe from Mexico, where it had been in use long before the arrival of the Spaniards.
- Madder. Another widely used red dye which is obtained from the roots of the madder plant, *Rubia tinctorum* L. The colorants in madder are alizarin and purpurin.
- Weld. This is a yellow dyestuff obtained from *Reseda luteola* L. or dyer's rocket, which was cultivated in northern Europe.

Many tropical trees also contain dyestuffs which can be used to dye textile to shades of yellow, red and blue. These colours are not, however, very lightfast. Brazilwood was often used to produce red colours. A blue-black colour was obtained from logwood, more specifically from the tree *Haematoxilin campecheanum* L., indigenous to North and South America.

Direct dyes

These dyes can be used to dye fabric without any pre-treatment. The colours are often not very lightfast or wetfast. An example is the yellow colour derived from the roots of the *Curcuma longa* (Indian saffron or turmeric); others are the dyestuffs from chestnut and red cabbage. Direct dyes can sometimes be used with mordants in order to obtain a better wetfastness.

1.6.2 Synthetic dyes

The more modern, synthetic dyes can be classified on the basis of their chemical properties and the way they are bound to textile. The first synthetic dyes had very poor fastness to light and water. These factors should be considered when conserv-

Figure 23 Cochineal insects (photo courtesy J.H. Hofenk de Graaff).

ing or exhibiting dyed objects. After the First World War, synthetic dyes become increasingly stable.

Basic dyes
Basic dyes are often referred to as cationic dyes because when dissolved in water they form positively charged ions (cations). It is because of this charge that they bind strongly to the negatively charged surface of some textiles such as cotton and linen. The oldest synthetic dye, Perkin's mauve, belongs to this dye class.

Acid dyes
Acid dyes work in exactly the opposite way to basic dyes. Their ions are charged negatively (anions) and therefore bind better to the positively charged areas of textile fibres which are present in wool, silk and nylon. Acids are added to the bath to donate protons to the amino groups in these fibres, resulting in a positively charged surface.

Direct dyes
Direct dyes are water-soluble dyestuffs that can diffuse directly from solution into the textile fibres and are particularly suitable for dyeing cellulose fibres. Salts are often added to the dye-bath in order to increase the swelling of the fibres and to make the dyeing process more uniform.

Disperse dyes
Disperse dyes are dyestuffs which are not soluble in water but are dispersed in the dye-bath with the aid of an emulsifier. They are mainly used to dye synthetic fibres.

Reactive dyes
Reactive dyes are synthetic dyes that bind chemically to textiles and therefore have excellent fastness to water.

Premetallised dyes
Premetallised dyes are metal complex dyes. The dyestuff binds itself to the fibres using the already incorporated metal ion, which acts as a mordant.

1.7 Textile finishes/after treatments

There are many different ways in which textiles were and continue to be improved in order to enhance their natural qualities. A complete list would be never-ending so only a few processes are described below that can be found in textile collections and which have direct effects on the preservation of the material (Table 5) (see section 2.5).

Calendering and mangling
Linen and cotton fabrics can be treated in order to give them a smoother, glossier appearance and to make them more dirt-repellent. A smoother, shinier appearance is important, especially with damask weaves, to enable the details in the pattern to be seen more clearly. In calendering, the fabric is passed between heavy, smooth, heated rollers but the achieved result is not fast to water. An additional shine, which improved its fastness to water, was obtained by first treating the fabric with wax or rice milk (e.g. chintz) or by using gum arabic. When fabric is mangled, it is first wrapped around a roller before being rocked to and fro between two heated rollers.

Mercerising
Cotton fibres can be given more of a sheen by mercerising. For this purpose it is treated with an alkaline solution, which makes the fibres swell enormously. As the fibres swell in their width, they will shrink in their length; this shrinkage is prevented by keeping the cotton under tension, resulting in a certain gloss that is permanent. Mercerised cotton has a larger moisture regain and the fibres swell more than normal cotton.

Moiré
A watered effect in ribbed fabrics can be obtained by pulling a once-folded or doubled piece of fabric between heated rollers under pressure, while adjusting the tension continuously. A rippled or watered effect – which is random and not fast to water – is created in the fabric called moiré (Fig. 21).

Table 5 Textile finishes/after treatments.

Textile finishes	Brand name*
Moth-proofing	Eulan, Mitin
Fungicide finishes	Eulan-aspect, Sanitized
Waterproofing	Perlit, Persistol, Phobotex, DRI-SIL red
Water- and dirt-repellent	DRI-SIL blue, Zepel, Scotchguard, P-Silikon, Olcophobol
Flame-retardant	Aflamman, Proban, Pyrovatex Zirpro
Crease resistance	No-iron, Wash and Wear, Minicare, Sanfor-plus, Bell-o-fast
Durable press for wool	Siroset, Vouw Vast
Durable press (others)	Fixaform, Koratron
Anti-shrinkage	Santor, Superwash, Basolan, Dylan, Sironized

Distinct from later, industrially manufactured moiré, it often has a clear sharp crease down the middle of the fabric; the watered effect is mirrored. At the time of the Industrial Revolution, the effect was obtained with metal rollers in which the watered pattern was engraved. By rolling ribbed fabrics in this way a moiré effect was obtained but the fabrics were not fast to water unless treated with resin. This moiré can be recognised by a clearly repeating pattern. There are also imitations that are woven.

Starching
Starch is one of the most important aids to fixing creases and pleats as seen in, for instance, lace collars, bonnets and traditional costume. Starch is similar to cellulose, a water-insoluble poly-glucose, in this case built up from α-glucose units. Instead of a straight cellulose chain, starch consists of amylopectin and amylose – the latter has a helical molecule with a very open structure in which water molecules are easily held. This causes it to form a gel with water. Linen and cotton can be impregnated with starch before drying them in shape. The shape in which the starched fabric dries thus becomes stiff and fixed. Starch cannot easily be washed out by wet cleaning but can be adequately removed with an enzyme treatment. Starched three-dimensional textiles can cause a problem in storage (see section 6.3.5). Starched fabric is also dirt-repellent.

Weighted silk
Silk is often degummed, i.e. the sericin is dissolved from the pure silk (fibroin). This process causes a loss in weight of about 25% (see section 1.3.2). Traditionally, because it was sold by weight, silk was weighted in order to compensate for this loss. Silk was weighted with vegetable substances such as gum arabic or tannins, which resulted in an increase back to the original weight (à pari) or sometimes even 25% above the original weight (above pari). The advantages of weighting silk in this manner were an increase in volume, better preservation (comparable to the tanning of leather) and improved results with dyeing. Other water-soluble weighting materials were used such as sugar or animal glue which had no improving effect on the preservation.

In the 19th century there was an increase in the demand for silk, and silk fabrics with a heavy drape and a rustling sound became popular and fashionable. Because the natural weighting of silk was not sufficient, processes were sought to weight the silk even further. Using tin salts, silk could be weighted up to 300% above pari by using a process in which it was alternately dipped in tin chloride and tin phosphate baths, with a final dip in a solution of sodium silicate. This process, often referred to as the dynamite process of weighting, resulted in extremely vulnerable silk that quickly degraded in storage and sometimes even combusted spontaneously. In the 20th century, the weighting of silk became less important as semi-synthetic and synthetic fibres emerged (although initially rayon was sometimes weighted). Unfortunately, due to the disastrous effects of tin weighting, only relatively few silk costumes from the end of the 19th and the beginning of the 20th century are still preserved in our collections. Where they do exist, they are often in poor condition (see section 2.5): extremely brittle, fragile (many slits can often be seen in either the warp or weft direction of the weaves, and even at an angle) and are often not capable of carrying their own weight (Fig. 24).

Moth-proofing agents
After the Second World War, woollen fabrics were treated with chemicals that deterred the caterpillars of moths from feeding on the wool (e.g. Élan and Mitin). These materials are wetfast and can also be dry cleaned. These chemicals can also be found in historic textiles such as tapestries and carpets, which were treated after the Second World War (see section 5.4.3).

Waterproofing agents
There has always been a need for making fabrics water-repellent, for example, in the fishing industry. Specially treated fishermen's clothing has been preserved from the 19th century and the beginning of the 20th century: linen shirts, sou'westers, etc. were coated with linseed oil to make them waterproof.

Figure 24 Detail of degraded weighted silk (photo courtesy ICAT textielrestauratie b.v., collection Drents Museum Assen).

This type of clothing is difficult to preserve: as the oil becomes hard it often stiffens the underlying textile.

Natural rubber was also used, applied as a very thin layer on top of the fabric (e.g. raincoats). This layer can often be seen to have crumbled with time. At present, synthetic materials are used to make textiles water- and even dirt-repellent such as DRI-SIL and Scotchguard.

Flame-retarding agents
Cellulose fibres are especially inflammable. This is one of the reasons why fire regulations demand that furnishing textiles and textiles used in exhibitions (not the textile objects themselves) are made fire-retardant. By the 17th century, research was being carried out into flame-retarding agents for textiles used in theatres. An English patent from 1735 describes the use of alum, borax, vitriol and copperas to make textiles and paper products fireproof. In 1913, the so-called 'Non-Flam' treatment was invented; fabric was treated with sodium stannate and then ammonium sulphate, followed by washing and drying (Lyons 1970: 166). After the Second World War, extensive research was carried out to improve fire retardants. Current treatments include:

- For cotton; the use of ammonium phosphates, silicates, borates and other salts added to fabric by submerging it in a bath. After treatment, the tenacity of the textile is reduced by 10%. In addition, acid products remain after treatment that will accelerate the natural degradation of the material. The most commonly used fire retardant is tetrakis (hydroxymethyl) phosphonium chloride (THPC). Another is n-methylol dimethylphosphonopropionamide (Pyrovatex CP). Textiles treated with either material become stiffer and the tenacity of the fibres is adversely affected.

- For wool; ortho- and metaphosphoric acid, sulphuric acid, ammonium borate and potassium percarbonate are used. These materials are usually sponged onto the textile, but can also be added in a bath. They can cause up to 22% shrinkage and will embrittle and weaken the textile. Other treatments involve the use of insoluble materials such as Zirpro (zirconium and titanium) or tetra-bromophthalic acid (TBPA). Fabrics treated with these tend to yellow more quickly.

Because of the adverse effects of the above-mentioned treatments, they are only intended for textiles used in the decoration of an exhibition and not for objects, although some tapestries and wall-hangings may have been treated in the past (Boetzelaer-Korotkova 2000).

Crease-resisting agents
The disadvantage of cotton, and particularly linen, is the fact that they crease. Industry has found an answer in non-iron fabrics by treating cellulose materials with urea-formaldehyde synthetic resins, which make the fabric stiffer by means of adapting their three-dimensional structure thus reducing creasing. Other agents for making cellulosic and polyester fabrics crease-resistant are melamine formaldehyde, dimethylol-ethylene urea (DMEU) and dihydroxy-dimethylol-ethylene urea (DHDMEU). These materials fill the amorphous area of the textile fibre (Timar-Balazsy and Eastop 1998: 106). The disadvantage is that the tenacity of the textile decreases and it can cause yellowing, especially if the textile is stored in plastic.

Durable press agents
Durable press agents make pleats in textiles resistant to normal usage, washing and/or dry cleaning. Finishes of similar chemical type as the above-mentioned crease-resisting agents have been used.

2

Degradation of textiles

Textiles are composed mainly of organic materials, characterised by polymers which have been built up from carbon chains (see section 1.1). These are subject to 'ageing'. Fibres processed into textiles will eventually turn to dust. Both natural and man-made fibres are subject to degradation. Inorganic fibres such as asbestos, glass fibre and metal thread suffer less from natural degradation processes and therefore have a longer life expectancy.

Three types of chemical reaction play a role in the degradation of organic materials: (photo-)oxidation; hydrolysis and cross-linking. These reactions are accelerated or delayed by environmental conditions; in addition, textiles can also degrade due to physical-mechanical forces (damage caused by tension, stretching, etc.). While these processes are discussed individually in the following subsections, it should be realised that in reality they can all contribute to the deterioration of textiles. Chemical degradation reactions are discussed for each fibre type, followed by findings on physical-mechanical processes.

2.1 Natural decay of cellulose

The chemical degradation of all plant fibres, and those semi-synthetic fibres made from cellulose (for example, viscose), occur according to three reaction types; (photo-)oxidation, hydrolysis and cross-linking. These reactions start in the amorphous areas (the most accessible parts of the fibre) and continue with extreme degradation in the crystalline areas. These chemical reactions are accelerated in the presence of moisture, light, air pollution and raised temperatures.

2.1.1 Oxidation

Oxidation is the process in which the hydroxyl or alcohol groups (C-OH side groups), which are present in the cellulose chain, are turned into aldehyde, ketone or even carboxyl groups (depending upon the position of the hydroxyl group within the glucose ring) in the presence of oxygen. When oxidation proceeds further, the glucose ring finally breaks (Fig. 25).

The results of these oxidation reactions on the appearance of the cellulose fibre can be observed with the naked eye. Plant fibres, such as cotton and linen, will turn yellow in due course. This yellowing is an indication of the formation of aldehyde and ketone groups, which are also referred to as chromophoric (i.e. colour-rendering) groups. The yellow colour of degraded plant fibres is furthermore caused by the presence of aromatic impurities. Old cellulose material often has an acidic smell caused by the acidic degradation products resulting from chain scission (a breaking of the bond between two glucose rings), which in turn is the result of extreme oxidation. It should be noted here that when advanced oxidation occurs, the material eventually turns lighter again. This 'bleaching' is

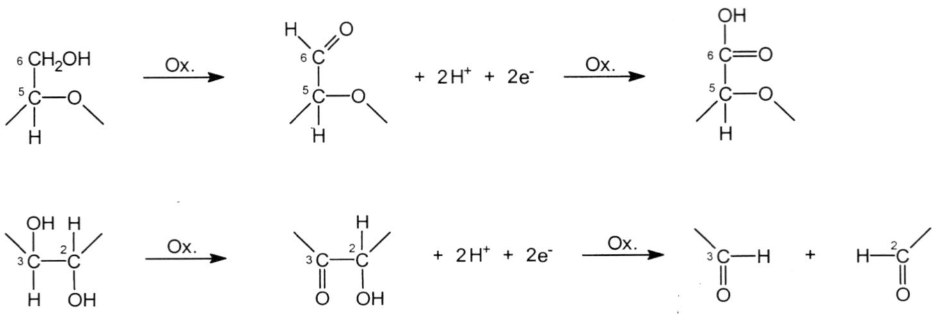

Figure 25 Oxidation of the different hydroxyl groups in cellulose (courtesy L.J. Pedersoli jr., Netherlands Institute for Cultural Heritage).

the result of advanced oxidation of both chromophoric aldehyde and ketone groups to colourless side groups.

Extreme oxidation has another disadvantage for cellulose: with the reduction in the degree of polymerisation (DP), the tenacity of the material will decrease; in other words, the material weakens.

2.1.2 Hydrolysis

Hydrolysis causes chain scission, but can also result in ring scission (a break within the glucose ring) (Fig. 26). In this context, hydrolysis is the absorption of water which results in the breakage of ether bonds. This reaction is catalysed by hydrogen ions, moisture content and temperature; hydrogen ions can be released in the above-mentioned oxidation reactions.

Scissions in the cellulose chain will result in a decrease of the degree of polymerization (DP) and a loss in strength. When ring scission occurs, more terminal hydroxyl groups are formed, which in turn are more sensitive to oxidation.

2.1.3 Cross-linking

There are many different ways in which the polymer chains of cellulose can cross-link but the end result is that adjacent chains become connected by chemical bonds. The most obvious cross-linking is the formation of hydrogen bonds between hydroxyl groups in adjacent cellulose chains. Although hydrogen bonds are relatively strong non-covalent bonds, they can be broken and formed in new positions. The ether (covalent) bonds are a lot stronger and consequently considerably more energy will be needed in order to break them (Fig. 27).

Textile material becomes noticeably stiffer and more brittle as a result of cross-linking. Extremely cross-linked cellulose material feels like paper to the touch and is very fragile. Inappropriate handling of such material can cause a lot of damage; the textile can easily split along folds and creases and it may crumble when touched.

2.1.4 Influence of environmental circumstances

The decomposition of cellulose due to the above-mentioned three processes is stimulated by oxygen

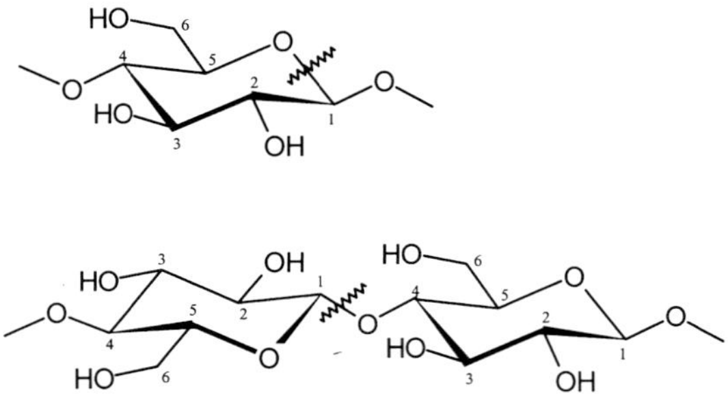

Figure 26 The hydrolysis of cellulose resulting in ring scission (above) and chain scission (below) (courtesy L.J. Pedersoli jr., Netherlands Institute for Cultural Heritage).

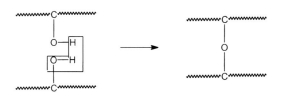

Figure 27 The formation of ether bonds (cross-linking) (courtesy L.J. Pedersoli jr., Netherlands Institute for Cultural Heritage).

in the air (oxidation), the presence of moisture (hydrolysis) and is further accelerated by raised temperatures. Light, both visible and invisible (ultraviolet (UV) and infrared (IR) radiation), also speeds up these chemical reactions (see Ch. 4). UV radiation delivers enough energy to start oxidation. IR radiation delivers energy in the form of heat, which accelerates degradation reactions. Some fibres become more sensitive to degradation under the influence of light, e.g. viscose, to which pigments may have been added during manufacture. Some of these pigments propagate degradation reactions.

Pollution in the atmosphere or in the textile itself also stimulates deterioration. Traces of metals such as iron, copper and manganese can act as catalysts in oxidation. Air pollutants such as nitrogen oxides (NO_x) and sulphur oxides (SO_x) form strong acids in the presence of moisture and thereby accelerate the hydrolysis of cellulose.

In addition to the chemical degradation processes described above, cellulose suffers from another form of decay, namely biological degradation. When environmental conditions are favourable, fungi and bacteria can attack cellulose. These microorganisms secrete enzymes that can break down otherwise indigestible cellulose into matter that they can digest (see section 5.2).

2.2 Natural decay of proteins

The degradation of protein fibres such as wool (hair), silk, fur and feathers is caused by influences similar to those that contribute to the decay of cellulose. The composition of proteins is more complex than that of cellulose, and it is beyond the scope of this book to discuss degradation reactions in detail. Proteins are composed of different amino acids, with a great variety of side groups in the polymer chains. In general it can be stated that silk degrades more quickly than wool. The greater sensitivity of silk to UV radiation and visible light compared to wool, for example, is accounted for by these differences in structure.

2.2.1 Photodegradation

Of all the natural fibres, silk is the most sensitive to light. The amino acids tryptophan, tyrosine and phenylalanine, which are present in silk, absorb light with a wavelength of 220 to 370 nm (i.e. in the UV region). The energy of the absorbed light is used in the oxidation of these amino acids, and causes the formation of chromophoric groups (Fig. 28). The results can be seen with the naked eye as silk becomes yellow or sometimes even light pink. Free radicals are formed which can cause chain scission, leading to a decrease of the degree of polymerisation (DP) and cross-linking. The silk changes colour, becomes brittle and weakens. Photodegradation – degradation caused by light – is influenced strongly by the acidity (pH) of the silk and its environment (Timar-Balazsy and Eastop 1998: 45, 46).

In wool, light causes oxidation that results in a yellowing and a loss in strength; furthermore, the

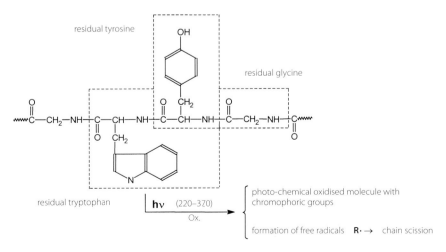

Figure 28 Degradation reactions in wool/hair and silk (courtesy L.J. Pedersoli jr., Netherlands Institute for Cultural Heritage).

free radicals cause chain scission and, in turn, form new cross-links, as a result of which the wool eventually becomes stiffer and brittle (Timar-Balazsy and Eastop 1998: 51, 52) (Fig. 28).

2.2.2 Hydrolysis

The protein chains are not only damaged by oxidation but also by hydrolysis. This can occur in both acidic and alkaline conditions. In an acid environment, salt linkages and hydrogen bonds break; protein chains break at the common peptide bond (the bond that links the amino acids together). This results in a decrease in the degree of polymerisation (DP), which causes a loss in strength. The amino acid cysteine present in wool and hair contains sulphur, which makes these materials more resistant to acid hydrolysis.

In an alkaline environment, the hydrolysis of protein fibres affects the ends of the protein chains. Cross-linking is encouraged between specific amino acid side chains. The rupture of salt linkages and hydrogen bonds caused by the alkali can result in a changed structure and hence less resistance to further deterioration. Wool and silk do not lose their strength as such but become stiffer and more brittle in mild alkaline conditions. More concentrated solutions of alkalis cause more serious damage to protein fibres and may even dissolve them.

2.2.3 Influence of environmental circumstances

The presence of oxygen, moisture and pollutants also plays a part in the degradation of wool and silk. It is known that wool will photodegrade ten times faster in humid conditions than in dry conditions (Timar-Balazsy and Eastop 1998: 51). Wool and silk are also subject to biological degradation. Most of the microorganisms concerned are not capable of breaking down wool and silk into digestible products, as is the case with cellulose. Even so, fungi and bacteria can grow on protein fibres, especially if there is enough nutrition present in stains and soiling, for example, to feed these organisms. Insects, however, represent a greater threat to protein fibres: the larvae of moths and different types of beetle can feed on wool, silk (less attractive than wool) and other animal materials such as feathers, skins etc., especially when soiled. It is assumed that the larvae secrete a substance, which pre-treats the material to make it digestible (see section 5.1).

2.3 Natural decay of other fibre material

Chemical degradation of semi-synthetic fibres follows more or less the same reaction process, which causes the raw materials to decay. The degradation of rayon and acetate fibres is therefore similar to that of cellulose, bearing in mind that these semi-synthetic fibres often have a lower DP and will therefore lose their strength more quickly.

During the production of these fibres, some materials may have been added, such as antioxidants, which slow down natural decay. In the course of the 20th century, synthetic fibres were developed with a very high resistance to degradation. In the early days of their development this was not the case. The early synthetic fibres were very difficult to preserve and are today often in a bad condition. The largest contributory factor in the decay of these early synthetic materials has been light. Synthetic materials have become more resistant to photodegradation as their production processes have developed.

Polyamide fibres (such as nylon) however, are still the most light-sensitive of all synthetic fibres. As polyamide fibres resemble proteins in a chemical sense, they will show similar chemical degradation. Nylon, for example, cannot withstand acids and alkalis very well – resulting in yellowing and a loss in strength.

Polyester fibres are extremely resistant to degradation, partly due to their high crystallinity. It is only when these fibres are exposed for a long time to, for example, light, acids and alkalis, that chemical degradation will occur.

By far the most resistant to light are acrylic fibres; even when exposed to sunlight these fibres lose very little strength. This is because during this process, ring structures are formed which are very stable (Gohl and Vilensky 1987: 97). It should also be noted that acrylic fibres are very crystalline.

In theory, synthetic fibres do not suffer from biological degradation by microorganisms or insects because the material is totally indigestible. Even so, biological decay can occur; fungi, bacteria and even insects can feed on dirt or a finish which could be digestible. Sometimes insects or rodents can gnaw their way through indigestible material in order to reach food beyond.

2.4 Physical-mechanical processes

The physical-mechanical processes described below contribute to the degradation of textiles.

2.4.1 Response to moisture

All fibres can absorb and release moisture to a certain degree depending upon: the fibre type; the relative humidity (RH) and the temperature of the environment. This moisture is partly chemically bound (structural water) and partly present as condensed liquid water in the fibre. The moisture present in the fibre acts as a plasticiser in the amorphous regions of the polymer, as it allows the polymer chains in the fibre to move in relation to each other without causing damage.

The moisture in the fibre constantly tries to maintain an equilibrium with the moisture content of the surrounding atmosphere. When the RH decreases, the fibre will release moisture in order to restore the equilibrium; on the other hand, when the RH increases, the fibre will absorb moisture. As a result of this absorption and release of water, the shape of the fibre constantly changes; fibres swell when they absorb and shrink when they release moisture. Fibres will wear and eventually break due to constant changes in their shape. When fibres are processed into threads and fabrics, they will rub against each other and consequently may cause damage to themselves (see section 3.1.2).

It is important to discuss a second phenomenon here, namely hysteresis. When a fibre absorbs moisture in dry conditions, the process of absorption will, at first, proceed quickly and then slowly level out until equilibrium with the environment is achieved. When the same fibre is then forced to release moisture, due to a decrease in the RH, this process will also proceed more quickly at the beginning and eventually level out when the new equilibrium is reached. When these two processes are represented on a graph, it can be observed that more moisture remains in the fibre at a certain RH when the fibre is releasing moisture, than at the same RH when the fibre was absorbing moisture. This phenomenon is called hysteresis (Fig. 29).

With regard to the conservation of historic textiles, this phenomenon can be used to treat extremely dehydrated and brittle textiles. By exposing such materials to a high RH, or even a wet treatment, a higher moisture content will remain in the fibre after treatment, restoring the flexibility of the fibre to a certain extent. The decision to treat a textile in this way should be left to the professional textile conservator as other unwanted effects can occur besides the desired hysteresis, such as mechanical damage due to swelling, dye bleeding, removal of finishes, etc.

2.4.2 Response to mechanical forces

One of the characteristics most appreciated in textiles is their flexibility. This flexibility of a finished textile is partly determined by the characteristics of the fibres used, such as the degree of crystallinity (see section 1.1.2). For example, a linen fabric will crease more easily than a similar fabric made from wool. The ultimate flexibility of a material is influenced by the method by which the fibres are processed into a textile, to be precise, the twist and ply of the threads and the way in which threads are interwoven, e.g. by weaving or knitting. A loosely woven fabric will be more supple than a densely woven fabric, and a knitted fabric will be more flexible than most woven fabrics.

All fibres, yarns and fabrics will respond in a specific way to mechanical forces, which can be present in textiles in the form of folds, creases and their own weight. In the following paragraphs, the term 'textile' is used when referring to fibre, yarn or fabric.

A textile can be stretched by different forces including its own weight. The mass of an object is pulled by the forces of gravity; the larger the mass, the greater the force. A tapestry stretches under its own weight when it hangs on a wall. The fabric of a dress with a heavy skirt which has been hung on a coat hanger will be stretched at the shoulders. A textile can also be stretched locally in, for example, folds, pleats and creases. Sometimes a textile is stretched under tension deliberately, e.g. embroidery stretched on a frame or upholstery on furniture.

When expressing the elongation of a textile on a graph against the force applied, the curve shown in Figure 30 is obtained. There is an obvious yield point illustrated in this curve and structural changes in the textile occur when this yield point is passed. Within fibres, the polymer chains

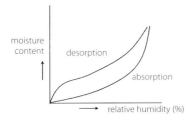

Figure 29 Hysteresis in the absorption and release of moisture by a textile fibre. At the same relative humidity, the moisture content when absorbing moisture is constantly lower than when releasing moisture.

slide alongside each other and chemical bonds are broken; in yarns, the fibres slide alongside each other. If the force is released before it reaches the yield point, the textile will return to its old shape; however, once the yield point is passed, although the textile can partly return to its old shape owing to its flexible character, there will remain some degree of permanent deformation. If the forces applied are too great for the textile it will eventually break.

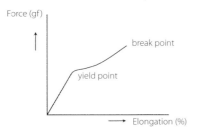

Figure 30 The elongation of textile (after Graaf 1980: 55).

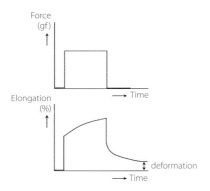

Figure 31 The elongation of textile due to long-term stress (after Graaf 1980: 57).

Figure 32 Damage occurring alongside a fold (photo courtesy ICAT textielrestauratie b.v.).

In the case of a tapestry hanging on a wall or a dress on a coat hanger in storage, the forces present will have the effect shown in Figure 31. At first, the textile will be stretched out fairly quickly, but in time this will level out. If the weight or force applied is reasonably large (about three-quarters of the tenacity of the material), there is a chance that the textile might eventually break; however, if the tension applied to the textile is released before this happens, the textile will partly return to its former shape and a permanent deformation will have occurred.

2.4.3 Response to tension

The question that arises now is how does tension influence the preservation of textiles? The answer is that textiles under tension will degrade more quickly than those that are relaxed. The consequences of long-term stress can often be seen in historic textiles. A textile will break first at its pleats and folds (Fig. 32). Slits can occur over a period of time in embroideries that are mounted on a stretcher frame. The top part of a tapestry that hangs on the wall is often in worse condition than the bottom part. It should be taken into consideration that in some tapestries the top part, representing the sky, is often woven mainly in silk that has usually been bleached. Fumes from burning sulphur (sulphur dioxide) have been used for bleaching since the Middle Ages, a process which has proved to be extremely aggressive. These light silk areas are therefore not very strong and are ultra-sensitive to degradation. The silk becomes brittle and powdery, resulting in fibre loss, and splits may also occur.

2.5 Intrinsic decay

The different characteristics of weighted silk (as described in section 1.7) and bleached silk lead us to one of the most important factors in the degradation of textiles: the method by which they are produced, processed and manufactured. For centuries, textiles have been manipulated in diverse ways in order to give them certain characteristics. Dyeing or printing processes using mordants introduce various metals into the textile. Some of these metals act as catalysts in the degradation of textiles, accelerating the degradation process. An example of this can be seen in some chintzes, where the black outlines of the motifs are often in poor condition

Figure 33 Detail in a patchwork blanket showing damage caused by mordants (photo courtesy ICAT textielrestauratie b.v.).

and sometimes even completely lost (see section 1.7 and Fig. 33). When chintz is made, the mordant tannin (derived from oak apples, oak bark and certain plants) is applied locally (by painting or printing). Following this, a solution of iron(II) sulphate is applied. The iron ions are oxidised to form black iron(III) tannate with the tannin. If the textile is not rinsed properly after this process, harmful substances remain. Damage is caused by sulphuric acid, which is formed from the remnants of iron(II) sulphate in combination with moisture from the atmosphere. The metal ions act as catalysts in the oxidative degradation of textiles.

Another example of intrinsic decay is that which occurs in the silk American flags made during the Civil War. The white stripes are often in very bad condition; they have turned a brown colour and display many slits. In the red stripes, the silk is in a somewhat better condition, but also displays yellowing and slits. The blue silk, however, is often in almost pristine condition. How is it possible that the same material (silk) in one object can degrade in such a variety of ways? Research showed that an explanation could be found in the bleaching of silk. Natural silk is not white but has a yellowish hue. This colour was not acceptable for the white stripes of the national flag, which is why the silk had to be bleached. The bleaching method used was very aggressive and consequently this affected the silk during the bleaching process. Due to an excess of acid, which remained in the silk, decay was accelerated over time. In order to dye a deeper colour red for the red stripes, the silk only had to be slightly bleached; but for dyeing blue, unbleached silk could be used – hence the differences in degradation (Boersma 1993, 1996).

There are many more examples of degradation inherent in an object. Sometimes the conservator can slow down further decay; in the case of the American flags from the Civil War, the excess of acid was rinsed out in a wet treatment. In the case of the black outlines in the chintz, premature support of weak areas could have prevented the loss of textile fragments. In many cases, however, there is no known remedial conservation treatment to prevent this inherent degradation. In these instances only preventive conservation can make a difference: care should be taken to keep these types of object under the best possible conditions.

2.6 Other factors

As stated at the beginning of this chapter, the deterioration of textiles is a complex matter involving several different types of degradation reactions, which, in turn, are influenced by other factors. Listed below are those factors mentioned earlier, together with those not yet discussed. Very often the cause of damage cannot be seen directly, but it is important to be aware that all damage is cumulative!

Light
Light is extremely harmful to textiles. In addition to visible light, UV and IR radiation also damage textiles (see Ch. 4).

Moisture
A certain amount of moisture is necessary to maintain the flexible character of textiles. When the moisture content is too high, degradation accelerates and the growth of microorganisms is stimulated. On the other hand a low RH will dry out the textile, resulting in a loss of flexibility. Strong fluctuations in RH are detrimental to the optimum preservation of textiles (see Ch. 3). The effects of fluctuating RH can be observed in, for example, the brown edges of folded white linen sheets which have been kept in a wooden cupboard for too long. The constant absorption and release of moisture (referred to as a 'wet/dry' interface) causes degradation reactions to take place, which produce a brown discoloration. As water diffuses due to fluctuating RH, these degradation products are transported to the surface of the textile, where the concentration of these coloured products will become visible.

Temperature
Temperature has a direct influence on the speed of degradation reactions: the higher the temperature, the more quickly reactions take place. In general, it can be said that each temperature increase of 10 °C

may result in the doubling of a reaction's speed. This is one of the reasons why ironing is not recommended for historic textiles. Dry heat also causes desiccation and physical degradation of textiles (Timar-Balazsy and Eastop 1998: 16).

Temperature can also influence the development of insects. In northwest Europe, which has a temperate climate, those insects that represent a real threat to textile collections will reproduce more slowly at temperatures below 15 °C.

Air pollution
Apart from the well-known industrial pollutants such as sulphur and nitrogen oxides, other pollutants may also be present. For example, organic acidic vapours can be released from wooden showcases or cupboards (see section 6.2.2).

Intrinsic degradation
Intrinsic decay of an object can be due to: an unfortunate combination of materials (an iron frame in a silk parasol); the decoration technique (the iron-gall outlines in chintz); or the production process (weighted silk). Certain decorations or accessories such as those made from cellulose nitrate and cellulose acetate can produce harmful acidic degradation products (see section 6.3.6). Preventive conservation is often the only means of slowing down such decay.

Soiling and stains
The majority of objects in most textile collections will be soiled to some degree; clothing has been worn, interior textiles such as carpets have often been used extensively, and ethnographic textiles often still carry the 'aroma' of the country of origin. This dirt is not always unwanted – soiling and stains can contribute to a better understanding of an object and its historic authenticity – but there is one type of dirt that can be largely eliminated: 'museum dust'. One of the characteristics of textile is that air passes through it and it will catch and retain particles from the air, which make it dirty. Dust is hygroscopic and absorbs air pollutants; it can provide nutrients for (harmful) organisms.

Soiling and stains contribute to the decay of textiles. Dust may contain small, sharp particles which can work their way between the fibres, slowly cutting through the material as the textile moves. Stains may be hard and can make a textile brittle. Soiling and stains can also cause chemical degradation as they are often acidic and stimulate hydrolysis. Dirty textiles are more attractive to insects and microorganisms. The damaging effects of insects and fungi on textiles are discussed in Chapter 5 (see also section 10.4.1).

Handling
People are probably the biggest cause of damage to textiles. It appears to be so easy to move a textile object: just fold the object several times and carry it on one arm, leaving the other free to open doors. This approach is wrong and can cause irreversible damage (see Ch. 7).

Calamities and disasters
Severe damage can be caused by fire and water. Most textiles are flammable materials which burn easily when subjected to fire. Floods are often less destructive, but still happen all too often and cause irreparable damage. A burst water pipe, a clogged drain or a malfunction in the sprinkling system can cause irreversible damage. Prevention is better than cure! Other types of calamities or disasters include vandalism, crime or even war (see section 12.3).

2.7 Identifying degradation

There are several signs, or indicators, for degradation in textiles.

Fading
Light affects not only the fibres but also the dyes that are used to colour a fabric. The fading of colours is an exponential process which at first occurs rapidly and eventually slows down but will continue until the colour is completely faded. The original colour of a textile can often be seen on the

Figure 34 A locally faded dress (photo courtesy ICAT textielrestauratie b.v., collection Stedelijk Museum Kampen).

reverse which may have been protected against the influences of direct light (Fig. 34). In tapestries, the difference between obverse and reverse can be quite startling.

Yellowing
In undyed textiles, especially those made from cellulose, a yellowing or browning is a clear indication of degradation.

Loss of strength
The loss in a textile's strength only becomes apparent once damage has occurred. Before handling any textile, loss of strength should be anticipated and small visible indicators should be searched for, i.e. small splits in the fabric, fibre loss and a dusty appearance. Thus, all textiles should be handled with the greatest care.

Loss of flexibility
It may be possible to feel if a textile has become less flexible, although great care should be taken if assessing this by touch. Loss of flexibility may be caused by embrittlement or desiccation of the material, or by the degradation of decorative layers (such as paint layers) or textile finishes/after treatments. Conservation treatments may also affect the flexibility of a textile: applying a support often reduces an object's flexibility.

Acidity
A 'stuffy' or 'musty' smell is often an indication of degraded textile. Objects made from animal fibres (e.g. tapestries) can sometimes release an almost pleasant smell of stock or broth; this may be noticeable when tapestries that have been rolled and packed for a long time are unrolled.

3

The museum environment

The lifespan of a textile depends largely on the environmental conditions in which it is kept. Twentieth-century banners, such as those of trade unions or local brass bands, which were previously carried outdoors in parades, are today in poor condition. They were often stored after a parade while they were still wet or damp, which led to damage from fungi and insects, bleeding colours, 'blooming' of paint layers (a general term used for describing a paint layer which has become opaque), detached parts, tears, stains (ring marks) and oxidised metal parts (Fig. 35).

The longevity of a textile collection is influenced by the properties of the environment to which it is exposed. The temperature and relative humidity (RH) and the degree of pollution in the air all play an important part in the degradation processes of organic and inorganic materials.

Figure 35 Front and reverse of a banner damaged by water, which resulted in the bleeding of colours and stains (ring marks) (photos courtesy ICAT textielrestauratie b.v., collection H.V.B.V. 'De Tien', personnel division of the Haarlem Fire Brigade).

3.1 The properties of the environment

3.1.1 Temperature

Temperature is a measure of the average energy of molecular motion in a substance. Heat is the total energy of molecular motion in a substance. In general, as heat energy increases, thereby increasing the vibration, rotation or forward motion of the molecules, the temperature will increase. Temperature is measured in degrees Celsius, Fahrenheit or Kelvin. Heat is measured in joules or calories (1 calorie (cal) = 4.186 joules). A calorie is the amount of heat needed to raise the temperature of one gram of water by one degree Celsius. Heat can be transferred from one place to another by three methods: conduction (in solids); convection (of fluids (liquids or gases)) and by means of infrared radiation. Sources of heat in a museum may include the sun, heating systems, machinery, lights and people. The radiant heat of the sun and artificial light sources can cause the temperature to rise markedly in small and enclosed spaces, e.g. showcases.

In general, the lower the temperature at which objects are kept, the less they are at risk from damage by chemical or biological factors. Furthermore, it is very important to control fluctuations in temperature, as changes in temperature cause changes in the RH of the environment (see section 3.1.2). Most objects are sensitive to changes in RH. Keeping a textile collection at a low temperature may not be very practical – apart from the high costs involved in maintaining a low temperature, it is also more difficult to control the eventual move of a textile object from storage to exhibition. A practical compromise is to keep textile collections at a temperature between 16 and 18 °C, both day and night (Michalski 1992a; Paine 1998: 36). Slow temperature changes as a result of the changing seasons are acceptable. Extreme fluctuations should be avoided.

The temperature of the environment can cause damage to objects by three different processes:

- Physical processes influence the behaviour of a material without changing its chemical structure; a model made of wax for example, can melt. Materials expand when they warm up and shrink when they cool down, and the extent to which they do this depends on the material. This phenomenon can lead to internal stresses in objects composed of different materials such as banners, costumes, shoes, etc. and will eventually result in damage.
- Chemical processes change the chemical composition of a material. In general, the speed of chemical reactions doubles when the temperature increases by 10 °C. In the case of materials made from cellulose, the speed of chemical reactions more than doubles if the temperature rises by 5 °C (Thomson 1978: 41).
- The biological processes of living organisms such as insects and fungi, can damage organic materials. Every insect species has an optimum temperature for its metabolism (see Ch. 5).

3.1.2 Relative humidity

The maximum quantity of moisture that the air can contain is dependent on its temperature. The term 'relative humidity' (RH) is used to describe the moisture content in the air. It is the relationship between the quantity of moisture actually present in the air (expressed in grams per m³) and the maximum quantity of moisture that the air can contain at the same temperature (this is not, however, the complete picture as no consideration has been given to the atmospheric pressure). This relationship is expressed as a percentage. At any given temperature, air which contains the maximum amount of moisture has an RH of 100%. An RH of 0% means that the air is completely dry. This is expressed in a formula as Equation 1 (below).

As the temperature rises, the air can hold more moisture. In a closed space, when the temperature rises the amount of moisture present remains the same – the RH, however, decreases. Conversely, in a closed space, if the temperature decreases and the amount of moisture remains the same, the RH increases (see Fig. 36b). When a person wearing spectacles enters a warm room from the cold, the glasses will steam up if they are below the dewpoint, i.e. below the temperature at which water vapour starts to condense from the surrounding warmer air. This is because the air cools down

$$RH = \frac{\text{weight of moisture present in the air}}{\text{maximum potential weight of moisture in the air at the same temperature}} \times 100\%$$

Equation 1

when it comes into contact with the cold glasses upon which the moisture, which the cooled air can no longer hold, condenses on the surface of the glass. Once they warm up, the glasses will become clear again as the condensation evaporates.

Absolute humidity (AH)
Figure 36 shows 1 m³ filled with air at a temperature of 20 °C. Assuming that 17 g of water vapour is added to saturate the air, then condensation will occur if even more moisture is added. This process depends on the temperature, as warm air can hold more water vapour than cold air. The absolute humidity (AH) is the amount of water vapour in grams per m³ of air (or g/kg dry air). A volume of air is characterised by the following parameters: temperature, RH and AH. By using a psychrometric chart (see Fig. 41), it is possible to predict the changes that will occur when one of these parameters changes. It can also be used to identify a particular indoor climate and to establish which measures are necessary to improve it.

Damage to textile objects caused by changes in RH and levels of RH
All organic materials respond to changes in RH because they are porous, hygroscopic and in many cases hydrophilic. This means that these materials will release moisture into the environment at a low RH as a result of which they will shrink. Conversely they will absorb moisture at a high RH, thereby swelling or expanding. Objects do not shrink and swell evenly; a material will respond more quickly to changes in RH at its surface than internally. This can cause internal stresses, resulting in damage. The risk of damage is greater:

- the greater the difference between the original and final RH;
- the more hygroscopic the material;
- the more complex the construction of the object, for example, when solid parts are combined with hollow ones;
- the less the flexibility of an object or when an object is constrained, an example being an embroidery mounted on a stretcher frame.

High RH
Most organic materials swell at a high RH, e.g. a piece of wood or paper. Textiles behave slightly differently; the fibres of textiles will swell in their width when they absorb moisture, but this process is inhibited by the fact that fibres are usually twisted and plied into threads, which are often restrained in a fabric. Because fibres swell in their width a contraction is caused, which results in a tighter twist of the threads. As a result, threads and fabrics shrink at a high RH (Fig. 37). When

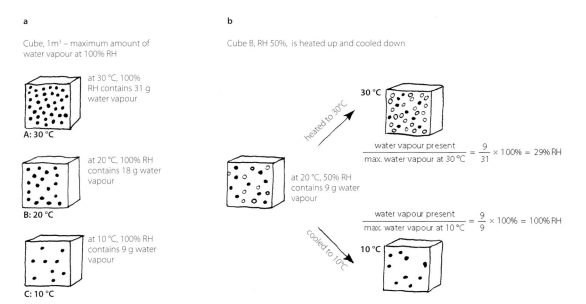

Figure 36 a. The relationship between temperature and relative humidity. **b**. The relationship between temperature and relative humidity; the moisture present in the air remains the same, however changes in temperature result in higher or lower RH.
Key: ● = represents 1 gram of moisture; o = available space for 1 gram of moisture to create a RH of 100%

the moisture is released into the air, the fabric will expand again (Hedley 1993: 113). This phenomenon is strongly influenced by the fibre type (some synthetic fibres hardly absorb water), weave tension, type of cleaning and drying, after treatments, etc., to the extent that the end result may be that a fabric actually expands in high RH, as weave tension is being released.

The colours of dyed textiles may fade more quickly at a high RH. In this case the reaction is indirect; the damage is actually caused by the effect of light on the textile (see Ch. 4). A high RH can also decrease the mechanical resistance of a textile, which can absorb so much moisture that it will deform and sometimes even break under its own weight.

Also, fungal growth may occur on organic materials at an RH higher than 65%. This growth will be further enhanced by both static air and a higher temperature (Fig. 38).

Inorganic materials such as metals do not absorb moisture, but can react in different ways to moisture in the atmosphere. An RH of less than 45% is recommended for the preservation of metals. High humidity, especially in combination with polluted air, can cause rapid metal corrosion. In textile collections, a high RH can cause problems when textiles are combined with metal, as is sometimes the case with the buckles, sequins, buttons, etc. found on clothing and accessories.

Low RH

Materials that absorb moisture easily will shrink when the RH is lowered. Textile fibres themselves will shrink but, since they are usually plied into threads and worked into fabric, the fabric itself may expand (see above). A low RH (roughly below 35%) will cause the embrittlement of organic materials and can also lead to deformations, especially when an object is thin and has a large surface area (such as paper, leather and parchment). Fresh animal skin remains flexible and is not influenced by a low RH: its chemical composition and fat content give it its elasticity. Vegetable and animal adhesives, on the other hand, are sensitive to a low RH; they dry out, becoming hard and brittle. They also lose their adhesive power, which may cause problems in the construction of an object.

Fluctuating RH

Organic materials contain a certain amount of bound water (see section 2.4.1). There will be a constant exchange of moisture between the object and the surrounding air in order to maintain equilibrium. Constant fluctuations in RH will cause abrasion between fibres and threads. If the fluctuation in the RH is great, it may cause a lot of tension in the material and could therefore lead to more rapid decay. It should be noted that organic materials need time to adjust to a new RH in the environment, and that it may take several days to weeks before a new equilibrium is reached. Therefore, rapid fluctuations over several hours will have little effect, provided the RH returns to the level to which the object is accustomed. A rapid change leading to new RH conditions is, on the other hand, very damaging. This, for example, can be seen in historic houses where central heating was installed at some point in time. Heating

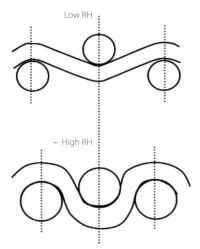

Figure 37 Shrinkage in a fabric at a high relative humidity (cross-section).

Figure 38 Fungal growth on organic material.

in the winter resulted in a rapid change to much dryer conditions, causing severe damage. This can clearly be seen in cracks that developed in wooden furniture. The damage to textiles is often less visible instantly, but will become noticeable over time.

Fluctuations in RH are particularly damaging to composite objects, i.e. objects composed of different materials, which respond to the changes at different rates. Internal stresses are caused because each material shrinks and swells differently, and may result in tears, crazing and distortions. This can be seen, for instance, in fans with ivory ribs. This also accounts for objects that are constrained such as embroideries which have been tensioned on a frame.

RH and temperature in microclimates
Organic materials are often used for their buffering qualities to help stabilise RH levels inside enclosed spaces. They have the capacity to absorb or release moisture (see section 3.5.2). The use of these RH-buffering materials may, however, have an adverse effect when used in microclimates. Research carried out at the former Central Research Laboratory for Objects of Art and Science in Amsterdam (now the Netherlands Institute for Cultural Heritage) has proven that the relationship between RH and temperature in microclimates is somewhat different from that known in larger spaces, where RH and temperature counterbalance (when the temperature increases, the RH decreases and vice versa). A study was made of the unexpected and unwanted effect of browning in paper objects (prints, drawings, etchings, etc.), that were mounted in subframes and packed together in archival boxes. It was found that the RH inside the window cut-out of the subframe behaved unpredictably in response to changes in the temperature of the surrounding atmosphere. A rise in temperature caused an increase in RH inside the window cut-out, and, conversely, a drop in temperature caused a decrease in RH (Hofenk de Graaff 1993).

A similar phenomenon was observed in sealed wooden showcases. In this instance, an increase in the temperature of the surrounding atmosphere had an almost immediate effect (within approximately two hours) on the RH inside the microclimate. On the other hand, the response to changes in the RH of the environment was found to be very slow, and it could take up to one week before the RH inside the microclimate was affected.

Apparently, the moisture content of the organic materials present in the microclimate influences the reaction to temperature changes. The ratio of the amount of organic material to the volume of the microclimate is important: the described reversed effect is believed to take place when this ratio is approximately 30% or more. Under these circumstances, a rise in temperature may cause an increase in RH.

Fluctuating temperature, which is often used as a means of maintaining a constant RH in a museum or archive, can therefore have an undesirable effect. It would be better to maintain a constant temperature and also to use a preponderance of organic material for packaging and mounting in order to control the RH. In addition, the use of localised air-conditioning units such as (de)humidifiers may assist in maintaining appropriate humidity levels (see section 3.3.2).

In conclusion, both a constant RH and temperature are important in the safekeeping of organic objects. Acceptable ranges and limits of RH need to be established based on the local climate, the nature and condition of the materials constituting the collection, the RH levels to which the materials have been acclimatised, the structure of the building and other relevant factors. An average RH of between 45 and 55% is a good starting point for the preservation of textiles. RH levels below 65% should always be maintained in order to reduce the potential for mould growth – but above 35% to prevent desiccation and shrinkage of organic materials. Slow changes as a result of the changing seasons are acceptable. Fluctuations that occur repeatedly over a period of a few days are potentially damaging and should be avoided.

3.1.3 Air pollution

The most harmful air pollutants are the acidic and oxidising gases sulphur dioxide (SO_2) and nitrogen dioxide (NO_2), the reducing gas formaldehyde (HCHO), ozone (O_3)) and fine dusts, such as soot and metal (oxide) particles. Examples of sources of pollution inside a museum include:

- nitrogen dioxide: internal combustion engines, gas-fired appliances (water heaters and cooking equipment);
- ozone and soot (toner): electrostatic copy machines, printers;
- formaldehyde: chipboard and some medium density fibreboard (MDF) (see section 6.2.2);
- acids: cleaning agents, wood and boards;
- soot, tar: smoke from cigarettes and cigars;

- hydrogen sulphide (H_2S): rotting of organic material, substances containing sulphur may emit hydrogen sulphide

Most pollution comes from outside. The presence of harmful chemical pollutants such as nitrogen dioxide and sulphur dioxide in the atmosphere has increased enormously since the 18th century due to the burning of coal, brown coal, peat and oil; and in the 20th century from the use of petrol and the production of plastics. The introduction of natural gas to replace coal and oil has reduced air pollution, but the acidification of the environment is still a factor to be considered. Air pollutants accelerate the natural degradation processes of organic materials. The exposure of museum collections to these harmful substances should therefore be reduced as much as possible. National environment agencies can usually give details of the air pollution in a particular area. They should be able to provide measurements of sulphur dioxide, black soot, fine dust, nitrogen dioxide, nitric oxide, ozone, oxidants and carbon monoxide.

3.2 Measuring and recording the museum environment

In order to implement measures to improve the interior climate of a building it is necessary to record temperature and RH as well as their fluctuations. Special measuring instruments are required to carry out this process. Measurements should preferably be taken continuously, but at least for one full year, so that the influence of seasonal changes on the indoor climate can be recorded. The environment within the building should be monitored using 24-hour recording devices during a full calendar year. An external sensor, to provide ambient readings, is essential to assess the performance of the building fabric. Such a survey may quickly identify the existence of differing environmental conditions within different zones of the building. Survey results should be analysed before major alterations are undertaken or expensive air-conditioning systems are installed. Some measuring instruments show the temperature and/or RH at a specific moment (spot monitoring), whereas others show the changes over a given period of time (continuous recording). The latter are preferred by museums as it is important to know what the fluctuations are and when they occur. It is also important to keep a logbook so that recorded data can be interpreted.

Hair hygrometer

The hair hygrometer is a (mechanical) RH meter which measures the RH without the storage of data. The meter essentially consists of hair that expands and contracts as the humidity fluctuates. Attached to this is a pointer that indicates the equivalent RH in percentage format. The hair hygrometer is fairly inaccurate and has to be regenerated and calibrated regularly. Its greatest disadvantage is that it doesn't store data – it only shows the RH at the moment at which a reading is taken. In order to record changes of the RH over time, several readings will have to be taken at regular intervals.

Thermohygrograph

A thermohygrograph records the temperature and RH on graph paper. Depending upon the type used, it registers these readings over a period of one day, one week or one month. The advantage of this type of recording is that an insight is gained into climatic changes. One of the two pens in the meter registers RH – this pen is attached to natural hair, which elongates and shrinks depending upon the changes in RH. The other pen registers temperature and is attached to a bimetallic strip (made from two dissimilar metals welded together). The two metals expand at different rates when heated – the metal with the greater expansion will bend the one with the lesser expansion to a degree proportional to the rise of the temperature (see Fig. 39).

The thermohygrograph has to be regenerated at least every three months and should be calibrated every six months. If this is not done, there may be inaccuracies in the measurements. Regeneration can easily be achieved by wrapping a wet cloth around the device for approximately three hours; the hair will regenerate and thus respond better to changes

Figure 39 Thermohygrograph (photo courtesy Erfgoedhuis Zuid-Holland).

in RH. The device can then be calibrated 24 hours later. Calibration involves adjusting the pointer to the correct RH which can be done with the aid of an electronic thermohygrometer, which measures both temperature and RH. Electronic RH meters are fairly accurate, but should also be calibrated. This is done by using salt standards of a known humidity which are placed over the sensor of the apparatus. Salt standards with a value of 11 and 75% RH are common and are fine for adjustment but for calibration of a sensor for use in a museum, a salt standard with an RH near 50% is essential. The electronic meter can only give a reading at a moment in time and is therefore less suitable for monitoring an indoor climate. It can, however, be used as a control instrument. The traditional whirling sling psychrometer can also be used as a calibrating instrument – it is not necessary to calibrate this hygrometer, although care should be taken not to soil the cotton wrapping on the wet bulb thermometer.

A thermohygrograph is not very accurate – the RH pen can give defective readings outside the central range of 40 to 70% RH – but it is a useful indicator as it registers fluctuations and is easy to read. Thermohygrometers with synthetic hairs are also available. The advantage of these is that the hair does not require regeneration but the disadvantage is that they are even less accurate, although still useful in indicating trends in climatic changes.

Data loggers

The modern equivalent of the thermohygrograph is a small programmable data logger: a recorder of temperature and RH which stores the measurements. The sensor for RH is much more accurate than the thermohygrograph, but should be calibrated at least once a year. In addition to measuring temperature and RH, some data loggers also measure light levels and even more advanced systems are available that can be linked to security alarms, smoke detectors, etc.

The frequency of the measurements can be set and can vary from one per minute to one every few hours. The stored data are retrieved by means of a computer; the measurements are downloaded and can be illustrated in graphs using the software supplied. The data can be downloaded manually but this requires assistance as the data loggers have to be physically moved from their positions and linked to a computer by a cable; they can be downloaded *in situ* using a laptop. There are also systems that make use of radio signals whereby data loggers send their data to a computer elsewhere in the building. The advantage of these is that no personnel is required in order to retrieve readings.

Pros and cons of data loggers

Some data loggers cannot be read directly without the use of a computer. They lack a display which would enable a passer-by to notice any unusual readings. This problem can be overcome by continuously linking data loggers to a computer (by wiring or by radio signalling). The software can then be used to set off an alarm which would alert staff if measurements exceeded preset values. Some data loggers have a built-in alarm light which comes on when the preset minimum and maximum values are exceeded. There are also data loggers available with small display windows, which allow visual control.

Most data loggers do not have to be calibrated more than once a year when the equipment may be returned to the manufacturer who will calibrate the sensor inside a special climate chamber, which can be costly. It is also possible to calibrate data loggers *in situ* using available software: temperature and humidity can be calibrated for some models at up to three points. A humidity reference can be provided by the external connection of industry standard salts, which are pushed onto the sensor (see above). It is important, however, to be alert to possible defects. To check the readings of the data logger's sensors, it is advisable to walk around with a calibrated electronic thermohygrograph every six months.

One of the great advantages of temperature and RH data loggers is that they can be packed with an object for transportation so that the conditions en route can be monitored. They can also be used to monitor climatic conditions for objects on loan. Many museums nowadays will send along a data logger to be placed near their objects in order to monitor climatic conditions. Insurance companies have also shown an interest in these developments.

3.3 The control of environmental conditions

The benefits of maintaining proper environmental conditions are manifold, but in practice, values of temperature, RH and levels of radiation etc. are often found which differ from those shown to be favourable for the long-term preservation of textiles. One of the reasons may be that a museum has to fulfil a variety of functions, not least the different requirements of people and artefacts. The human body responds to an RH lower than 30% with a tingling feeling in the nose, throat and eyes, and to one higher than 70% with a clammy feeling. Maintaining an RH well within these boundaries benefits both people and objects. Humans are even more sensitive to temperature; 18–22 °C is perceived as a comfortable temperature in which to work. For the preservation of objects, lower temperatures are more beneficial. Humans need ventilation to supply oxygen and remove body odours and carbon dioxide (CO_2). A certain amount of ventilation is also necessary for objects in order to remove decomposition products (gases) and to reduce the risk of fungal growth in microclimates, however, too much air movement can increase the distribution of dust and air pollution.

3.3.1 Division into zones

The different demands of humans and objects in indoor climates can be met by creating two different types of climatic zones ('non-critical' and 'critical') within a museum building. The non-critical zone is aimed at people and contains rooms used as offices, shops, and cafeterias. A pleasant temperature is most important; the adjustment of the central heating only needs to be set for working hours. This type of zone is referred to as 'non-critical' as it only requires adjustment of temperature, which can be achieved easily. Objects sensitive to climatic changes should not be placed inside this zone.

The critical zone consists of storage and exhibition spaces, and conservation studios. It is here that objects are kept. The necessary climate for the safekeeping of museum objects is much more difficult to realise. Both temperature and RH have to be kept at a constant level; a central heating system alone is unlikely to be able to achieve this, so possible fluctuations of RH will need to be constrained by either humidifying or dehumidifying the atmosphere.

Microclimate
The term 'microclimate' is used when a small area within another space has different environmental conditions compared to the rest of that space. Microclimates may be used deliberately in order to create a more stable environment (see section 3.3.2) or to create specific conditions favourable for the preservation of certain objects, such as a low-oxygen environment to retard degradation processes or eradicate insects (see section 5.4). The use of RH-buffering materials however, may have an adverse effect when used in microclimates (see section 3.1.2).

Unwanted microclimates can be formed, e.g. in enclosed areas with little ventilation when temperature changes occur – a situation that often exists in museums. An example of this would be a microclimate inside a framed sampler hanging directly on an outside wall. The cold outside wall causes a lower temperature inside the frame than in the room. RH increases inside the frame and can even exceed saturation point, thereby leading to condensation on colder parts such as the glass. Such microclimates provide attractive conditions for fungi: a high RH, still air and nutrients (textile, adhesive, dust and impurities). One solution to reduce the risk of fungal growth inside the framed sampler would be to create a small distance between the object and the wall, for example by placing pieces of cork at the back of the frame to allow air to circulate behind the object.

3.3.2 Conditioning of the environment

In northwest Europe, the outside atmosphere has an average RH of approximately 82%. The level within a museum with a textile collection should ideally be between 45 and 55%. It is obvious that something has to be done in order to achieve this level. The shell of the building is very important, i.e. the roof, walls (with windows and doors), the floors and foundations. It should be well insulated in order to separate the atmosphere outside from that inside. Once the shell has been properly insulated, measurements should be taken of the environment inside. The starting points for treating the atmosphere are: first, establish the demands of the collection; second, measure the current environmental conditions, and finally, improve the conditions that do not conform to the standard set. If the environmental conditions have to be adjusted, local mechanical equipment, such as humidifiers and dehumidifiers or an air-conditioning system may be used. The two main advantages of air conditioning are: filtering of the outside air and moisture regulation in museum spaces. A constant RH is not easy to establish, especially in old buildings, which is often where museums are located. In theory, it should be established which spaces have the most constant temperature and RH – these are therefore the most suitable for preserving collections (stores and exhibition spaces). They should be designated as a critical zone because less energy and finances are necessary to adjust their climate to the demands of a collection. Sometimes, good results can be achieved by creating compartments inside spaces. Another solution is to store collections in purpose-built storage facilities at an external location.

Heating and cooling elements

If the heating system within the critical zone of the museum is connected to a thermostat, it is important that there is no day and night rhythm in the adjustment which would cause the temperature and RH to change every evening and morning. In some of the National Trust properties in the UK, the heating systems are connected to a humidistat instead of a thermostat (Staniforth 1994: 123); this adjusts the temperature to the demands of the objects and not to human comfort. The temperature is set to a maximum of 18 °C and the humidistat, which is connected to the central heating system, regulates a constant RH. RH becomes the trigger for the heating system: the system turns itself off when the humidity drops below a certain limit and switches on when it exceeds a set maximum. This of course requires some extra provision, for example when outdoor temperatures below freezing require the heating inside to be turned on even though the RH is already very low. In this instance, the risk of frozen pipes is greater than the risk of damage from a low RH. Good insulation is a way of avoiding sudden changes in RH.

Cooling can be achieved by using room equipment for local cooling or by adding a cooling unit to the air-conditioning system. Always be aware that when a space is being cooled, it will affect the RH.

Humidifiers and dehumidifiers

Most museums will be equipped with a heating system. Additional measures to control an indoor climate should address the issue of maintaining the required RH level. This can be achieved by using movable humidifying and dehumidifying units. The capacity of these appliances should correspond to the volume of the space, i.e. the volume of air. Furthermore, a space will have to be enclosed as there is no point in humidifying a passageway where all the conditioned air will escape immediately. In rooms with extremely high ceilings, the conditioned air will spread significantly and, as a result, the effect of the treatment will hardly be noticeable. In order to decide on

Figure 40 Room with a lot of hygroscopic material which serves as a buffer in maintaining a constant climate. The walls are covered with tapestries and wooden panelling. There is a wooden floor, and ceiling, and the room is furnished with wooden furniture (photo courtesy Simon van Gijn – Museum aan Huis, Dordrecht).

the type of equipment necessary, always keep in mind the air circulation and the buffering capacity of the building materials used in ceilings, walls and floors (see section 3.5). Organic materials, such as wooden panelling and/or furniture, textile wall hangings, wooden ceilings and/or floors, have a significant influence on the behaviour of RH inside a room (Fig. 40). Humidifiers and dehumidifiers have to be placed away from all other equipment and objects in the room, and should not be placed next to each other, in order to achieve an optimal effect. It is also vital that they are left on 24 hours a day.

Humidifiers

In a temperate climate the heating is turned on during the winter, and as a result, extra water vapour is often necessary to maintain a proper RH. This can be achieved by means of a humidifier and there are several different types available (Table 6).

For museum purposes, only the cold moisture ventilator with a closed water tank (which is linked to a humidistat) is suitable. The larger types are equipped with a ventilator and air filters. The humidistat works as a sensor and turns the evaporator on when the atmosphere is too dry; it turns the evaporator off when the required humidity level has been reached. The water in the tank has to be kept topped up but the equipment can also be attached to the water supply so that a constant refilling process can take place. Some humidifiers can potentially be a source of *Legionella* bacteria. Humidifiers that work on the basis of misting (atomisation) can present these problems. Humans can contract Legionnaires' disease by breathing in water droplets contaminated with *Legionella* bacteria. The cold moisture ventilator, however, releases moisture that is immediately taken up by the atmosphere as water vapour, and as a result, no actual water droplets are formed. Furthermore, the bacteria need a higher temperature than is present in this equipment for their development. Fungi can also grow inside a humidifier but the use of chemicals to prevent fungal growth is not recommended as these chemicals are often harmful to the collection. To help overcome this problem, the humidifier can be equipped with an active carbon and dust filter. It is necessary to clean the inside of the apparatus regularly using soap or chemicals, followed by a thorough rinsing. The filters should be changed annually.

The positioning of a humidifier in a museum environment is of great importance. It should never be placed in close proximity to museum objects tucked away, in a corner or immediately against the wall (a distance of at least 15 cm away from the wall is recommended). Small water containers which hang from radiators have no effect on the humidification of a room. They also need to be cleaned regularly in order to avoid the growth of algae, bacteria and fungi. For these reasons such water trays are not appropriate for museum purposes.

Dehumidifiers

In cases where the RH is constantly too high and structural improvements of the building are not

Table 6 Different types of humidifiers (source: de Guichen *et al.* 1998: 22).

Type	Advantages	Disadvantages	Care
Atomisation	Sturdy apparatus Easily available Simple to operate High RH easily obtained Compact model	Humidification forced & abrupt With tap water, risk of deposits on objects Avoid copper tank and copper pipes	Empty tank when not in use Add biocide to minimise build-up of microorganisms Regenerate the ion-exchange column producing demineralised water on regular basis
Evaporation	Simple, strong apparatus Can disinfect while it humidifies No risk of deposits of salts on objects Comes in a compact model	Humidification is forced, but less abrupt than with atomiser Produces hot vapour Without biocides there is a risk of microorganism build-up due to hot, humid air	Empty tank when not in use Use tap water, not distilled water, to facilitate flow of electric current
Ventilation (cold moisture)	Natural and gentle humidification Improved type with filter compensates for lowering of temperature by heating and sterilisation	Fragile machine with moving parts Care very important A good quality model occupies considerable space in a room Hard to achieve RH above 80% Without sterilisation microorganisms will grow	Empty tank when not in use Clean sponge and change filter once a month Clean drum and grids once every three months Add tablets to prevent scale on a regular basis

resolving this problem, then a dehumidifier can provide some relief. There are several different types:

- Using a desiccant: the dehumidifier sucks in the moist air over a desiccant, usually silica gel attached to a rotating drum. The desiccant is continuously regenerated by warm air. This warm air can, however, increase the temperature of the environment surrounding the equipment by approximately 2 °C. The water that is removed from the atmosphere is collected in a tray, which has to be emptied regularly. This type of dehumidifier is more effective in cold, unheated rooms.
- The cooling dehumidifier removes the surplus water in the air by passing it over a cold surface. The moisture in the air condenses and is collected in a tank. The dried cold air is warmed up and released back into the environment. The tank has to be emptied and cleaned regularly in order to avoid bacterial growth. This type of dehumidifier does not work at temperatures below 8 °C.

A dehumidifier needs to be equipped with a humidistat which turns itself off when the desired RH has been reached. It is possible to connect a dehumidifier to the drainage system so that the water collected is constantly removed. The use of building dryers should be avoided because they cannot be adjusted and have a restricted capacity. They can, however, be used in the event of disasters, such as floods, providing that the situation is constantly monitored.

Humidifiers and dehumidifiers are often used in combination with each other. The humidifier should be set at 45%; the dehumidifier at 55%. This results in an overall acceptable museum climate. These machines should not be positioned adjacent to each other as they will constantly switch each other on and off.

Passive buffers

Passive buffers can be used to condition small spaces (i.e. microclimates). The principle is as follows: the buffering material, such as paper, cotton wool, silica gel, Art Sorb, or Pro Sorb (see section 9.2.8) is placed in an area adjacent to the space that needs buffering. These materials buffer the RH inside the microclimate by absorbing or releasing moisture when the RH inside differs from the one at which they were conditioned. This type of buffering may be used in those showcases which require a different microclimate from the surrounding atmosphere. The use of buffering materials demands a special type of showcase that is built from conservation grade materials and is airtight (Chaplin 1994; Cassar and Graham 1994; Lafontaine 1984).

Passive buffers have many different uses including the use of acid-free cardboard boxes for storage, special crates made for the transportation of objects, and microclimate boxes for paintings (Wadum 1998). The undesired effects of microclimates when used in environments in which the temperature fluctuates should be considered (see section 3.1.2).

Air-conditioning systems

The indoor climate of a museum can also be controlled by means of an air-conditioning system. Museums that have to deal with a lot of internal warmth, moisture and air pollution may consider using air-conditioning systems. The installation and use of air-conditioning systems is expensive for the following reasons:

- The installation requires a large capital investment;
- In existing buildings, radical alterations are often necessary;
- When used daily, maintenance costs are high;
- Costs for the replacement of obsolete equipment is ongoing.
- The air-conditioning system in museums should give priority to the control of RH. In modern buildings, air treatment involves ventilation, cooling and dehumidifying the atmosphere, without any attempt to achieve a constant RH. It is therefore important to make sure that the special requirements for a museum climate are set and implemented at an early stage in the development of a museum.

An air-conditioning system works by sucking in the outside air and treating it; it is purified, and then, depending on requirements, heated or cooled, dried or humidified. In order to save energy, existing circulating air can be mixed with fresh air from outside – the standard is a ratio of 1:1 (recirculating air to fresh air). If the air is extremely well filtered and, providing human comfort is not a major issue, this ratio can be adjusted – to as much as 9:1. The advantage of this is that the filters will last longer as the recirculating air is already purified.

In a two-zone system (see section 3.3.1), the air-conditioning system of the critical zone (storage and exhibition spaces) can sometimes use as much as 95% recirculating air, which is also environmentally friendly. The non-critical zone, however, needs an increased amount of fresh air during daytime, but can be switched to low-energy recirculation at night.

There are disadvantages to air-conditioning systems other than the high costs:

1. A large amount of space is needed to house the apparatus and ducts.
2. The risk of potential problems that may arise, e.g. due to power failure or fungi growing inside the installation.
3. Temperature and RH need to be monitored inside rooms in order to collect measurements independent of those taken by the installation. This will result in better control of the indoor climate.

Measures to contain the influence of harmful substances
The influence of harmful substances in museums must be limited as much as possible. This can be achieved by restricting the sources of pollution (see section 3.1.3) and by carrying out the following:

- Check storage materials and systems for the emission of harmful substances (see sections 6.2.2 and 9.1);
- Remove those materials that emit formaldehyde (see section 6.2.2);
- Place copying machines in separate ventilated spaces;
- Establish separate ventilation for the non-critical zone (offices, restaurants, toilets) and critical zone (museum spaces). This is particularly important if part of the air is recirculated in the air-conditioning system;
- Place rubbish bins (especially those of catering facilities) outside the building.

The entry of unfiltered air from outside should be minimised by:

- Reducing the infiltration of unnecessary outdoor air via cracks in the shell of the building – seal as many cracks and seams as possible and build airlocks at all entrances to the building;
- Making use of filters to remove nitrogen (di)oxide and sulphur dioxide from the polluted outside air and position high-efficiency filters to trap soot and metal particles;
- Laying special carpet or doormats in the entrance hall to bind particles of dust and air pollution;
- Positioning the fresh air inlet carefully, i.e. away from car parks/traffic routes (acid oxides and soot from car exhaust fumes).

Objects can also be protected from harmful influences by placing them inside storage systems (cupboards, boxes, slipcovers); this helps to create an extra barrier between the objects and the environmental conditions. In this instance, the registration of a collection is essential for the retrieval of objects (see Ch. 11).

3.4 Summary

Three parameters are important when describing the condition of the atmosphere: temperature (T), relative humidity (RH) and absolute humidity (AH). If these variables are to be kept under control, it is extremely important that the building has an adequate shell and sufficient ventilation. The conditions necessary for the preservation of artefacts in a museum are very specific. Special measures are often necessary to achieve these conditions; these vary from using microclimates to air-conditioning systems. A suitable indoor climate for preserving textiles would be:

1. Constant RH in the critical zone;
2. Low temperature;
3. No air pollution.

A cold, hermetically sealed chamber filled with an inert gas with a fixed RH would be perfect. Although this is technically possible (and may be an option for items in storage) it is neither practical nor desirable for a museum's exhibition area. A safe indoor climate can be achieved by setting certain tolerance levels for RH, temperature, light and air pollution. An RH of between 45 and 55% suffices for most objects. Higher temperatures increase the rate of chemical processes, especially the oxidation of organic materials. Pollutant gases, such as ozone, nitrogen (di)oxide and sulphur dioxide, should be eliminated. The use of filters made from active carbon has proved to be effective. Small particle pollutants (dust and soot) should be removed using high-efficiency air filters. Last but not least, it is important for museums to ensure that set procedures are followed for cleaning, regenerating and calibrating equipment, and for changing filters.

3.5 Appendix

3.5.1 Psychrometric chart

The moisture content of a volume of air is characterised by temperature (T), relative humidity (RH) and absolute humidity (AH) (see Table 7). Their relationship is presented in a psychrometric chart (Fig. 41). The points mentioned in Table 7 are drawn in the psychrometric chart; A, B, C, and D are positioned on the saturation line. Temperature is set along the horizontal axis; absolute humidity along the vertical axis. The curved lines represent lines of equal relative humidity.

Two of the three parameters are necessary to establish the climatic conditions of a volume of air. When two parameters are known, the third one can be read from the chart without the need for calculations (de Guichen *et al.* 1998).

Monitoring changes using the psychrometric chart
Temperature and RH fluctuate continuously inside a room – a small change in one of these parameters will have an immediate effect on the other. This relationship is presented in the psychrometric chart. It can help to predict unfavourable circumstances such as changes in RH due to heating up/cooling down and changes in AH due to the addition or removal of water. This will allow corrective measures to be taken in time to prevent possible problems.

For example, using the starting point (A_0 in Fig. 42): T_0 = 20 °C, RH_0 = 60%. The room is heated up to T_1 = 25 °C by an electric radiator. What is the effect on the RH? First locate point A_0 in Figure 42; from the graph it can be read that the AH is equal to 10 g/m³. When the temperature rises, the amount of water vapour in the atmosphere (the AH) remains constant, therefore point A will move along a horizontal line until it reaches the new temperature, point A_1. At this point the graph shows that the RH will be 43%.

A similar example can be given for changes in RH: how much water would be necessary to raise the RH in a room of 5 × 10 × 4 m from 40% to 55% (assuming the temperature is 20 °C, the room is empty and the air remains still)? In order to increase the RH to 55%, 2 g of water is necessary for every m³, a total of 0.4 litres of water for 200 m³.

Several rules can be extrapolated from the psychrometric chart:

- When T drops and AH remains constant, RH increases;
- When T rises and AH remains constant, RH decreases;
- When AH increases and T remains constant, RH increases;
- When AH decreases and T remains constant, RH decreases;
- In order to maintain a constant RH when T decreases – reduce AH;

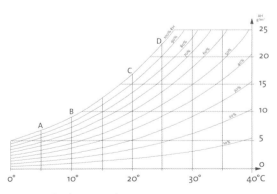

Figure 41 Psychrometric chart.

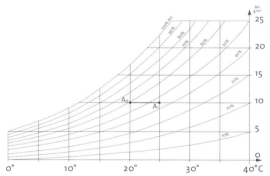

Figure 42 The use of the psychrometric chart.

Table 7 Absolute humidity (AH) of the atmosphere at given temperatures and at 100% RH.

Temperature	5 °C	10 °C	20 °C	25 °C
RH = 100%	AH = 7 g/m³	AH = 9 g/m³	AH = 17 g/m³	AH = 22.5 g/m³
Points	A	B	C	D

- In order to maintain a constant RH when T rises – increase AH;

The psychrometric chart can also be used to predict changes when some of the parameters change (e.g. the risk of condensation when the temperature drops) and clarify how the indoor climate of a space should be adapted in order to make it acceptable as a museum space for objects.

3.5.2 Materials and their equilibrium moisture content (EMC)

Organic materials, such as wall-hangings, wooden panelling and wooden furniture, have a significant effect on the RH in a room. For example, if the wooden elements in a room of 5 × 10 × 4 m weigh approximately 500 kg, considerably more moisture will be necessary to increase the RH of the space from 40 to 55%. How much moisture is necessary can be calculated with the aid of the EMC curve, which presents the equilibrium between RH and the bound water in the material at a certain temperature.

The water vapour present is divided and constantly exchanged between the material (e.g. wood) and the surrounding atmosphere. These changes are in fact a dynamic equilibrium. When the amount of water that evaporates from the wood per second equals the amount of water vapour that is absorbed by the wood, equilibrium will exist. The EMC graph for wood (and other materials capable of absorbing and releasing moisture) shows a curved line (Fig. 43), which expresses the amount of moisture present in a material that is in equilibrium with the RH of the surrounding atmosphere. The amount of bound water in hygroscopic materials can be calculated from the EMC graph if the weight of the dry material is known using the following formula:

$$\frac{\text{weight of water} \times 100\%}{\text{weight of dry material}} = \% \text{ of bound water}$$

EMC curves of natural materials

All materials have a particular behaviour in absorbing and releasing moisture; this is characterised by their EMC curve (see Fig. 43). As can be seen from the graph:

- There is quite a difference in behaviour between organic materials (1, 2, 3, 4 and 7) and inorganic materials (5 and 6): the first group of materials is porous and hygroscopic and will have much higher moisture content in equilibrium with the atmosphere than the latter group;
- In comparison to other materials, leather is capable of absorbing the most moisture;
- Not all organic materials have a linear correlation;
- An example is the curve for cotton (see Fig. 44); this curve can be divided into three parts, A, B, and C, each one with a different gradient:

    A: an increase in RH from 0 to 10% causes the moisture content of cotton to increase by 3 g;
    B: an increase in RH from 10 to 70% has a more gradual effect on the increase in the moisture content of cotton, namely by 4 g;
    C: an increase in RH from 70 to 100% again results in a high increase in the moisture content of cotton – 7 g.

In other words, cotton is more sensitive to fluctuations in RH in the ranges of 0–10% and 70–100%, and is less sensitive to fluctuations in the range of 10–70%. It is important to understand the EMC curve in order to anticipate the behaviour of a material when the RH changes.

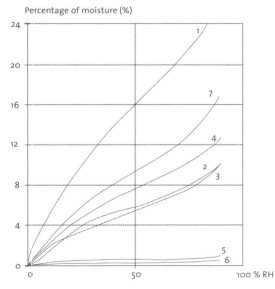

Figure 43 EMC curves for different materials: 1. leather; 2. linen; 3. paper; 4. starch; 5. chalk mortar; 6. brick; 7. oak (de Guichen et al. 1998: 9).

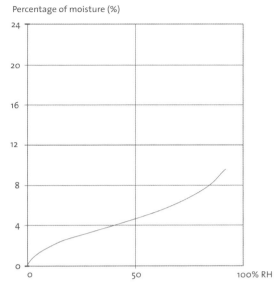

Figure 44 EMC curve of cotton (de Guichen *et al.* 1998: 10).

3.5.3 The effect of organic materials on the changes in the indoor climate

An empty space will respond differently to changes in temperature than a space in which hygroscopic materials are present. In the first instance, the RH of the atmosphere changes immediately according to the curve in the psychrometric chart. When organic materials are present, the RH will respond much more slowly and will affect the final reading, depending upon the type and mass of the hygroscopic materials. A closed system will always give a reaction different to that of an open system. In a closed system with fluctuating temperature, if only a small amount of hygroscopic material is present, the AH in the atmosphere remains the same; if a lot of hygroscopic material is present then the RH remains the same.

Temperature
In a room filled with tapestries and furniture, it takes longer to increase the temperature by 10 °C than in an empty room. The presence of objects has a delaying effect on temperature changes.

Relative humidity
When the RH in a room has to be increased the amount of moisture required depends on the contents of the room. Thomson explains that in a showcase with a volume of $1 \times 1 \times 0.1$ m with a base of 10 mm thick plywood 'the wood holds about 800 times as much water as the air' (Thomson 1978: 128).

4
Light

Our starting point is that any light must be seen as a concession.

David Saunders, National Gallery (Cassar 1994a)

4.1 Introduction

Some of the risk factors for the safekeeping of textile collections can cause rapid degradation – insects and fungi. Other risk factors – environmental conditions and light – are always present and continuously affect collections. When the relative humidity (RH) changes, a textile can often recover and establish a new moisture equilibrium with its environment. In contrast, damage caused by light is irreversible and cumulative. Some knowledge of the actions and effects of light is therefore important when dealing with the preservation of textile collections.

The structure of the human eye determines the way in which light is experienced. When light enters the eye, a signal is passed to our brains allowing us to recognise objects by their shape and colour. Our vision is, however, more advanced than that of a camera: for example, our brains are capable of correcting the changes in daylight conditions. This explains why we see snow as white even though it is fairly blue under bright skies. Our eyes are also capable of adapting to changes in light intensity. At low light levels, colours lose their brilliance, and at extremely low levels we can hardly distinguish colours. Our eyes deteriorate as we age: a 60-year-old man needs ten times as much light in order to differentiate between colours as a 16-year-old.

Familiarity with the working of the human eye is important when designing lighting for an exhibition – in order to understand the possibilities and restrictions of lighting. It is especially important to be aware of the harmful properties of light which cause degradation of materials. The speed of degradation depends upon the energy (wavelength), light intensity, time span and the kind of material from which the object is made.

4.1.1 Electromagnetic spectrum; wavelength

Light (also called visible radiation) is an electromagnetic radiation with a wavelength of 400–780 nm. Only a small part of the radiation emitted by a light source consists of light (see Table 8). The sun and artificial light sources also emit infrared (IR) radiation (wavelength between 780 nm and 1 mm) and ultraviolet (UV) radiation (wavelength 100–400 nm) both of which can also cause damage to materials albeit in a slightly different way from visible radiation (see sections 4.3 and 4.5).

When light travels through a prism it separates out into its component colours called the spectrum. Each colour has a different wavelength, from blue at 400 nm to red at 780 nm. The shorter the wavelength, the greater the energy and the more severe the damage caused by light.

4.1.2 Light intensity, luminance and reflection

Illuminance is the light energy falling on a surface at a certain rate, measured in lux (lumen per square

Table 8 Schematic classification of part of the electromagnetic spectrum.

Name	Wavelength
Ultraviolet radiation	100–400 nm
UV-C	100–280 nm
UV-B	280–315 nm
UV-A	315–400 nm
Light	400–780 nm
Infrared radiation	780–1 mm
IR-A	780 nm–1.4 μm
IR-B	1.4–3.0 μm
IR-C	3.0 μm–1 mm

metre). Luminous intensity is the amount of light emitted by the source travelling in a given direction and is measured in candelas. The quantity of light falling on a surface depends on its distance from the source. As the distance increases, less light will fall on a surface (see section 4.3.3).

The light reflected from a surface, as seen by the eye, is known as the luminance and is one of the most important considerations in lighting design. Although technically, luminance refers to the light leaving a surface after it is reflected, it is used here as the visual appearance or brightness of a surface when illuminated. The luminance is dependent upon the nature of the surface finish and its reflectance. For the application of luminance to design, the essential principle is that luminance is not affected by a change of distance between the lit surface and the observer: an illuminated surface will have the same brightness for two people viewing it from different distances. Brightness correlates with luminance although the actual impression or perception of brightness is influenced by how well the eyes adapt, by the surrounding contrasting levels of brightness and by the information content of the viewed surface. In considering the lighting design for exhibitions it is essential to remember that we observe *luminance* not *illuminance* (see section 4.7).

Light incident on a surface can be absorbed, transmitted (with refraction) or reflected. Incident light is fully or partially reflected depending on the reflecting coefficient of the surface. The reflected light will have different characteristics according to the nature of the surface on which the light falls.

4.1.3 Damage

The damaging effect of light on objects depends not only on the illuminance but also on the length of exposure. The general rule, also referred to as the law of reciprocity, is:

Damage = illuminance × length of exposure

Using this general rule, it can be calculated that an object exposed for 10 hours at 200 lux is subject to the same amount of damage as if it were exposed for 40 hours at 50 lux (both resulting in 2,000 lux-hours). Objects on display made from light-sensitive materials should be exposed to minimum lighting conditions only during the opening hours of a museum and for a restricted number of days; for example, an exposure of 50 lux for 125 days at eight hours a day results in 50,000 lux-hours per year. Objects made from materials that are less light-sensitive may be exposed for 480,000 lux-hours per year (200 lux × 200 days × 8 hours per day).

It should, however, be noted that any exposure to light, even at these restricted levels, will cause cumulative damage to objects.

4.2 Measuring devices

The illuminance of a surface is measured in lux; one lux is defined as an illumination of one lumen per square metre. Lumen is a unit for measuring the flux of light being produced by a light source or received by a surface. Examples of suitable lighting conditions:

- 20 lux is often sufficient in corridors;
- In a living room, a mean lighting of 200 lux is perceived as satisfactory;
- 500 lux is necessary to read a book.

On a bright and clear day the light intensity can reach 20,000 lux. Direct sunlight reflected from a sheet of white paper into our eyes is too strong for us to perceive as pleasant.

4.2.1 Lux meter

Light intensity can be measured *in situ* with a lux meter (Fig. 45) for direct and reliable data. In order to obtain an average lux value for a room, it is necessary to measure the light levels throughout the entire day at different locations. Some modern electronic data loggers can measure light levels and UV radiation in addition to temperature and RH. This type of equipment takes measurements at preset intervals. The collected data can then be downloaded onto a computer and presented as a graph.

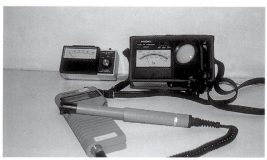

Figure 45 Lux meter, UV meter and an electronic thermohygrometer (photo courtesy Erfgoedhuis Zuid-Holland).

4.2.2 UV meter

The energy of radiation is inversely proportional to the wavelength: the shorter the wavelength, the greater the energy. Invisible UV radiation, a shortwave radiation, initiates (chemical) reactions. It is therefore important to determine the level of UV radiation present. The most commonly used UV meter in museums is the ratio detector; it measures the energy of the UV radiation (in microwatts) per lumen of visible light. Until recently, the maximum value allowed for museum collections was set at 75 µW/lm (Thomson 1978). This was based on a pragmatic consideration: it represents the UV radiation of a standard light bulb. Nowadays, however, it is possible to eliminate nearly all UV radiation with a wavelength shorter than 400 nm. The maximum value allowed is now set at 10 µW/lm, which is the current detection limit (di Fraia 1997; Michalski 1992b). Note that UV should be measured after light levels are adjusted to the recommended setting.

4.2.3 Blue wool standard

The blue wool standard is a strip of cardboard to which eight dyed woollen fabric samples are attached. The dyes are arranged so that each dye will fade twice as fast as the previous sample (Fig. 46): sample one is the most sensitive to light, sample eight the least sensitive. The lightfastness of dyed materials is recorded on a scale from one to eight according to ISO Standard 105. Using the blue wool standard, a visual indication can be obtained of the effect of light over a period of time and is a useful tool for investigating the effects of light on objects (Feller and Johnston-Feller 1981). The blue wool standard can be positioned in, for example, a showcase, to record the effects of lighting. Part of each dyed woollen sample is covered during exposure. After exposure, the covered parts of the samples are compared to the exposed parts. Depending upon the rate of fading, extra precautions can be taken to reduce the light intensity or the exposure time. This is a simple test (it can be carried out by museum staff) that provides a graphic demonstration helping to convince management to implement the necessary measures.

4.2.4 LightCheck strips

Recently a new tool has been developed for monitoring the cumulative illumination to which a light-sensitive object has been exposed. As a result of the European Commission funded project, 'A light dosimeter for monitoring cultural heritage: development, testing and transfer to market', two types of light dosimeters have been developed based on the same principle: a light-sensitive coating on a substrate gradually changes colour as it absorbs light. An estimate of the amount of light absorbed is determined by comparing the progressive variation in the colour to a colour scale. Both types of dosimeters are more sensitive than the traditional blue wool standard. LightCheck Ultra 'LCU' is designed to monitor the exhibition of very light-sensitive objects (and short exposure times up to 120 megalux-hours) whereas LightCheck Sensitive 'LCS' is applicable for more durable objects and longer exposure times up to 400 megalux-hours.

Figure 46 Example of a blue wool standard after exposure. The fading of the blue colour can be seen at the top where the samples were exposed to light (photo courtesy J.H. Hofenk de Graaff, ICN).

4.3 Visible light

4.3.1 Damage to materials

Light can damage objects in different ways. UV radiation (see section 4.4) and visible light set off chemical changes in paper and textiles, which weaken and discolour them and causes inks, dyes and pigments to fade (Fig. 47). IR radiation is less energetic than both UV radiation and visible light and heats materials. This can cause them to expand, leading to mechanical stresses. It can also cause chemical changes to progress more rapidly. IR radiation adds to the destructive effects of visible light and UV radiation (see section 4.5).

Some objects are more sensitive to the effects of light than others. Organic materials, such as textile, paper, wood and leather are the most vulnerable. More often than not the original colours will have faded or changed – if the original colours are still present it is probably because they have had little exposure to light. An example of the effect of light on dyestuffs is the blue colour commonly seen in old tapestries, especially where trees and shrubs are depicted. The original green colour was obtained by first dyeing the wool threads blue and subsequently yellow. In general, yellow dyestuffs are considerably more sensitive to light than blues and consequently fade more rapidly, changing the overall colour from green to blue. Research into the light sensitivity of dyestuffs (Padfield and Landi 1966) revealed that natural yellow dyestuffs and the red dyestuff obtained from redwood were destroyed within 50 years of exposure at low light levels.

When taking precautions, it is important to base these on the most sensitive material present in an object. Colours obtained with natural dyestuffs on silk and cotton are more light-sensitive than those on wool (Henderson *et al.* 1991).

4.3.2 Light sources

It is recommended that the illumination of extremely light-sensitive objects should not exceed a maximum of 50 lux. This is easier to obtain with artificial light than with daylight. Unless daylight is excluded completely, it is very difficult to keep the lighting below 50 lux. The human eye can still see colours at light levels of approximately 30 to 35 lux, but elderly people often perceive this level as too dark, especially when there is a change in light levels from one room to another. In order to help visitors to adjust to low light levels more easily when they enter an exhibition where these levels are used, the basic lighting should be gradually adjusted prior to entry. Carefully placed spotlights can be used to highlight objects or details in objects. In exhibition rooms with large windows through which sunlight can enter, the lighting conditions

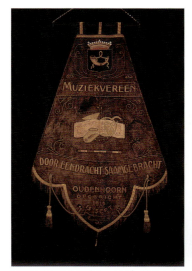

Figure 47 Front and reverse of a Society banner. The lining and reverse show discoloration. The original green colour of the lining, now faded to orange, can be seen when folding away the side flaps (photos courtesy Erfgoedhuis Zuid-Holland, collection Oudheidkamer Geervliet).

will vary according to the weather. On a cloudy day, less light will enter the room than on a bright day. Measures should therefore be taken to prevent direct sunlight from entering before stabilising the lighting conditions. This can be achieved by fitting filters, blinds or shutters to the windows. It is important to monitor the light levels and the UV radiation at regular intervals and to adjust the effects of daylight where necessary.

4.3.3 Measures to reduce light levels

In order to reduce the harmful effects of daylight and to regulate lighting levels, certain measures have to be taken. There are three ways to reduce light levels:

- Shortening the time span of exposure: an effective way to ensure that exhibited objects will be exposed for a shorter period of time is to rotate the objects with similar items from storage. Time switches can also be installed to control the lighting in a room or showcase. To ensure that a showcase is only illuminated when it is actually being viewed, contact mats or movement sensors that regulate the lighting can be used. A more old-fashioned but still effective method is to cover the showcases with curtains that can be pulled aside in order to view them. This method does have the disadvantage that viewers will need an incentive to encourage them to look at the exhibited objects.
- Reducing the illuminance at the surface. Illuminance obeys the inverse square law, one of the most important characteristics of light and application to design. The quantity of light falling on a surface depends on the distance from the source. This quantity varies inversely with the square of the distance between the source and the surface receiving the light. By increasing the surface between the light source and the object, less light will fall on its surface. If the distance between a point light source (e.g. a light bulb) and an object is doubled, the amount of light reaching its surface will decrease to 25% or by a factor of four. For a light bulb positioned 1 m from an object which yields an illumination of 200 lux on the object, the illumination from the same light bulb will be reduced to 50 lux if it is placed 2 m from the object.
- The use of photocells: light sensors linked to shades, blinds, light sources, etc. These light sensors register when a light level exceeds a previously set level. Shades may automatically be lowered or artificial lights may be turned on, depending on the situation, by a signal from the photocell.

4.4 UV radiation

Of the sun's radiant emittance (approximately 1351 W/m^2), only 900 W/m^2 reaches the earth's surface as some of it is absorbed by the atmosphere. The action of the atmosphere, especially the ozone contained in the stratosphere, is crucial, as it drastically absorbs the ultraviolet component of solar radiation, in particular UVC (100–280 nm) and UVB (280–315 nm). The maximum UVA (315–400 nm) component measured is 70 W/m^2, while the maximum UVB component is 2.5 W/m^2; ultraviolet C is totally absorbed and does not reach the earth's surface. The radiation that reaches the earth's surface varies during the day, with the highest values during the central hours of the day.

UV radiation has short wavelengths and is therefore extremely harmful. Although UV radiation represents only a relatively small part of sunlight, it is, however, responsible for the most damage. In general, the amount of damage to objects caused by UV radiation is greater than that caused by visible light.

4.4.1 Damage to materials

UV radiation causes molecular changes in organic materials. In textiles, light accelerates degradation processes such as oxidation and cross-linking, especially in the amorphous areas of the polymers (see Ch. 2). For example, cotton loses 50% of its strength when exposed to full sunlight for four months. Paper is also extremely sensitive to UV radiation, particularly lesser quality paper that contains lignin, e.g. the older type newspaper, which turns yellow and disintegrates quickly when exposed to sunlight. Vegetable fibres containing lignin (such as jute) also have an increased sensitivity to photo-oxidation. Damage to textiles caused by light can furthermore be accelerated by the presence of pollution and certain dyes.

4.4.2 Light sources

When exhibiting textiles, special attention should be taken to avoid sunlight entering exhibition spaces through windows. The UV radiation in direct sunlight is much higher than the recommended maximum exposure of 10 µW/lm. Curtains and blinds may be used to reduce the amount of sunlight that can access a room; although they reduce light levels, they seldom filter out the UV radiation. Some fabric blinds are available (through commercial outlets) treated with a coating that will reduce IR radiation. Artificial light sources that emit low levels of UV radiation should be used; where possible UV filters can be placed in front of the light source, although not all filters are suitable for a museum environment – some filter out one or more colours, which results in incorrect colour rendering of the objects. Incandescent lights, halogen lamps and fluorescent lights (often referred to as tube lights or fluorescent tubes) will have to be tested for the emission of UV radiation prior to use.

Since UV radiation is the most energetic and destructive form of light it might be assumed that if UV light is eliminated, visible light is of minimal concern. This is not true – all wavelengths of light can cause significant damage (see section 4.3).

4.4.3 Measures to filter out UV radiation

When sunlight cannot be avoided, UV radiation from outside should be excluded, for example, by the use of special glazing or by the application of UV filters on the windows. The latter can be covered with a special sheet material, such as Perspex VE or VA, Plexiglas 201 or 209, and Lexan 9034 (note that ordinary Plexiglas or Perspex does not filter out UV). In some instances it may be possible to replace window glass with laminated glass which has a UV filter incorporated. Special UV-filtering foil, which has to be applied directly to the glass, can also be used. A suitable filter should not allow more than 1% of the radiation of 380 nm wavelength to pass through and not more than 50% of the radiation at 400 nm (Martin 1997). It should be noted that UV barrier materials are susceptible to ageing therefore their blocking capacity will decrease over time. It is also possible to apply UV barrier foils to the glass of showcases particularly when objects require additional protection from UV radiation.

4.5 Infrared radiation

IR radiation is the radiation that we perceive as warmth. It has a wavelength of 780 nm to 1 mm.

4.5.1 Damage to materials

The energy of IR radiation can be harmful. It can have a mechanical effect or increase chemical reactions. Shrinkage and cracking are mechanical changes, e.g. a spotlight aimed at the top of a lace bonnet will make the temperature rise locally and therefore the RH will decrease (see section 3.1.2). The lace will then release moisture in the area that has been warmed up and consequently the material dehydrates. Tensions caused as a result of this could eventually lead to tears in the lace.

Localised heating by light sources is particularly problematic when thermoplastic adhesives have been used in the conservation of an object as they become sticky at higher temperatures.

The rate of chemical reactions is increased by the heat of IR radiation. Cellulose, for example, will degrade 2.5 times as rapidly when the temperature is increased by 5 °C (Thomson 1986: 43).

4.5.2 Light sources

Sunlight contains a high level of IR radiation. Measures such as shutters and blinds on the outside of windows provide the most effective protection against the radiant heat of sunlight. If it is not possible to use these types of materials, curtains on the inside of windows provide an alternative. Of all the artificial light sources, incandescent lights and halogen lamps give off the most IR radiation. An incandescent light bulb yields only limited amounts of visible light; halogen lamps are more efficient, especially those that run on mains voltage. These types of lamp should never be used in an enclosed space, such as a showcase, unless a special separate compartment with a ventilator is available.

4.5.3 Measures to eliminate IR radiation

If the distance between an object and a lamp is increased, this reduces the heating up of the object. When it is not possible to increase the distance, lamps with dichroic-coated reflectors can be used. These reflect most of the heat generated out through the back of the lamp.

4.6 Light sources

When choosing light sources, the following should be considered:

1. The amount of UV and IR radiation emitted by the light source.
2. Colour rendering. In order to render colours correctly it is important that all wavelengths between 400 and 780 nm are present in the light source (continuous spectrum). Sunlight contains a complete and continuous spectrum as a result of which all colours present in objects will be rendered correctly when illuminated by the sun. Some artificial lights also give acceptable colour rendering, which is expressed by the colour rendering index R_a. In general, incandescent lights and most halogen lamps have an R_a of 100, which means that all colours are represented as they would be if illuminated by sunlight. For fluorescent light sources, the colour rendering index varies with the phosphor type. When objects are exhibited, artificial light sources should have an R_a of at least 85.
3. The colour temperature. The colour of light depends upon the temperature of the light source: the higher the temperature of the light source, the whiter the light. The colour temperature is expressed in degrees Kelvin (0 °K = −273.15 °C, absolute zero) (Table 9). An incandescent light bulb has a colour temperature of approximately 2,700 °K and appears yellow when compared to the blue of a clear sky (15,000–30,000 °K).

   It is difficult to give the colour temperature of discharge lamps such as fluorescent tubes, energy-saving lamps and neon lights. The type of gas and its pressure, and the fluorescent powders inside the lamp determine the colour temperature of the emitted light.

   When illuminating a room, the colour temperature of the light used should be considered. Light emitted by a light source with a low colour temperature at a low light level is perceived by humans as 'warm'. When dimming an incandescent light bulb, the colour temperature is lowered in addition to the reduction of the light level. Using light of a higher colour temperature at low light levels makes colours look more vivid. Higher light levels are required in offices and laboratories, and in these situations it is best to use neutral white light of approximately 4,000 °K.

4. Lamp life (maintenance). An incandescent light source has a lamp life which varies from 1000 to 4000 hours depending on the type. Discharge lamps, however, will last much longer: 8000 to 12000 hours.
5. Efficiency (energy costs). Efficiency is expressed in the amount of lumen per watt. For instance, a tungsten halogen lamp has an efficiency of 22 lm/W (depending on the type) and a fluorescent lamp may have an efficiency up to 93 lm/W.
6. Ability to be dimmed. To reduce the lux level it can be useful to use a light management system. It is important to use light that can be dimmed. An incandescent light source, for example, can be dimmed very easily with a dimmer and fluorescent tubes can be dimmed by using special control gear.

The sun

- Emits a lot of IR radiation (heat);
- Emits a lot of visible light;
- Emits a lot of UV radiation.

UV radiation is partly filtered out by glass. Extremely high lux values can be obtained and a room can be heated up significantly by direct sunlight. It should therefore be avoided at all times. Indirect sunlight can be used provided that the intensity of the light can be adjusted and that UV and IR radiation are blocked out as much as possible. Because daylight fluctuates it is important to monitor light levels regularly.

Incandescent light bulbs

- Emit a lot of IR radiation (heat);
- Emit relatively little visible light;
- Emit little UV radiation.

An incandescent light bulb is filled with an inert gas and contains a thin tungsten coil. When electricity is passed through the coil, it glows; the lamp emits light. The colour temperature of light bulbs (2,700 °K) is lower than that of halogen lamps and some of the fluorescent lamps; a light bulb gives off 'warm' light which is often experienced as pleasant, especially in combination with low light levels. The electrical power consumed by the lamp is mainly transformed into heat (94%) and when used in small spaces such as showcases and cabinets, the temperature can therefore rise significantly. In view of this, it is advisable to use other external light sources (see section 8.3.8). The colour render-

Table 9 Several light sources and their colour temperatures.

Light source	Colour temperature
Incandescent light	2,700 °K
Halogen lamp	3,000 °K
Fluorescent tube light	2,700–6,500 °K
Daylight on a cloudy day	Approximately 6500 °K

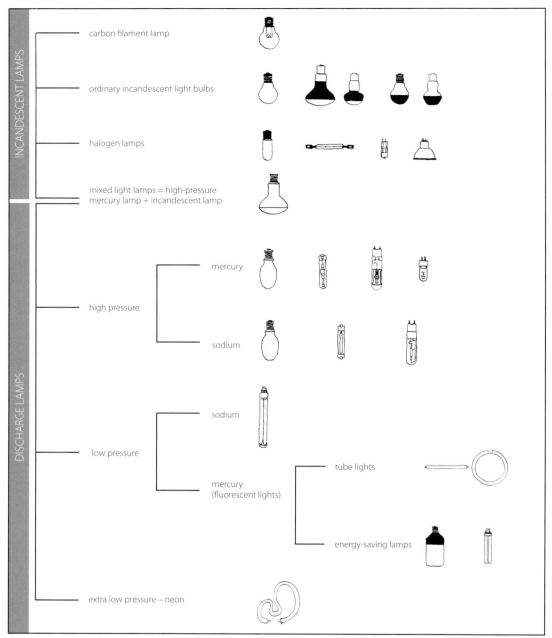

Figure 48 A schematic overview of different types of lamps (courtesy R. Visser, Technical Management, Amersfoort, The Netherlands).

ing of incandescent light is optimum with an R_a of 100. Light bulbs have an average life expectancy of 1,000 hours but the bulb emits less light over time as the tungsten vaporises and condenses onto the inside of the glass (black discoloration). This is less common with modern lamps.

Halogen lamps

- Emit a lot of IR radiation (heat);
- Emit more visible light than incandescent light bulbs;
- Emit a lot of UV radiation.

A halogen lamp is a variation upon the incandescent light bulb. The lamp is filled with halogen vapour in addition to the inert gas and, as a result, emits whiter light and has a greater performance than a light bulb. The lamp itself is usually made of quartz glass (rather than normal glass) in order to be able to withstand the higher temperatures – as a result halogen lamps emit more UV radiation than incandescent lights. If halogen lamps are used in museum settings, the UV radiation must be filtered out. This can be achieved by placing a UV-absorbing sheet glass in front of the lamp or by using a bulb with a coating which reduces the UV emission without affecting the colour rendering. At present, there are several different types of halogen lamps available with UV filters or coatings, often described on the packaging as UV block or UV stop. The colour temperature is around 3,000 °K.

The lifespan of a halogen lamp depends upon the type used, but is usually between 2,000 and 4,000 hours, i.e. considerably longer than an ordinary light bulb. In addition, the lamp does not become blackened and consequently emits light at its full strength throughout its entire life. The colour rendering is perfect with an R_a of 100.

Halogen lamps with UV filters are useful in museum settings as spotlights. There are two types available:

- **High-voltage halogen lamps** accept 230 volts and can be placed directly into a bracket (in industry often referred to as the luminaire). These lamps generate a lot of light but also more heat, and are less economical than low-voltage halogen lamps. For example, an efficiency of 15 lm/W for 230V high-voltage halogen lamps compared to 22 lm/W for 12V halogen lamps. High-voltage halogen lamps can be dimmed, which will cause a slight colour change.
- **Low-voltage halogen lamps** run off a 12 or 24 volts supply and therefore need a transformer. Electronic transformers are preferable since they can handle the peak loads which occur when the lamp is turned on. The lamps will therefore last longer. In addition, an electronic transformer uses less energy and gives off less warmth. Low-voltage halogen lamps can be dimmed. A special type of lamp – the cold halogen lamp – is fitted with a reflector that reflects most of the generated heat towards the back of the lamp. A disadvantage of this appliance is that, with an open luminaire, colours can be seen at the back of the lamp. The colour temperature of a cold halogen lamp is in general slightly higher at 3,100 °K.

Low-voltage halogen lamps are more compact, more efficient and have longer lifespans than high-voltage halogen lamps.

Discharge lamps (e.g. fluorescent tubes)

- Emit little IR radiation (heat);
- Emit more visible light than light bulbs;
- Emit a little or a lot of UV radiation, depending upon the type.

All discharge lamps work according to the same principle. The lamp is filled with gas (in fluorescent lights this is mercury vapour together with inert gases). An electric charge discharges into the gas at which point UV radiation and sometimes visible light are emitted. Fluorescent lights have special fluorescent powders (phosphors) on the inside of the glass tube, which change this radiation into visible light. The composition of these powders not only determines the colour of the light, but also the colour rendering of the lamp. Fluorescent lamps are extremely efficient, long-lasting light sources with broad applications. The discharge tube yields little heat, however, the starter becomes warm.

Different types of fluorescent lamps are available varying in wattage, length, shape and light colour. Not all fluorescent lamps have suitable colour rendering for museum purposes but there are some with excellent colour rendering, for example, nos. 927, 930 and 940, manufactured among others by Philips and Osram (the R_a of Philips' 800 series is higher than that of the 900 series, although the colour rendering is less good; this is due to the method by which the R_a is measured). These lamps are suitable for use in museums. Because the starter in these lamps becomes warm, they should not be placed in showcases unless the lamp is fitted in a separate ventilated compartment. Colour rendering is somewhat reduced with ageing so the lamps should be replaced before this happens. The colour temperature depends upon the type but lies between 2,700 °K and 6,500 °K.

Fluorescent lamps are now available that can be operated by electronic high frequency starters and have a colour rendering index of more than 90. This combination is of great interest to museums as there are several advantages, including:

- Increased lifespan (up to 12,500 to 16,000 hours);
- Low energy costs (approximately 25% less energy than conventional systems);
- No individual starters necessary;

- No flickering light as the light turns itself off automatically when defective;
- Minimum depreciation (relapsing light levels), approximately 5%;
- Easy to dim;
- Low maintenance costs.

Compact fluorescent lights
The discharge of the gas occurs in a number of small tubes which are connected to each other. They can be fixed in a compact fashion into a special lamp foot, making them almost as small as incandescent light bulbs. Compact fluorescent lamps have similar properties to the tubes (economical, long lifespan, choice in light colour).

These lamps are an economical alternative to incandescent lamps – they save energy (using 50 to 80% less energy) and have a longer lifespan (lasting 8 to 12 times longer). They can only be dimmed when an electronic starter is used. The colour rendering of most compact fluorescent lamps, however, is not good enough for museum purposes. From Philips, only the PL 'L' energy-saving lamp in the 900 series (18, 24 and 36 watt) with an R_a greater than 90 is suitable for museum use (the equivalent from Osram is the Dulux series). Note that the light levels (lux) should not exceed the desired level.

One particular energy-saving lamp has the tube, electronics and lamp foot compacted into one. As these lamps are similar in size to incandescent lamps, they can be used to replace ordinary light bulbs but their colour rendering is not good enough for exhibition spaces.

High-pressure discharge lamps: CDM (Philips), HQI (Osram)
In high-pressure discharge lamps, light is generated in much the same way as with fluorescent lights. Visible light is generated in a broad spectrum as the gas is under high pressure. CDM and HQI are both metal halide lamps, CDM has a ceramic element and HQI is the same lamp but with a quartz element. These lamps can be smaller than fluorescent lights; they take longer to warm up (up to four minutes) and to cool down when turned off. Although the colour rendering of most lamps is unsuitable for museum purposes, they all have an R_a of 80 or more. One of Philips' latest lamps is the CDM-T: the advantage of this lamp is that it maintains its colour rendering index with ageing. Many of the modern metal halide lamps are equipped with UV filters.

LEDs (light emitting diodes)

- Emit little IR radiation (heat);
- Emit a lot (relatively) of visible light;
- Emit little UV radiation.

LEDs are little coloured lights that are used in electronic equipment, toys, signs, etc. LEDs are different from ordinary light bulbs in that they do not have a filament to break or burn out. When a current passes across a diode (made from two different semiconductors) light is emitted. The colour of the light depends on a number of factors, including the type of materials used for making the LED.

Until recently, the light output from an LED was too low to be considered for practical uses such as replacing the incandescent bulb. Recent developments, however, have made these lights more useful and they have already found their way into museums for the illumination of objects in exhibition. They are very small, produce a lot of visible light and generate very little heat – they are also at least five times more energy efficient than their incandescent counterparts.

Red, yellow and green coloured LEDs have been around for some time, but other colours, including white are now also available. These have a colour-rendering index of 85 or greater. The colour temperature can range from 5,500 °K to as high as 8,000 °K.

4.6.1 Fibre optics

Fibre optics are not a light source as such but a means to bundle light and transport it over distances. The light sources can be placed separately and at a distance from the objects (Fig. 49). This presents enormous advantages from a conservation point of view. There is no localised heating near the museum objects and hardly any UV radiation reaches the objects. The disadvantage is that there is a loss of light. The lamp that is used most often inside the light box is a halogen lamp with a reflector or a high-pressure discharge lamp. The latter has a longer lifespan (6,000 hours) and proper light efficiency, but a colour rendering of just over 80 instead of 100. Fibre optics can be equipped with lenses, mirrors, reflectors and frosted glass in order to achieve certain effects.

Figure 49 A showcase for ecclesiastical textiles, which are illuminated with fibre optics (photo courtesy Karma Design, The Netherlands, collection Museum Kunst & Geschiedenis).

4.6.2 Energy efficiency

The energy efficiency of a lamp is expressed in the number of lumens per watt. Table 10 shows that the light efficiency of compact fluorescent lamps is higher than that of incandescent lamps. For this reason (outside a collection) it would be better to replace a 60 watt light bulb with an 11 watt energy-saving lamp. All discharge lamps have a high efficiency compared to incandescent bulbs. There is however one problem: in some lamps the colour rendering is affected by this higher efficiency. The fluorescent lamp with a proper colour rendering index (R_a = 90) has a lower efficiency. Note: it is extremely important to clean the luminaire, fittings and reflectors of the lamps regularly in order to maintain maximum efficiency. Note also that lamps made of quartz glass should not be touched with bare hands.

Although incandescent lamps remain an option, other more efficient light sources are available. Recent improvements in colour rendering as well as the possibility of dimming has increased the use of high frequency fluorescent lamps. Although the outlay costs are higher, they are cheaper to run due to low maintenance and energy costs. Museums should contribute to reducing energy consumption and preventing environmental pollution by choosing a lighting system that takes into account energy use, and the environmental effects of the production and waste disposal of lamps.

4.7 Presenting a textile collection

4.7.1 Lighting design

The illumination of objects for an exhibition is a complex matter, as many issues have to be addressed. Apart from reducing damage to objects to an accepted minimal level, the lighting design has to plan for the total visual environment. It has to suit the variety of activities that will occur in the space; the appearance of the space and the architecture and the atmosphere of the exhibition. It is therefore important that those responsible work together right from the start to achieve a good lighting plan.

A lighting design concept that is oriented primarily towards providing a recommended illuminance level (in order to reduce damage to objects) may not meet the safety criteria for persons using the space. It is therefore recommended that a lighting engineer should be consulted when designing a display.

Table 10 The energy efficiency of several types of lamps expressed in lumen per watt.

Incandescent light	100 watt	14 lumen per watt
Halogen 230V	100 watt	17 lumen per watt
Halogen 12V	100 watt	24 lumen per watt
Fluorescent light (900 series)	58 watt	65 lumen per watt
Energy-saving bulbs	26 watt	65 lumen per watt

Some suggestions to be considered are presented below (see also section 4.6 for the properties of several lamps):

- A spectrum with minimal UV and IR radiation;
- A colour rendering index $R_a > 85$;
- The colour of the light should resemble natural light, especially when it is used in combination with daylight.
- The possibility of using different types of light sources;
- The possible use of special filters;
- The flexibility of the design (e.g. the possibility of influencing the level of daylight);
- Simplicity in operation and maintenance;
- The integration of design and architecture should adhere to aesthetic criteria.

The distance between light source and objects
Nearly all objects are three-dimensional and this should be emphasised by the lighting. One of the methods often used for illuminating three-dimensional objects with artificial light is an ambient overall lighting scheme complemented by spotlights. These can be aimed at an angle of 45 degrees. Special care should be taken with shiny objects to avoid reflections that may make them difficult to see. The walls and ceilings should preferably be light-coloured (but not white), and the floor slightly darker. A high ceiling would simplify such a display. The type and colour of the objects also play a role.

Objects with a vertical surface are often more difficult to illuminate. If the light source is too close, it will give off a reflection; if it is too far away it will cast a shadow and obscure the texture of the object. A light source with an angle of 30 degrees in relation to the vertical plane presents a reasonable alternative when illuminating vertically positioned objects. The higher the ceiling, the farther away the light source should be placed from the object. With a 3 m high ceiling the light source should be 0.8 m from the wall; with a 4 m high ceiling this distance should be 1.35 m (Fig. 50).

The relationship between basic lighting levels and highlights
The lower the ambient lighting levels, the less light is necessary for the highlights to provide proper contrast. Therefore, make use of indirect light by reflecting light off walls and ceilings but avoid strong reflections from white walls, which can result in too great a contrast. Pay attention to the difference between dispersed general lighting and bundled lighting (spotlights). Ensure that objects are not exposed to light bundles that are too powerful as this can cause localised heating of the object. By increasing the distance between the object and the lamp, the illuminance and the heat generated are reduced. Alternatively, use low power lamps or lamps with reflectors.

Reflection and glittering
Daylight that enters through windows or badly aimed spotlights can cause unwanted reflections and localised glittering which may affect the pleasure of looking at exhibited objects. Visitors find reflections extremely annoying and the same is true for objects that are placed in the dark or are poorly illuminated. In most cases direct daylight can be diffused by curtains – in some cases it may even be preferable to completely block off a window.

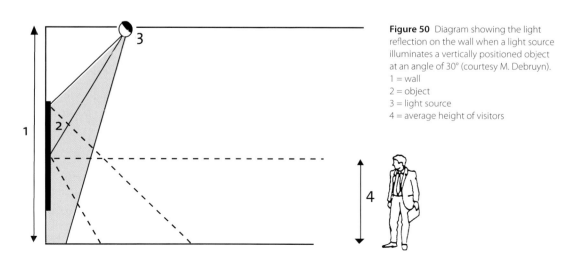

Figure 50 Diagram showing the light reflection on the wall when a light source illuminates a vertically positioned object at an angle of 30° (courtesy M. Debruyn).
1 = wall
2 = object
3 = light source
4 = average height of visitors

Diffused light causes very little shadow, which can sometimes make it more difficult to see details or texture. Employing additional spotlights can help to overcome this problem.

The effects of lighting

To avoid daylight falling directly onto museum objects, the angle at which the daylight enters a museum and reflecting the light from the walls and ceilings into the exhibition space can be adjusted. The colour of the exhibition space, and the structure of the walls and ceilings will determine the final effect of the reflected light. In general, light-coloured and smooth surfaces reflect more light than dark and structured surfaces. For example, raw concrete has a reflection rate of 20% whereas a smooth, white plastered wall yields a reflection of 80%.

In order to see clearly the details on objects, the contrast with the environment should not be too great. A dark object hung on a light wall appears as a silhouette; it is almost impossible to see its details. When details are less important it is possible to play with light and deliberately create dramatic effects based on strong contrasts. Theatre lighting designers are often involved to good effect in the design of lighting for special exhibitions. Any lighting design should always be discussed with a (textile) conservator.

4.8 Recent developments

The phrase 'permitted lux-hours per year' could be interpreted as meaning that each year starts with a clean slate, implying that an object can be permanently exposed provided that the number of lux-hours per year is not exceeded. This does not take into consideration the cumulative effect of light. The key question is: How many lux-hours can an object endure before unacceptable damage occurs? Some museums have tried to establish guidelines for their collections of paper and graphic documents (Colby 1998; Derbyshire and Ashley-Smith 1999). The objects were divided into categories depending upon their sensitivity to light (in a similar way as the blue wool standard). The 'just noticeable fade' (JNF), or 'perceptible change', of an object was recorded empirically (Table 11). A 'just noticeable fade' is the colour difference that can just about be perceived by the human eye and corresponds with a measurable colour difference of 1.6 CIELAB units (CIE 2004). Thinking in terms of 'just noticeable fade', a coloured surface will be completely faded after 30 JNF. An object that is attractive in display because of its colour will have lost its exhibition value after 10 JNF. So when an object is made of a material that has 1 JNF in 10 years, it will no longer be suitable to put on display after 100 years and is considered to be lost in roughly 300 years.

Table 11 shows the exposure time necessary to cause one just noticeable fade under two types of lighting: a spectrum similar to daylight through normal glass, containing a high amount of UV radiation, and light from which all radiation with a wavelength of 400 nm or less has been filtered out.

Materials can be categorised on the basis of their light sensitivity. ISO levels 1–4 for all light-sensitive pigments and materials of poor quality such as watercolours, portrait miniatures on ivory and parchment, pastels and coloured printing techniques; ISO levels 5–8 cover the more light-fast pigments and materials of good quality such as monochrome pencil drawings, black and white etchings and engravings. Once a division in ISO levels or blue wool categories has been created, it can be used to establish an acceptable rate of fading upon which exhibition schedules can be designed. The aim should be to opt for a shorter exhibition time, a lower number of lux-hours per year or a longer time span between periods of exhibition.

The fading of colours in textiles often levels out over time. Colours fade rapidly at first and much more slowly as time progresses until colour changes become barely noticeable. The colours in historic textiles are often already faded to such an extent that further fading is unlikely to be noticeable. It should be noted that light has another extremely harmful effect on textiles: the reduction in tensile strength. It would, therefore, be useful to create a similar division in textile materials, one based not only on colour fading but also on the reduction in tensile strength.

Table 11 Exposure time in 10^6 lux-hours (megalux hours or Mlx h), necessary to cause one just noticeable fade (CIE 2004).

Blue wool category	1	2	3	4	5	6	7	8
Light with high UV content	0.22	0.6	1.5	3.5	8	20	50	120
Light with low UV content	0.3	1	3	10	30	100	300	1100
Category of light sensitivity	High responsivity			Medium responsivity			Low responsivity	

The International Commission on Illumination (CIE) published a technical report (CIE 2004) which contains recommendations for lighting in museums. This suggests adding two further categories to those listed in Table 12:

- Zero tolerance: materials and objects that have never been exposed to light and are in original condition, for example a fabric sample book.
- Irresponsive materials and objects that are not damaged by light, such as stone and metal.

Table 12 shows an initial categorisation of materials according to their light sensitivity. In Table 13 an example is given as to how this categorisation can be used according to light sensitivity in practice (based on CIE 2004).

It should be noted that the value of these guidelines is somewhat limited as it is often not known how many lux-hours to which an object has already been exposed before it entered the collection, or even during its time as a collection item. A record of the lux-hours of every object on display should therefore be started as soon as possible.

Table 12 Categorisation of materials according to their light sensitivity (CIE 2004; Instituut Collectie Nederland 2005).

Category	General description	ISO level	Examples
Zero tolerance	Sensitive material that should never or only rarely be exposed to light	< 1	Unfaded textiles with original colours
High responsivity	Most historic vegetable dyes and lake pigments	1	Turmeric, saffron, sulphonated indigo, many modern dyes for paper, coloured textiles, coloured plastics, rubber
	Most insect extracts (lac, cochineal) Most early synthetic dyes (anilines)	2	Carmine lake, gamboge, quercitron lake, madder on cotton, old fustic
	Many cheap synthetic dyes	3	Madder on silk, cochineal on wool and cotton, weld, alum mordant on wool, indigo on cotton and silk, feathers
Medium responsivity	Some historic vegetable dyes (madder on wool, lake) Most furs, hairs and feathers	4	Bone, horn, mother-of-pearl, lac dye and seaweed on wool, weld tin mordant on wool, untanned leather, vegetable-tanned leather
	Paintings on canvas, wood	5	Alizarin (madder) lake tint, alizarin (madder) on wool
	Painted and untreated wood	6	Cochineal on silk Foxglove on wool
Low responsivity	Modern pigments for external use Artists''permanent' paints	7	Indigo on wool, alizarin (madder) lake, alizarin (madder) and water lily roots black on wool, vermilion, chrome yellow
	Structural colours in insects Few historic vegetable dyes (indigo on wool)	8	Permanent paints, cadmium red, orange and yellow
Irresponsivity	Most inorganic materials	>8	Stone Metal Glass Ceramic Carbon

Table 13 An example of how to use the categorisation according to light sensitivity in practice, exposure time in 10^6 lux-hours (megalux-hours or Mlx h) (CIE 2004; Instituut Collectie Nederland 2005).

ISO level	Exposure time for 1 JNF (Mlx h)	In practice	Consequences
<1	No UV	UV < 10 µW/lm Exposure to light to absolute minimum	Exhibit only in exceptional circumstances
1	0.3	6000 hours @ 50 lux will cause 1 JNF	If 1 JNF is acceptable within 10 years, the object
2	1	(6000h × 50 lux = 0.3 mlx h)	can be exposed for 20% of the time @ 50 lux, i.e. in
3	3		total for 2 years (2y × 365d × 8h × 50lux ≈ 0.3 mlx h)
4	10	67000 hours @ 150 lux will cause 1 JNF	If the object is exposed permanently @ 150 lux,
5	30	(67000h × 150 lux = 10 mlx h)	1 JNF will occur in approximately 20 years
6	100		(22y × 365d × 8h × 150 lux ≈ 10 mlx h)
7	300	1500000 h @ 200 lux will cause 1 JNF	If the object is exposed permanently @ 200 lux,
8	1100	(1500000h × 200 lux = 300 mlx h)	1 JNF will occur in approximately 500 years
			(510y × 365d × 8h × 200 lux ≈ 300 mlx h)
>8	>1100		Permanent, lux adapted to surrounding

5

Insects and fungi in textile collections

5.1 Insects

Insects play an important part in the natural degradation of organic materials; they make no distinction between rubbish and valuable objects. Textile collections represent a good source of nutrients for the larvae of moths, fur and carpet beetles. They have the ability to digest keratin, the main constituent of wool, fur and feathers. Cotton and silk are not usually attacked by the larvae of moths and carpet beetles, but when these materials are dirty or are used in combination with wool, they too can be damaged. Cockroaches (omnivores), silverfish and firebrats (sugar eaters) are harmful to textile collections to a lesser extent; drugstore beetles and cigarette beetles can also cause problems. Insects also seek shelter in textiles in order to pupate, causing damage without actually feeding on the material.

5.1.1 Characteristics

Insects are invertebrates. They have an external skeleton: their skin hardens to a shell of chitin to which their muscles are attached. Insects form the largest group within the Arthropods. Their legs consist of jointed segments and their bodies are divided in three segments: the head (with eyes, external mouthparts and antennae), the thorax (to which three pairs of legs are attached and often one or two pairs of wings), and the segmented abdomen. Insects are hexapod, i.e. they have six legs.

5.1.2 Development

Insects can be divided into two groups on the basis of their development. Cockroaches, silverfish, firebrats, lice, grasshoppers and crickets develop by incomplete metamorphosis (Fig. 51). From the egg, a small nymph hatches that already resembles an adult to some extent; it will continue to develop and grow through a number of stages. As it grows, it sheds its skin several times. After the last moult it has all the characteristics of the adult (wings etc.) and is fertile. This type of insect feeds during all its developing stages.

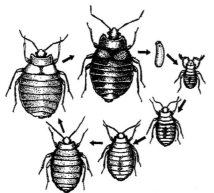

Figure 51 Incomplete metamorphosis.

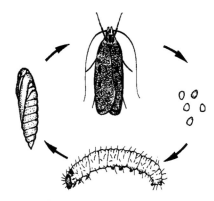

Figure 52 Complete metamorphosis.

around 70%; some species have adjusted to drier conditions while others need a high relative humidity (RH) (such as silverfish). Some species obtain all the moisture they need from their food – woodborers usually need a moisture content of more than 12%. Other species need a high RH because they feed on the fungi that grow on the objects.

Light is not a vital requirement but it affects the behaviour of insects. Adult carpet beetles, for example, fly towards the light, whereas silverfish, moths and cockroaches hide from it. This behaviour can play an important role when inspecting a collection for the presence of insects. Another factor important for the behaviour of insects is the need for shelter. Cockroaches, silverfish and firebrats crawl away into crevices and gaps.

Beetles, moths, butterflies, flies, mosquitoes, bees and wasps undergo a complete metamorphosis (Fig. 52). A tiny larva hatches from the egg; as it eats and grows, it sheds its skin several times. The larvae are thus the most harmful to textiles. When the larva is large enough it pupates, undergoing a complete change in appearance into an adult before finally emerging from its cocoon. The adult insects are responsible for the dispersal and reproduction of the species. They do not usually feed and therefore cause no damage to textiles. The complete cycle from egg to adult can take up to one year, with the adult insects usually appearing in spring or summer. If circumstances are favourable, this cycle can be shorter, resulting in two or more generations per year.

5.1.3 Requirements

In order to stay alive, insects need oxygen. They do not have lungs but take in air through a number of openings called spirades in their skin, which is then distributed through the tracheal system. Insects obtain the nutrients they need from organic material. Some insects are omnivores (e.g. cockroaches, drugstore beetles); others have a preference for vegetable material (larvae of woodborers and cigarette beetles); and some prefer animal material (the larvae of fur and carpet beetles and moths). Dirt, grease, dust, sweat and urine on textiles provide extra nutrients that make textiles more attractive to insects. Insects can stay alive at a temperature of between 5 and 45 °C, but for most species development is optimal at between 15 and 35 °C. Most insects can develop in a relative humidity (RH) of between 50 and 90%; the optimum is

5.1.4 Insects in textile collections

Although up to 30 damaging insect species may be encountered in European museum collections, only those most commonly found in textile collections are discussed here.

Moths

*Webbing clothes moths (*Tineola bisselliella*)*
In northwest Europe, the webbing clothes moth has problems surviving in an outdoor climate; it prefers the warmth of houses. Although it is possible for these moths to move independently from birds' nests to collections they are usually brought in with infested artefacts. A fertilised female can lay in excess of 100 eggs in a safe place; for example, under a collar, in a lining, in pockets or in the upholstery of furniture. The eggs are barely visible to the naked eye – often the frass and excrement are mistaken for eggs. Tiny white naked larvae hatch from the eggs and eat their way through the textile. They spin a cocoon of webbing around themselves and over the material to protect them from desiccation, which, in turn, fills with their excrement. Their droppings look like small pellets with a maximum diameter of 0.5 mm and have the same colour as the material eaten by the larvae. The larvae make irregular holes and produce a lot of waste – they are in fact rather messy feeders. An object under attack from this moth looks dirty with several holes, webbing and droppings.

After a period of weeks to several months, the larvae pupate. A uniformly golden-coloured moth, 5–7 mm long, emerges from the cocoon (Fig. 53). The adult moths are poor flyers that scuttle away from the light; they only live for a few weeks during which time they reproduce but do not feed. A characteristic of harmful moths is that while at rest they fold their wings over each other on their abdomen; they do not hold them upright like butterflies or spread out like other moths.

*Case-bearing clothes moth (*Tinea pellionella*)*
Case-bearing clothes moths can survive in a moderate outdoor climate and live in birds' nests, from which they often enter a collection (via chimneys, windows, etc.). Adult case-bearing clothes moths resemble the webbing clothes moth: they are somewhat larger with a length of 7–8 mm, also gold-coloured but with several dark spots on their wings (Fig. 54). The larvae can be clearly distinguished because they spin a small case around their bodies, which they drag along as they move about. The cases are of the same colour as the material on which they feed and thus serve as camouflage as well as protection. As they do not spin silk tubes, they produce less waste than the webbing clothes moth (Fig. 55). In particular, they graze the surface of a textile, and when in danger hide in their cases in which they also pupate. The case-bearing clothes moth has a preference for a somewhat higher humidity and is found less in heated environments.

*Tapestry moth (*Tricophaga tapetzella*)*
The tapestry moth can only live at relative humidity of about 80% and is no longer found very often in textile collections (Fig. 56). Tapestries hanging against a cold, damp outside wall can be vulnerable to attack by this moth. The larvae have a preference for coarser material and also spin cases around their bodies. When the moths emerge after pupation they leave the case behind in an upright position. Moths have a wingspan of 8–10 mm. From the shoulder their wings are approximately one-third brown, becoming cream in colour towards the end.

Carpet beetles

*Carpet beetles (*Anthrenus sp.*)*
Carpet beetles are small and round, approximately 2–4 mm in length, and similar in shape to ladybirds but only half the size. They have white/black/brown/orange scales on their wing cases (elytra) (Fig. 57). They fly well – usually towards the light. In summer they are often found on windowsills. Most species need to go outside to feed on pollen in order to become fertile. The beetles lay their eggs in birds' nests, where the larvae can eat feathers, hair and other animal matter. The active larvae can move easily from the nests into buildings and are of great concern to museums, where they not only feed on dead insects and mice, but also on museum objects (hence they are often referred to as museum beetles without making a distinction between the species); in fact, there is only one type that is officially called the museum beetle (*Anthrenus museorum*).

Figure 53 Webbing clothes moth (length 5–7 mm).

Figure 54 Case-bearing clothes moth (length 7–8 mm).

Figure 55 Damage to velvet caused by the case-bearing clothes moth (photo courtesy ICAT textielrestauratie b.v.).

Figure 56 Tapestry moth (wingspan 8–10 mm).

Young carpet beetle larvae are tiny and can crawl through the smallest gaps. They grow to between 4 and 5 mm in length, are torpedo-shaped with brown or black bristly hairs. This hairy appearance has given them their nickname 'woolly bears'. The larvae gnaw small, regular holes or graze areas bare without spinning webbing or cases. They eat quickly and voraciously. When attacking skins and fur, the larvae eat the hairs at their root, the damage only becoming visible when the fur is touched and the loose hairs fall out. While growing, the larvae shed their skins approximately six times. The most striking indication of the presence of active carpet beetle larvae are these hairy, cast skins.

*Two-spotted carpet beetle or fur beetle (*Attagenus pellio*)*
Fur beetles are somewhat more oval in shape than carpet beetles. They range from 3 to 6 mm in length and are black with a small white dot on their wing cases (Fig. 58). Just like carpet beetles, the adults may feed on pollen and lay their eggs in birds' nests. The larvae are hairy and resemble carpet beetle larvae, but are longer (4–10 mm) and more elongated with long tail hairs. They feed on animal matter and dead insects. When these larvae enter a collection they can cause a lot of damage.

*South American carpet beetle or cabinet beetle (*Trogoderma angustum*)*
The South American carpet beetle (known in the UK as the cabinet beetle) has found its way into European museum collections since the mid-1990s. Originating from South America, it was introduced into Germany along with imported goods. The beetles are black with two curved white bands over their wing cases; they are more oval in shape than the common carpet beetle (Fig. 59). The larvae are slim, 4–6 mm in length, hairy with long tail hairs. They feed on animal matter and are very mobile and destructive.

Cockroaches
Cockroaches, which exist in museum collections in northwest Europe, are often imported from warmer climates (they need heated buildings in order to survive). They undergo an incomplete metamorphosis; the nymphs look like the adults but without wings. The adult insects vary in length from 1 to 3 cm. They are brown to black and have two pairs of wings. The forewings are leathery and veined and are held flat over the back. Cockroaches are easily identified by their long whip-like antennae, the semi-round pronotum covering the thorax, and the long and spiky legs. Also characteristic are the two cerci, little pointed protrusions sticking out from the rear of the abdomen.

The female deposits an egg case (oothecea), which contains between 12 and 50 eggs, in a safe place – usually in cracks or behind skirting boards. Cockroaches are omnivorous and eat during all the developmental stages. They are usually found in dwellings or catering areas and consume all kinds of material, leaving their strong-smelling droppings behind. They are active at night and hide

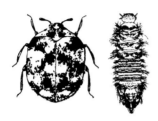

Figure 57 Carpet beetle (adult: length 2–4 mm; larva: length 4–5 mm).

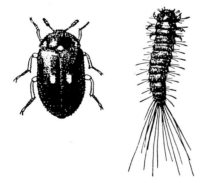

Figure 58 Fur beetle (adult: length 3–6 mm; larva: length 4–10 mm).

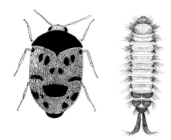

Figure 59 South American carpet beetle or cabinet beetle (adult: length 2.5–4 mm; larva: length of 4–6 mm) (reprinted from *A Guide to Museum Pest Control* by kind permission of the American Institute for Conservation of Historic & Artistic Works).

during the day, preferably in a dark, warm place. Cockroaches need either high humidity or drinking water in order to survive.

*German cockroach (*Blattella germanica*)*
This cockroach species is the one most commonly found in heated buildings in northwest Europe. The adult insects are approximately 1.5 cm in length. They are slender, light brown and have two dark stripes on their pronotum (Fig. 60). The eggs hatch immediately after the female drops her egg case.

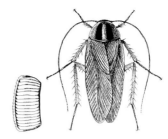

Figure 60 German cockroach (length 1.5 cm) and its egg case (reprinted from *A Guide to Museum Pest Control* by kind permission of the American Institute for Conservation of Historic & Artistic Works).

*Oriental cockroach (*Blatta orientalis*)*
The males of the oriental cockroach have wings; the females only have the stumps of rudimentary wings (Fig. 61). The adult insects are approximately 2.5 cm in length and are blunter in shape and darker in colour than the German cockroach. After the female lays her egg case, it will take several weeks or even months before the eggs hatch. Such a case could find its way into a collection unnoticed and hatch later. The insects need a high temperature to survive and are often found in kitchens and bakeries.

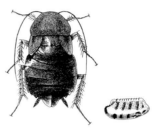

Figure 61 Oriental cockroach (length 2.5 cm) and its egg case (reprinted from *A Guide to Museum Pest Control* by kind permission of the American Institute for Conservation of Historic & Artistic Works).

*American cockroach (*Periplaneta americana*)*
The American cockroach is the largest cockroach species found in northwest Europe, with a length of approximately 4 cm. Both males and females have wings (Fig. 62). They need a high temperature and humidity to survive.

Bristletails

*Silverfish (*Lepisma saccharina*), grey silverfish or 'paperfish' (*Ctenolepisma longicaudatum*) and firebrat (*Thermobia domestica*)*
Silverfish, grey silverfish and firebrats belong to the most primitive group of insects, the bristletails. They undergo an incomplete metamorphosis; the nymphs resemble the adult insects. The adults are carrot-shaped and approximately 10–15 mm in length. The body is covered with shiny silver or grey-coloured scales. They have two long antennae, no wings and three long tail hairs. They move away from the light and are active at night. They are scavengers that feed on carbohydrate material and they can digest cellulose. In textile collections, they are particularly fond of synthetic cellulose materials such as cellulose acetate and viscose. Furthermore, they have a preference for starched materials and can graze the adhesive and starch from a surface. They can cause damage, for example, to sized, starched and calendered textiles, textiles with applications of gilded paper and tankas (Fig. 65).

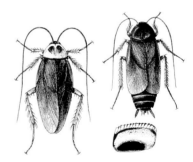

Figure 62 American cockroach (length 4 cm) and its egg case (reprinted from *A Guide to Museum Pest Control* by kind permission of the American Institute for Conservation of Historic & Artistic Works).

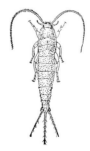

Figure 63 Silverfish (adult: length 10–15 mm).

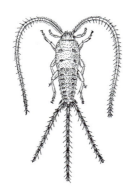

Figure 64 Firebrats (adult: length 10–15 mm).

Figure 65 Damage caused by silverfish: detail of a talismanic shirt (14th century, India), made from cellulose fibres, sized and embellished with verses in ink from the Qu'ran. The silverfish have eaten away the size (photo courtesy Textile Conservation Centre, University of Southampton, object in the collection of the Al-Sabah Collection of Islamic Art, Kuwait).

They have also been known to eat acid-free tissue paper and crumbs of food.

Silverfish can only live in humid conditions with a relative humidity above 70%. Their body is covered with silver grey scales and singularly positioned hair; their antennae are slightly shorter than their own body (Fig. 63). Firebrats can withstand somewhat drier conditions and have a preference for higher temperatures, with an optimum around 37°C. They have dark grey, spotted scales and antennae that are at least as long as their own body; in addition to this, their bodies are covered in tufts of hairs (Fig. 64).

Grey silverfish ('paperfish') have recently been found on a more regular basis and are often wrongly identified as firebrats. Grey silverfish also have dark grey scales and tufts of hair. Their antennae are as long as their body. They look very much like firebrats, but can survive fairly well in medium range temperatures and humidity. They lead a marginal existence at temperatures of 16 to 18°C.

Woodborers
All woodborers are beetles. The female insects lay their eggs in crevices or old exit holes in wood. After several weeks, small larvae hatch from the eggs. While feeding they tunnel through the wood, producing bore dust which is a mixture of excrement and waste. Bore dust usually remains inside the tunnels but sometimes it falls out when the object is being handled or when the beetles fly out. Larvae can live for several years inside the wood. They look like little worms, hence the name 'woodworm', but unlike worms they have small legs. The larvae pupate when they are fully grown, usually just under the surface of the wood. A beetle emerges from the cocoon after a few weeks. In spring or summer, these beetles gnaw through the remaining wood until they reach the surface and fly out, leaving behind a small exit hole. In most cases, the beetles only live for a few weeks during which time they do not eat.

It is not easy to determine whether exit holes are old or fresh, but the best indication of a fresh hole is a small pile of bore dust. This will collect underneath an object, proving that an insect has been active. In order to detect woodworm activity, an object can be placed on a piece of (black) paper and monitored to see whether bore dust collects over a period of time. Another method of detecting activity is to check whether new exit holes have been made. This can be done by filling up existing exit holes with furniture wax or applying a piece of paper over the surface which will become perforated; any newly made holes can easily be identified.

Although in principle woodborers do not cause damage to textiles, they can be present in textile collections, for example in furniture and composite objects. Of the many dozens of woodborer types found in nature, only a few cause problems in collections, namely those which live in dead and dry wood. The most damaging types are the common furniture beetle (*Anobium punctatum*), also referred to as 'woodworm' or 'bookworm', the deathwatch beetle (*Xestobium rufovillosum*), and the powder-post beetle (*Lyctus brunneus*): all three can be found in objects and in buildings. The notorious house longhorn (*Hylotrupes bajulus*) is only found in the fabric of buildings.

*Common furniture beetle (*Anobium punctatum*)*
The common furniture beetle is dark brown, 3–5 mm in length and has its head tucked underneath the

thorax (Fig. 66). The beetles emerge in spring and summer (from April to August) and live for three to four weeks. The larvae are yellowish-white, 6 mm in length and C-shaped. They live for approximately three years in the wood before they pupate in springtime. The larvae eat both soft and hard wood and have a preference for the sapwood. The exit holes are round with a diameter of 1–2 mm. The bore dust is unicoloured, granular and cigar-shaped.

*Deathwatch beetle (*Xestobium rufovillosum*)*
The deathwatch beetle exists mainly in the timbers of buildings and has a preference for moist hardwood that has already been pre-digested by fungi. The beetles are dark brown, 6 to 9 mm in length, with yellowish spots, and also have their head tucked underneath their thorax (Fig. 67). The larvae are yellowish-white, 11 mm in length and C-shaped. They live for 4–10 years in wood before they pupate in autumn. They hibernate in wood as a beetle and emerge in spring (from March to June). The exit holes are round with a diameter of 3–4 mm. The bore dust is wood-coloured and consists of large pellet or lentil-shaped granules.

*Powderpost beetles (*Lyctus *sp.)*
The powderpost beetle is slender, reddish brown in colour, and 5 to 7 mm in length (Fig. 68). The larvae are yellowish-white, C-shaped with a length of 5–6 mm. For 10–11 months they live in wood. In spring, they pupate and the beetles fly round for approximately one week between May and September. The larvae are only found in the sapwood of starchy hardwoods, especially oak, tropical hardwoods and bamboo. The exit holes are round with a diameter of 1–2 mm, resembling those of *Anobium punctatum*, but the bore dust is very fine, talc-like and remains in the tunnels.

5.2 Fungi

5.2.1 Fungi in textile collections

The most common fungi in textile collections are those that live on the surface of a material and which are capable of digesting cellulose, therefore objects made from vegetable fibres are especially vulnerable to attack. Synthetic fibres are generally not affected by fungi, unless they are soiled or have a certain finish. Mould (mold) and mildew are types of fungi and are commonly used interchangeably, although mould is often applied to black, blue, green, and red fungal growths, and mildew to

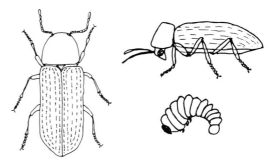

Figure 66 Common furniture beetle (adult: length 3–5 mm).

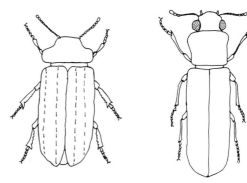

Figure 67 Deathwatch beetle (adult: length 6–9 mm).

Figure 68 Powderpost beetle (adult: length 5–7 mm).

whitish growths. The most common fungi species are: *Alternaria* sp. (olive green to black/grey mycelium), *Aspergillus* sp. (thick white/yellow to green/black mycelium), *Cladosporum* sp. (olive green/brown velvet-like mycelium), *Fusarium* sp. (white/yellow/pink to red-brown fleece-like mycelium) and *Penicillium* sp. (thick grey/green mycelium).

5.2.2 Characteristics and development

Fungi are microorganisms which form a separate kingdom alongside plants and animals. They are an indispensable link in the natural chain of decay and recycling of organic material. At the same time they represent a threat to museums because they can also affect the organic material present in collections. Most fungi consist of a mycelium (the fluffy part that can be seen at the surface). This mycelium is built up from threads – the hyphae – from which the fruiting bodies grow (Fig. 69). The fruiting bodies carry the spores which are responsible for disper-

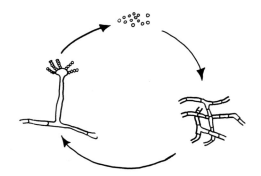

Figure 69 Life cycle of fungi.

sal of the fungi. The spores are small particles (1 to 10 µm) that can spread easily through the air. When conditions are favourable, spores can germinate and form hyphae, which in turn develop into a new mycelium. Encapsulated spores can remain viable for centuries and therefore present a risk when archaeological finds are being handled. These finds may contain fungal spores that could cause diseases.

5.2.3 Requirements

Fungal spores are present everywhere; it is simply impossible to create a sterile environment. Spores cannot just germinate and grow however; they require certain conditions and nutrients. First, spores need a growth medium. Fungi obtain their nutrients from the material on which they grow, in contrast to plants, which use the chlorophyll in their foliage to extract carbon from carbon dioxide in the air. Organic materials such as paper, leather, adhesive, wood and textile provide those nutrients. Furthermore, fungi need oxygen for their metabolism. The temperatures at which fungi can develop range from 4 to 40 °C with an optimum of between 24 and 30 °C. By far the most important condition for growth is moisture; fungi need an RH of between 70 and 100% in order to develop, though the spores of some fungi species can germinate at a lower RH. Other species can continue to grow after germination at a lower RH because they can produce their own water. In general, there will be no fungal growth at an RH below 65%, therefore the most efficient and effective way to avoid fungal growth is to maintain an RH below 60%, providing a small safety margin.

5.2.4 Damage caused by fungi

Fungi cause damage to objects in a variety of ways. First, they cause direct damage by their growth; fungi growing on the surface of an object can obstruct the view of an underlying object. As they penetrate, the hyphae damage the structure of the material, breaking down the material with the aid of enzymes in order to obtain nutrients. Fungi can also cause indirect damage as they produce acidic or coloured metabolites. Another phenomenon often associated with fungi is 'foxing', the collective term for the appearance of small red/brown/black spots on paper and textiles. The cause of these spots can vary: small rusty iron particles, bacterial activity, fungi and the effects of moisture. Last but not least, fungi present health hazards ranging from allergy and irritation of the skin and the respiratory system to diseases. Only a few species are found in museums that have the potential to cause diseases, but proper precautions should always be taken when working with material affected by fungi to ensure personal safety (see section 5.4.2). As mentioned above, extra care is needed when dealing with archaeological material.

5.2.5 Active or not?

The mycelium of an active fungus is often soft and moist in appearance in contrast to inactive fungi, the appearance of which is often dry and powdery. Active fungi should be treated immediately otherwise there is a danger that they may spread through the rest of the collection. This risk is much smaller when dealing with inactive fungi. If in doubt, remove the mycelium and wait for two weeks to see if new growth occurs indicative of the presence of a viable and active fungus. Samples can also be examined by a specialist to determine the species and its activity.

When 'fluffy' or hair-like growth is observed on an object, determine first of all whether or not it is a fungus – fluff or stains could also be dust, salt crystals or the recrystallising oils of waxes. Remove some of the fluff/stain, put it on a microscope slide and carry out the following tests on the sample to aid identification.

Materials required
- Microscope slide (glass plate, tile)
- Scalpel
- Tweezers
- Magnifying glass
- Distilled water

- Vinegar
- 96% ethanol (alcohol)
- Tissue paper
- A heat source (light bulb, flame)

Tests

1. Examine the fluff/stain under a magnifying glass. Are the threads loose with no connection to each other? Do they criss-cross the surface?
   Yes = dust
   No = proceed to step 2.
2. Scrape off a small sample of the fluff/stain, put it on a microscopy slide and add a few drops of distilled water. Does the sample dissolve within five minutes?
   Yes = salt
   No = proceed to step 3.
3. Add a droplet of vinegar to the water. Does the sample fizz or dissolve within five minutes?
   Yes = salt
   No = continue with step 4.
4. Remove the water and vinegar by applying tissue paper to the side of the droplet. Place a drop of ethanol on the sample. Does the sample dissolve within five minutes?
   Yes = an organic compound or salt
   No = proceed to step 5.
5. Place the sample above a heat source (e.g. light bulb or flame). Does the sample melt within five minutes?
   Yes = oil or wax
   No = probably a fungus.

5.3 Integrated pest management

Until the 1990s the battle against insects and fungi was largely fought using pesticides. These poisonous chemicals were dissolved in a (organic) solvent or used directly as powder, gas or vapour. Gradually, as insects and fungi became more resistant to these pesticides and because these products proved to be hazardous to humans and the environment, the old pesticides were replaced by new ones. Although these are supposed to be safer, they are still toxic formulations that can be harmful to humans and museum objects.

As a result of stricter laws, old pesticides such as dichlorodiphenyltrichloroethane (DDT), lindane (HCH), pentachlorophenol (PCP) and naphthalene have been replaced by the less hazardous and more biodegradable pyrethroids such as permethrin and deltamethrin. Many of the poisonous gases used in the past have been banned. Since the 1980s ethylene oxide, often used for the disinfection and disinfestation of museum objects, has only been allowed for the sterilisation of hospital equipment in many western European countries. Methyl bromide has been banned in industrialised countries since 2005. Intensive research has been carried out in recent years into effective, clean and safe alternative pest control methods and some very interesting ones have become available (see section 5.4).

Relying on the 'perfect' pest control method to treat biological attack, however, is the wrong approach. In most cases of insect infestation or fungal infection, the problem can be traced back to poor handling of objects within the museum at an earlier stage. Many problems can be prevented by taking correct preventive measures in the first place, saving both time and money. Regardless of the treatment method, preventive measures will also have to be taken in order to prevent the problem recurring within a short period of time.

In order to lessen the chances of an infestation or infection arising – and to deal with them in an efficient way should a problem arise – the concept of integrated pest management (IPM) has been developed. IPM is a strategy that aims to reduce the use of harmful pesticides to a minimum by taking the appropriate preventive measures and by responsible handling of the collections. When, despite all the precautions, a fungal or insect attack needs to be treated, a method must be found that is both safe and non-toxic for humans, the environment and museum objects – toxic pesticides should only be used a last resort.

5.3.1 The five steps of IPM

IPM consists of five steps that follow each other in a logical order. The strategy is based on preventive measures and on monitoring. Providing there are no signs of active infestation or infection during monitoring, only the proper preventive measures need be continued. Only if monitoring shows damage to objects, or the presence of an actual pest, should active disinfestation measures be taken. The five steps are:

1. Avoid
The storage conditions should be made as unattractive to pests as possible so that insects and fungi do not 'feel at home'. Low temperatures and RH slow down the development and reproduction of both types of pest. Make sure that the RH remains below 60% to avoid fungal growth and the development

of lice and mites that feed on fungi. Avoid microclimates and local condensation; make sure there is sufficient air circulation and ventilation. Inspect the water reservoirs in humidifiers and dehumidifiers regularly.

Dust and dirt are the icing on the cake for insects and fungi. Good housekeeping is the starting point of all preventive measures. Clean and dust-free rooms and objects are not particularly attractive to pests. It may not be possible to thoroughly clean some objects – the cleaning of objects is subject to ethical and technical considerations – therefore, always consult a conservator (see section 10.4.1). Keep food away from the collections; remove all rubbish, especially from restaurants and kitchens, and store it far from the collection areas, preferably in a closed container.

Position furniture so that the room can be cleaned easily. Locate bottom shelves and cupboards approximately 15 cm above the floor. This will enable cleaning underneath and provides a response time in case of flooding. It also makes it more difficult for crawling insects to reach the objects.

The building should be the outer protective shell for the collections and not a source of insects and fungi. Building maintenance is, therefore, extremely important. Remove birds' nests, plants and rubbish close to the building. Check that gutters and drains are kept clean and repair leaks immediately.

2. Block
Whatever lives outside a museum building should remain there. Make sure that insects cannot enter the building. Keep windows and doors closed or provide them with screens. Repair holes and cracks in the walls, seal openings around pipes and ducts, and place fine screens or filters in front of ventilation holes, pipes and drains. Inspect the building twice a year (spring and autumn). Monitor and replace the filters of air-conditioning units and clean ducts regularly. Check filters, mats and reservoirs of (de)humidification equipment. Make sure that staff and visitors do not unintentionally bring insects into the museum. Do not allow coats and bags inside storage and study areas. Store packaging materials such as cardboard boxes, crates and pallets away from the collections.

The most important route of entry for insects and fungi into the collections is probably newly acquired objects, loans or objects returning from loan. All incoming objects must be inspected. When in doubt, keep suspect objects in quarantine for two to six weeks. Place the objects in a designated quarantine room or – in case such a space is not available – place them in a well-sealed cardboard box or seal them inside transparent plastic. Always take great care with moist material because of the risk of fungal growth.

3. Detect
Regular inspections and constant monitoring are necessary to verify whether the preventive measures are appropriate. During visual inspections objects are checked for signs of insect infestation or mould infection. To complement visual inspections a monitoring system for insects can be implemented using traps (see section 5.3.2).

When insects are found they must be identified in order to determine whether they may cause damage to the collection. Ideally fungi should also be identified, especially in cases of archaeological finds, inexplicable sources and other possible health and safety risks. Every inspection and find should be recorded in a logbook, noting down place, date, type, number, the name of the inspector and the action taken (Table 14). In this way it is possible to monitor whether there are fungi or insects present, and to locate and identify the species.

4. Confine
When an infestation is detected, it is important to prevent it from spreading by locating all affected objects. Inspect all the objects in the direct vicinity of those affected and isolate them. If at all possible, remove them from the area and place them

Table 14 Example of a logbook.

Location	Object	Date	Method	Observation	Quantity	Inspected by	Action taken
Room 1 under chair	Chair (1973.415)	30 May 2003	Visual	Bore dust holes 1 mm	Small pile 4 holes	YY	Chair isolated for further inspection
Room 4	Floor carpet	30 May 2003	Trap	Webbing clothes moth	6 adults	XX	Thoroughly vacuumed carpet, replaced trap
Store 3 cupboard 2	Costume (HK-123.a)	30 May 2003	Visual	Carpet beetle *Anthrenus*	8 larvae	XX	Costume isolated and frozen, cupboard cleaned, traps placed

in a dedicated quarantine room. Also track down any objects which arrived with the same transport but were placed elsewhere in the collection. Avoid dispersal of fungal spores or insect escape during transport to the treatment area. Move objects only in boxes or wrapped in plastic. If a major infestation occurs, seal off the infested area from the rest of the collection and always use the same route for evacuating the affected objects.

It is very important to determine the source of the infestation or infection and eliminate it. Only then should the collection and the display or storage area be thoroughly treated.

5. Treat
When an infection or infestation has been detected, the objects and area must be treated. Determine what needs to be treated and the treatment options available. The choice should be based on a preference for safe and clean non-toxic methods (see section 5.4), but be realistic – sometimes it is necessary to resort to using toxic pesticides. Whichever method is chosen, make sure it is effective and conducted correctly.

Finally, clean treated objects (see section 10.4.1) and the area in which they were kept – only then should objects be returned to their places. Spaces in which fungi were present can be cleaned with a disinfectant based on quaternary ammonium compounds (always follow the directions for use). Clean all surfaces with this disinfectant using a cloth, mop or brush. Allow the disinfectant to work for 15 minutes before cleaning the surfaces with water (unless the directions for use state otherwise). Work from top to bottom, cleaning ceiling, top shelves, cupboards, walls, skirting boards and floors from the back of the room to the door.

5.3.2 Detection

Visual inspections
The visual inspection for insects and fungi in a collection is continuous. Look out for signs of pests every time a cupboard or drawer is opened. Random checks should be made in those parts of the collection that are not used regularly, especially in spring and summer when insect activity is at its peak. Inspect quiet, dark corners and cupboards, and check any objects made from materials that are particularly vulnerable to insects such as fur and feathers. Also check any objects that cannot be cleaned (often the case with ethnography). Look for:

- Damage to objects;
- Frass and excrement underneath objects;
- Live and dead insects;
- Cast larval skins;
- Fluffy surface growth and coloured stains.

Cleaners, security staff and users of the collection can become valuable extra eyes if they are given instructions as what to look for and report finds to a designated person.

Insect traps
Insect traps can complement visual inspections; they are a useful tool for monitoring insect populations, but are not a disinfestation method. They must be used correctly (i.e. the right trap in the right place) and they need to be checked regularly. Traps can be used for the general inspection of buildings and collection areas, or more specifically for monitoring a certain type of insect or an allotted area.

Various types of insect traps are available. Sticky traps, such as those for cockroaches and the Delta trap (Fig. 70) consist of a simple construction with

Figure 70 Delta trap (photo courtesy of Agnes W. Brokerhof).

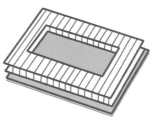

Figure 71 Window trap (courtesy M. van Breemen).

Figure 72 Diamond trap for moths (photo courtesy of Agnes W. Brokerhof).

a sticky bottom on which any passing insect will be caught. The traps are placed alongside skirting boards, near doors and windows and on shelves near sensitive objects, as this will increase the chance of catching crawling insects. They give a general overview of the insects that are present in the building – provided of course, that they get caught in the trap. The window trap (Fig. 71) makes use of the fact that certain insects like to crawl into small spaces. This particular type of trap is not very useful for catching the common textile pests.

Sticky traps can be made more attractive to insects by placing a lure in them such as food or a pheromone. Pheromones are chemical messengers used by insects to communicate; females secrete sex pheromones to attract males. These pheromones are species-specific and quite a number have been synthesised. They enable the targeting of a particular species. For the webbing clothes moth (*Tineola bisselliella*) the Delta trap and the diamond-shaped moth trap (Fig. 72), charged with *Tineola* pheromone, have proved efficient in attracting this specific moth; sometimes *Tinea* is also trapped. Lured traps should not be placed near doors and windows as they could attract insects from outside.

Electrical traps (with UV light as a lure) make use of the fact that some insect species, for example carpet beetles, are attracted by UV light. The lamps must emit UV light and not just blue-coloured light. These traps have the disadvantage that UV light causes damage to the materials in a collection, so they can only be used in spaces where objects are placed inside cabinets or boxes or are covered by a densely woven (cotton) fabric.

Every find has to be recorded in a logbook (see Table 14). When the traps show large numbers of insects in one particular place, or when the same insect species is found regularly, there is something structurally wrong. When only one or two insects are found in spring or summer, this usually indicates an odd hibernator or passer-by.

5.4 Disinfestation and disinfection methods

5.4.1 Insects

There is a range of effective methods at our disposal to control the museum insect pests that are usually found in temperate climates, in all their developmental stages (see section 5.4.4). It should be noted that these methods do not kill fungal spores and are therefore not suitable for disinfecting objects affected by fungi. These methods can, however, affect the mycelium; as a result mould growth can often be slowed down and 'fluff' can be more easily removed mechanically.

Low temperature treatment – freezing

Insects die when exposed to low temperatures for a certain period. In general, a treatment requires a minimum exposure of one week at −20 °C. Systematic research into the effects of low temperatures on museum objects is scarce; however experience has shown that the treatment of most organic material with a normal moisture content should not present any difficulties. Inorganic materials (e.g. glass and metal), on the other hand, cannot absorb moisture – during freezing, condensation may form on the surface – but provided sufficient organic material is present to absorb this moisture, there shouldn't be any problems.

Materials that expand differently in length, width and thickness as a response to changes in temperature (referred to as anisotropic materials such as ivory, bone and wood) may cause problems, especially when used in combination with other materials and when their movement is restricted.

It should be noted that materials are always more fragile at a low temperature than at room temperature therefore a safer method may have to be considered for extremely delicate objects.

In general, the freezing of wet material is not recommended and should only be done in emergencies (such as flooding) in order to avoid explosive fungal growth. In these instances a combination of freezing and drying under vacuum can be used. This so-called freeze-drying process can be carried out by special salvage companies (see section 12.3.2).

Before a freezing treatment, the objects are sealed in plastic. As much air as possible should be removed from inside the bag for two reasons: (1) the risk of condensation will decrease if there is less moisture-containing air inside the packaging and (2) when the frozen objects are left to thaw, condensation will only be formed on the outside of the packaging. Until the packed objects are treated, they should be kept sealed at room temperature so that the temperature change (and shock) will be as great as possible.

The sealed objects are placed inside a freezer. To ensure rapid cooling, the cold air should be able to circulate around the objects; they should be stacked loosely and the freezer only loaded to 70% of its capacity. To achieve a maximum cooling rate, the temperature of the freezer should be −20 °C before being loaded. The treatment time starts when the objects inside the freezer have reached −20 °C. An average load of textiles will need approximately 9–12 hours to reach this temperature. In the case of large carpets or tapestries the freezing process can be speeded up by rolling the object from either side onto two tubes, so that its bulk is divided over two thinner rolls; these will cool down faster than one thick roll.

Sometimes a double exposure is used. For example, when the insects are known to be tolerant to low temperatures or when it is difficult to monitor the temperature during treatment. After the first week of freezing, the objects are allowed to warm up to room temperature and left in their packaging for one or two weeks, after which time they are frozen again. The insects that survive the first treatment will have been urged to develop into a less tolerant stage by the temperature shock; they will be killed during the second exposure.

After freezing, the objects are removed from the freezer and left to warm up slowly. The object should not be unwrapped until it has reached room temperature and there is no condensation present on the outside of the bag. The objects can then be cleaned to remove all traces of infestation. If this is not done, there is a chance that the object will be identified as being infested when inspected in the future and might be treated again unnecessarily.

Large objects, such as carpets and tapestries, can be frozen in commercial cold stores. These often offer a temperature of −40 °C, which is fine. The method of preparing objects for treatment remains the same. Always accompany an object to the commercial facility and leave clear instructions about the type of object and the correct way to handle it. It is also possible to lease large freezer containers or even trucks on site, allowing more direct control and reducing the risks.

High-temperature treatment – heat treatment
Exposure to temperatures above 45 °C effectively kills insects in all developmental stages within several hours: the higher the temperature, the faster total mortality occurs. To ensure the object's integrity, the temperature should not be too high. An acceptable compromise is 55 °C, which requires an exposure time of one hour to achieve total mortality of museum pests.

A simple application of heat is to seal the object in plastic (polyethylene), place it in an oven or heated space, and slowly increase the temperature to 55 °C. After the core has been kept at 55 °C for at least one hour the object is allowed to cool slowly to room temperature. It is also possible to control the RH of the air during heating and cooling in such a way that the moisture content of the objects will not change (the thermo lignum method). For museums in warm climates, a heat treatment using the sun as an energy source (solarisation) provides an inexpensive but effective method of disinfesting museum objects. Solarisation uses solar radiation to increase the temperature of (dark) materials covered by a transparent plastic film or glass (Brokerhof 2003).

A heat treatment is an effective, quick, clean and safe method – not only for humans but also for the environment. In addition, large quantities of material can be treated simultaneously. Currently, the method is not commonly used to disinfest objects, mainly because not enough is known about the possible adverse effects on collection materials. Objects containing materials with a melting point or a glass transition temperature of less than 80 °C and constructions under stress should not be treated with heat. As freezing often suffices, heat treatment is rarely considered as an alternative; nevertheless it has potential in those situations requiring a fast treatment.

High carbon dioxide concentration – CO_2 fumigation
Carbon dioxide (CO_2) is a gas that is released when organic components decompose. Our atmosphere contains roughly 0.03% CO_2. At a concentration of more than 20% it causes death to most sensitive insect species. For pest control purposes, objects are treated with carbon dioxide concentrations of 60% in air. For a successful treatment exposure times of five weeks at 20 °C, four weeks at 25 °C, and three weeks at 30 °C are recommended.

Fumigation using carbon dioxide is relatively safe for humans, the environment and museum objects. This treatment is carried out in an enclosed space, for example, in a gas chamber or in a specially constructed tent (a 'fumigation bubble'). The area surrounding the bubble should be monitored to ensure that levels of CO_2 do not exceed safe limits. The leaking of carbon dioxide is not a problem for the bubble as long as gas is added regularly and the concentration of carbon dioxide is maintained at a minimum of 60%.

This method has several disadvantages. First, it is slow. Secondly, the relative humidity in the treatment space can become too low when dry carbon dioxide gas from cylinders is used. The gas should therefore always be humidified. Thirdly, carbon dioxide may react with the added moisture in the atmosphere to form carbonic acid (H_2CO_3). Experience, however, has proved this risk to be insignificant.

In most countries, carbon dioxide treatments can only be carried out by licensed companies. Some companies have mobile bubbles or tents which can be used on site. In this case, museum staff should be responsible for placing the objects in the bubble/tent to avoid damage during handling. The company can then seal the bubble and flush it with carbon dioxide. During treatment the company should monitor the conditions – it is important that the temperature and carbon dioxide concentration are measured continuously during treatment so that the treatment time can be adjusted accordingly.

Low oxygen concentration – nitrogen fumigation
Normal air consists of 79% nitrogen (N_2), 20.9% oxygen (O_2), 0.03% carbon dioxide (CO_2), and a few other gases. Insects need oxygen; when the oxygen concentration drops below 1% insects become inactive, their metabolism slows down drastically, their development stops and eventually they die. In this process insects also lose moisture and as a result they dehydrate: the higher the temperature, the faster the treatment. On the basis of published results, a treatment with <1% oxygen will take five weeks at 20 °C, four weeks at 25 °C and three weeks at 30 °C.

Of all the disinfestation methods, treatment with low oxygen concentrations is the safest for objects, people and the environment – in fact it is the only method in which a component is removed from the air instead of something being added to it. As the remaining nitrogen is an inert gas there are no adverse effects.

An experienced conservator can carry out a low oxygen treatment, but it is also offered as a commercial treatment. As with high carbon dioxide concentrations, the treatment is carried out in a sealed space, either a specially built chamber or any airtight bag. Plastics with a low oxygen permeability (barrier plastics) such as laminates of polyethylene (PE) with a coating of polyvinylidene chloride (PVDC), polyvinyl alcohol (PVOH), ethylene vinyl alcohol (EVOH) or aluminium can be used as packaging. Bags can be shaped to any dimension or size by welding the plastic together with a heat-sealer. The bag should be made as small as possible but sufficiently loose to avoid damaging the object and to minimise the amount of air inside.

The bag is flushed with nitrogen to eliminate most of the oxygen. Next, small sachets of oxygen absorber (see Ch. 9) are placed inside the bag after which the opening is sealed. When treating small objects, a surplus of oxygen absorber is sufficient to lower the oxygen concentration and nitrogen flushing can be omitted. The oxygen concentration is measured with an oxygen meter or with an indicator (e.g. Ageless Eye) (see Ch. 9). After the necessary treatment time has elapsed, the object can be unpacked, cleaned and replaced within the collection but while there is a danger of the infestation recurring, the object should be left sealed in its packaging.

Methyl bromide fumigation
Methyl bromide (CH_3Br, MeBr) is a highly poisonous, colourless nerve gas. It is effective in treating all developmental stages of insects and has been used frequently in the disinfestation of woodworm, both in objects and in entire buildings. Because methyl bromide affects the ozone layer, its use is now banned in industrialised countries (Montreal Protocol).

The main disadvantage of methyl bromide for museum objects is that it reacts with materials containing sulphur, producing an unpleasant smell. The largest supplier of methyl bromide (Dow Chemical) has compiled a list of materials that cannot be treated with methyl bromide: materials containing protein, such as leather, parchment, skin, feathers, hair and wool; sulphite paper, such as newspaper and recent archival materials; paper with a silver finish such as photographic material; and rubber (vulcanised). Methyl bromide can soften resins and darken lead-containing pigments.

Methyl bromide fumigation can only be carried out by professional pest controllers. Fumigation is fairly rapid, but objects have to be packed and transported to and from the treatment facility. Following the treatment the objects need to be allowed to off gas, which results in a total treatment time of at least one week.

5.4.2 Fungi

Fungal growth indicates that the RH has been over 65% sufficiently long (usually in still air) for the spores to germinate. This clearly indicates that something has gone wrong in the preventive cycle (steps 1 to 3 of IPM). The most effective method for reducing, or even stopping fungal growth, is to lower the RH. In the case of a fungal explosion, the cause of the high RH should always be established first and eliminated. The next stage is to reduce the RH to less than 60%, preferably down to 40–45%. This can often be achieved with dehumidifiers. Ventilation and air circulation can help the drying process, but care must be taken to avoid dispersing the infection. In many instances, these measures are sufficient to slow down fungal development and allow enough time to remove the infection. Always seek professional advice when dealing with explosive fungal growth.

Dry, mechanical removal
The safest method of removing fungal growth is mechanical removal. This can be done by suction, using a vacuum cleaner with adjustable power or other suction equipment. When the fungal growth has embedded itself firmly in the material, it may need to be detached with a small brush, moving it towards the suction nozzle. Experience has shown that fresh mould can be removed more easily from objects after freezing, which kills and dries the mycelium.

When working with a vacuum cleaner, fungal particles and spores must be prevented from being blown into the room by the exhaust. A vacuum cleaner fitted with a high efficiency particle (HEPA) filter should be used; alternatively the exhaust air should be ducted out of the building. To prevent loose particles from an object being removed by the suction, place a piece of gauze over the nozzle (see section 10.4.1).

Whether or not fungal growth can be removed mechanically depends on the extent and the activity of the infection, the risk of dispersal of the infection, time pressure and total costs. The remains of an infection should always be removed, even following a sterilising treatment with fungicides or gamma radiation. The availability of labour, will affect the decision to sterilise or not. A small number of people will need more time to tackle an infection, time in which actively growing fungi can develop further. In this case a sterilising treatment may have to be considered just to gain time for removal and cleaning.

Freezing
Exposure to a temperature of −20 °C (freezing) will kill the vegetative parts (mycelium) of fungi but not the spores. Although freezing is not a disinfection method, it will stop active fungal growth and can thus be used to buy time for cleaning. In the case of a large fungal outbreak it is worth considering freezing the entire collection, thoroughly cleaning the collection space and then removing fungal growth from the objects in small batches.

Gamma radiation
Gamma (γ) rays are high-energy, electromagnetic rays which can penetrate deep into materials and are capable of killing microorganisms such as fungi and bacteria. Apart from ethylene oxide fumigation, gamma irradiation is the only method available for killing spores and disinfecting objects completely (sterilisation). Gamma rays can be compared with UV rays but contain a lot more energy. They are emitted by a radiation source, usually a cobalt source (^{60}Co) which itself is radioactive, but the radiation does not induce radioactivity in the treated material. Treatment with gamma radiation is carried out by commercial companies in specially designed facilities.

Large quantities of material with fungal growth can be treated in a short time without the need to unpack because gamma rays have such a deep penetration. This makes the cost of this treatment relatively low. The treatment is fast and effective and, as far as is known at present, no residues remain in the treated material. But research has shown that cellulose-based materials (e.g. paper, cotton and linen) are especially susceptible to gamma radiation. It breaks down the cellulose chains, resulting in accelerated ageing of the material. A treatment with 10 kGy (the gray (Gy) is the unit for the dose of absorbed ionising radiation; 1 gray equals 1 joule per kg) causes an acceleration of the degradation process by 10 to 50%. Furthermore, the damage is cumulative and each subsequent treatment will result in further acceleration of the ageing process. Gamma radiation should therefore be used only once and as a last resort. After disinfection the fungal remains have to be removed from the objects; they disturb the appearance of the object and, despite being dead, fungal particles can still cause sensitisation and allergies. In addition, material treated with gamma radiation is more susceptible to future fungal attack – the treatment degrades material, as a result of which it becomes an easier source of nutrients for fungi.

Figure 73 Personal protection in cleaning contaminated objects (photo courtesy Erfgoedhuis Zuid-Holland).

Personal protection while working with fungi
When working with objects affected by fungi in contaminated spaces, personal protection is necessary (Fig. 73). Only a few fungal species are harmful to our health, but exposure to large quantities of even a harmless fungus can cause irritation of the respiratory system and skin, sensitivity and allergies. Take extra care when working with textiles from archaeological finds because certain microorganisms and fungal spores may be present to which modern man has no resistance.

The basic personal protection consists of:

- *Laboratory coat:* in general a white lab coat is the most suitable as it shows clearly any dirt and stimulates regular washing. A lab coat should contain a high percentage of cotton; cotton absorbs moisture while synthetic fibres such as nylon let moisture pass through.
- *Gloves:* vinyl, latex or nitrile surgical gloves are suitable for handling infected objects. They offer the necessary protection against fungal spores and are relatively cheap, so they can be discarded after use. When using disinfectants, the use of nitrile or rubber household gloves is recommended as they provide better protection against solvents (see section 9.2.6).
- *Respirator and safety glasses:* respirators are divided into dust respirators and gas and vapour respirators (semi-facial and full facial). When working with fine dust, the P2 quality suffices; for fungi and old pesticide residues a P3 quality is required. The respirators should be discarded after use (see section 9.2.6).

5.4.3 Other methods

Washing and dry cleaning
Washing and dry cleaning are treatments that have some effect on insects and fungi in textiles. These treatments may not in themselves be lethal, but when objects are treated in one of these ways, there is a good chance that insect eggs, larvae and fungal mycelium will be removed. Since these treatments can also cause damage to textiles, always consult a professional textile conservator first.

Insecticides
Insecticide solutions, often based on pyrethroids (e.g. permethrin and deltamethrin), can be used for local control (particularly of woodworm) as an alternative to treatment of the entire object or structure. The insecticide is injected into the exit holes as deeply as possible. Take the necessary personal safety precautions, work in a ventilated room and always seek the advice of a wood or furniture conservator.

Insect repellents
Insect repellents are sometimes used to keep insects away from museum collections, although their use is discouraged. The best known are: mothballs, camphor, cedarwood, lavender, tobacco, sandalwood, impregnated paper strips (such as NexaLotte in Germany and the Netherlands) and Vapona cassettes. Some of these compounds act as an insecticide when applied in high concentrations. NexaLotte and Vapona cassettes contain insecticides but usually lethal concentrations are not reached and one can only rely on the repellent action of the lower concentrations, which is uncertain.

- The traditional mothball consisted of naphthalene or camphor; the modern versions contain para-dichlorobenzene. In general, the use of mothballs is discouraged as they give a false sense of security; they are damaging to objects and are harmful to humans and the environment.
- Naphthalene ($C_{10}H_8$) is a cyclic hydrocarbon obtained from coal tar. It sublimates from the solid phase straight into the gas phase. The gas is only effective when applied in a high concentration, which can be achieved in an enclosed space with large quantities of solid naphthalene. Beetles are less sensitive to naphthalene than moths; it is not clear if naphthalene acts as an insecticide, also killing the eggs. The gas can recrystallise on the surface of objects, where it is known to soften and dissolve fats and a range of other organic polymers. Naphthalene is harmful to humans. The substance can enter the body by inhalation, ingestion or via the skin. It can cause dizziness, headaches, kidney and liver problems and abdominal pains. Dust particles containing naphthalene are known to irritate the eyes (Knell 1994: 235; Timar-Balazsy and Eastop 1998: 293). The use of naphthalene in museum collections is strongly discouraged.
- Para-dichlorobenzene (PDCB, $C_6H_4Cl_2$), also known as Paracide and Paradow, sublimates like naphthalene. It is more effective than naphthalene, but only in high concentrations. Para-dichlorobenzene appears to kill only the adults and larvae of the moth, and not the eggs. There is doubt as to whether it is effective against carpet beetles. Para-dichlorobenzene can affect the

colours in textiles and can also act as a solvent for the binding media in painted textiles. Plastics, in particular polystyrene, can soften or shrink when exposed to para-dichlorobenzene. Para-dichlorobenzene is harmful to humans; it can cause headaches, dizziness, eye irritation, sore throat, irritation to the nose and respiratory problems (Knell 1994: 234; Timar-Balazsy and Eastop 1998: 294). The use of para-dichlorobenzene in museum collections is strongly discouraged.

- Camphor ($C_{10}H_{16}O$) and the essential oils that evaporate from cedarwood, lavender and other natural products can, in high concentrations, repel insects. These concentrations are difficult to achieve in practice. The commercially available blocks of cedarwood with their pleasant smell are often impregnated with extra cedar oil; the oil migrates in due time to form a thin layer on the outside of the wood, so direct contact with the objects must be avoided. Apart from enjoying the pleasant smell, the effectiveness of these products as repellents is not proven.
- NexaLotte strips are strips of paper impregnated with chloropyrifos. Insects should die from contact with the strips while evaporation of the pesticide should generate a lethal concentration of vapour in an enclosed area. Experience has shown that the strips are not always effective but it may well be that insects are becoming tolerant to this insecticide.
- Vapona cassettes contain the insecticide dichlorvos (DDVP; 2,2-dichlorovinyl-dimethyl phosphate). The substance is absorbed in liquid form by cardboard or another support, which is placed inside a PVC cassette. The insecticide evaporates slowly. The gas is extremely toxic to insects provided that the correct concentration is reached. In practice, such concentrations can only be reached in enclosed spaces. Dichlorvos is harmful to humans: it can cause headaches, dizziness, shaking, cramp, dribbling and pain in the chest. It is known to cause colour changes in textiles and it has a corrosive effect on metals. Dichlorvos is not recommended for museum use. It is banned in the UK but still approved in many other European countries. In the past, infested objects were sometimes treated in a plastic bag together with a Vapona cassette or strip ('bagging'). Because of the harmful effects of the vapour, this method is no longer used.

Insecticides and fungicides used in the past
It is very likely that historic textiles have been treated in the past with chemicals to deter insects, particularly ethnographic and costume collections containing a lot of wool, silk and fur (military uniforms) and for tapestries and carpets. Most of the substances used previously are now prohibited because they are harmful to human health and the environment. It has also been accepted that insecticides should not be applied directly to museum objects as there is evidence to suggest that they damage fibres, dyestuffs and finishes. Preventive conservation (i.e. good housekeeping) has been proved to be far more effective in the long term.

- Thymol (2-hydroxy-1-isopropyl-4-methylbenzene), a phenol compound, previously used for killing insects and fungi. Thymol crystals were sublimated by heating (above a lamp) and the affected object was exposed to the vapour. The vapour has a very low penetration and due to the harmful effects on objects (dissolving of oil paint, inks and varnishes, recrystallisation of the vapour and yellowing of cellulose) it is no longer in use. Remains of thymol from previous treatments will slowly evaporate over time (Timar-Balazsy and Eastop 1998: 294).
- Arsenic compounds (arsenic trichloride, di-arsenic trioxide, rat poison) were used in previous centuries to prevent insect infestation, especially in taxidermy. These compounds are no longer permitted but may still be present on older objects. Sometimes they can be seen as a fine, white powder on the surface. Arsenic compounds are very toxic to humans – they can enter the body by ingestion and also inhalation and skin contact. Therefore, always handle suspect objects with gloves and wear a lab coat and respirator. Place the objects in a plastic bag and prevent the spread of the powder. Arsenic powder should be carefully removed by a conservator who must adhere to strict health and safety guidelines.
- DDT (dichloro diphenyl trichloroethane) was often used in the past as an insecticide. It was applied to historic textiles either as a solid (powder) or in watery solution. In most industrialised countries it has been prohibited since the 1970s because it degrades very slowly and builds up in the food chain. DDT is often found in military, furniture and ethnographic collections where it can sometimes be seen as colourless or white crystals on the surface of treated objects. Also Lindane ($C_6H_6Cl_6$) was widely used, particularly as a wood treatment and moth proofing agent on textiles. Always handle suspect objects with gloves. DDT crystals should be carefully removed

by a conservator who must adhere to strict health and safety guidelines.
- Many different types of Eulan were sold by the Bayer AG (CN extra, NK, WA and BLN), but the most commonly used was Eulan U33 (also known as Edolan U), a chlorophenyl ether with a chloromethane-sulphonamide group applied in watery solutions. It was used as a mothproofing agent, applied to fibres in the production process to make the textile indigestible for moths and carpet beetles. Sometimes these products were used directly on historic textiles (Ballard 1984). The older types of Eulan have been replaced because they were extremely harmful to the environment. The present formulation of Eulan is based on the currently much used pyrethroid insecticides.

5.4.4 Choosing the most appropriate disinfestation method

The disinfestation and disinfection methods discussed here present a range of options from which to choose when confronted with a pest problem. The final choice of the most suitable option depends upon:

- The condition of the object or collection;
- The type of insect or fungus to be controlled;
- The material composition of the object or collection;
- Practical considerations such as cost, necessary facilities, equipment and transport.

The condition of the object determines whether it can be treated directly or needs a pre-treatment. The object should be strong enough to withstand the handling required for treatment and it should be air-dry. Some pest control treatments can have adverse effects on wet materials. The type of insect determines which treatment is the most effective. For harmful moths and beetles (whose larvae can live in or on an object) heat treatment is the fastest and most effective, but the risk of adverse effects is high. Therefore, freezing is generally the best option. This method is effective, relatively quick, safe, simple to carry out in-house and inexpensive. Although toxic fumigation methods are effective they are not faster than freezing, and since they have to be carried out in gas chambers, they are not more efficient. Treatment with high carbon dioxide or low oxygen concentrations is effective and safe, but less efficient as these methods require long treatment times.

In order to kill insects inhabiting the building, causing damage to objects while they move about – such as cockroaches, silverfish, grey silverfish and firebrats – the space itself needs to be treated. Silverfish can be controlled by lowering the RH. To control firebrats, the temperature can be lowered. In some instances pesticides may have to be used on skirting boards or in cracks and crevices in the room (always follow the instructions for use). Dessicant dusts are often effective on insects in cracks and crevices in buildings. It is often wiser to call on the help of professional pest control companies in which case it is important to make sure that the objects do not come into contact with the insecticide.

All insects (dead or alive) found in a museum space should be removed, even if they are not directly harmful to the collection. Their source should be established and eliminated. The entry of insects from the outside should be prevented by means of appropriate measures. If harmless insects can enter the building so can harmful insects. In addition, the remains of harmless insects will attract scavengers such as carpet beetles; when they have dealt with the corpses, they will move into the collection.

The material composition of the object will have a strong influence on the choice of treatment method but the general guidelines are:

- Do not freeze or heat treat fragile objects, layered structures or constructions under stress (paintings, gilding and marquetry);
- Do not heat treat materials with a melting point or glass transition temperature below 80 °C, especially constructions that are under stress (e.g. glued joints);
- Do not heat treat those materials whose protein structure has yet to be determined (natural history study collections, archaeological objects);
- Do not use methyl bromide (now banned in industrialised countries) on protein-containing materials (e.g. leather, parchment, skin, feathers, hair and wool), sulphite paper (newspaper and recent archival materials), paper with a silver finish (photographic material), rubber (vulcanised) or lead-containing pigments.

Finally, when determining the treatment required, practical considerations will be decisive. Does only one object require treatment or an entire collection? How much money is available for the treatment? How much time is available? Are facilities available for in-house treatment? Can the object or collection be transported to a treatment facility?

Are there insurance issues to be considered?

When going through the decision-making process, be guided by your conscience and try to work with a method that is safe for humans, the object(s) and the environment while maintaining a realistic and practical approach.

6

Storage

The majority of many museum collections is kept in storage; only a small percentage is on display to the public at any given time. Often the least appropriate areas of a museum building e.g. the attic or cellar, are traditionally allocated for the storage of museum objects, and it is costly to make major changes to this situation. More often than not, use has to be made of the available space as effectively and efficiently as possible, while constantly bearing in mind the preservation of the collection.

6.1 Storage facilities

6.1.1 General guidelines

Storage facilities for textiles should comply with a number of general guidelines. First and foremost, there should be a stable indoor climate, i.e. a constant relative humidity (RH) between 45 and 55%. Always maintain RH levels below 65% to reduce the potential for fungal growth and above 35% to prevent the desiccation and shrinking of organic materials. Slow changes as a result of seasonal variation are acceptable. Fluctuations that occur repeatedly over a period of a few days are potentially damaging and should be avoided (see section 3.1.2). Staff should not be working for long periods in storage areas, so the temperature can be kept lower than normal room temperature, for example between 16 and 18 °C, both day and night (Michalski 1992a; Paine 1998: 36).

A stable indoor climate can often be achieved by the use of proper insulation. Dehumidifiers and humidifiers can control RH locally where necessary (see section 3.3.2). If a constant climate cannot be guaranteed by these measures, consider installing an air-conditioning system. The advantages of air-conditioning systems are that they filter the air and regulate moisture levels in museum spaces; the disadvantages are the high costs involved in the installation, running and maintenance of the system. In order to save energy, existing circulating air can be mixed with fresh air from outside – a ratio of 9:1 can be achieved for storage areas (see section 3.3.2). Be aware that air-conditioning systems are vulnerable to mechanical failure and power cuts and can bring about drastic climatic changes when malfunctioning. Museum staff should be trained to deal with such events; these should be included in disaster planning (see section 12.3). If there are no areas within the building which can be brought up to an adequate standard, consideration should be given to relocating the stores to purpose-built external facilities.

Daylight should not be allowed to enter the storage facilities – any windows should be completely blocked. UV-free artificial light should be turned on only when someone is present in the store. It is advisable to divide the lighting into sectors so that parts of the store can be lit separately. Special sensors for movement can be installed to turn the light off automatically so that it can never be left on unintentionally. Emergency exit signs and lighting should be located away from the objects, especially if objects are stored on open display shelves.

There should be no water pipes running through the store – the risk of leakage due to cracks, corrosion, freezing etc. is unacceptable. Any doors should open towards the outside to allow optimum use of storage space; this will also reduce the risk of damage to any object placed too close to the door. Doors can never be wide enough. It is useful to have two doors in each 'gateway'; one door for normal access and the other to be opened if extra wide access is needed.

It is important that objects can be transported easily from storage areas to other parts of the museum such as the photography lab, loading dock and exhibition rooms. Ideally there should be no obstacles in corridors, staircases, etc. Doors should open in such a way as to provide easy access for objects being transported (see section 7.2). Corridors should be sufficiently wide to allow the doors to open fully (180 degrees); sliding doors are also an option.

The storage facilities must be easy to clean; dust is a source of nutrients for fungi and insects. This can be achieved by using smooth finishes on walls and floors. Concrete and wooden floors should be coated with durable varnish, which should not itself give off harmful substances (see section 6.2.2). The varnishing of floors should be carried out prior to placing a collection in store and enough time must be allowed for the varnish to dry fully (a minimum of two weeks, but preferably eight weeks, is recommended). Floors can also be covered with synthetic materials. The composition of these should be known and it is advisable to test a sample for the possible release of harmful substances over a longer period of time (see section 9.1).

White surfaces provide an extra stimulus for cleaning and these are therefore preferable to darker colours. Light-coloured surfaces also reflect the light better, as a result of which more energy-friendly lamps with a lower wattage can be used. The storage facilities should be cleaned regularly by specially trained staff. A strategy for cleaning and a list of permitted cleaning agents and methods should be compiled by the conservator and/or storekeeper.

6.1.2 Preventive measures

Insects and fungi
In order to identify an insect pest or fungal growth in good time, a proper integrated pest management (IPM) plan should be in operation (see section 5.3).

IPM is a strategy based on preventive measures and monitoring. Provided there are no signs of active infestation or infection during monitoring, no action is needed other than to continue with the correct preventive measures. Only when monitoring shows damage to objects or the presence of an actual pest, should steps towards active de-infestation or disinfection be taken (see section 5.4).

Fire
Fire detectors should be present in all storage facilities. There are several different types available; some detect smoke, while others respond to a rise in temperature. Smoke and ionisation detectors are the most sensitive types. Ionisation detectors, which are the most expensive, are able to detect the minuscule charged particles which are released in combustion. A fire in a museum store can be fought in different ways. The installation of water or gas sprinklers is one possibility. The so-called 'wet' sprinkler systems are not suitable for museum purposes as water is always present (under pressure) in the pipes that run from the reservoir to the sprinkler heads, with the attendant high risk of leaks and the possibility of accidental discharge. 'Dry' sprinkler installations are preferred because the pipes do not contain water. In the event of a fire, a valve is opened allowing water to run from the reservoir to the disaster area. The sprinklers should be fitted with sensors so that water is only released in areas affected by the fire. They should also turn off automatically as soon as the fire is extinguished.

Gas sprinkler installations are also an option provided that museum staff is properly trained in their use. It is however likely that the use of gases in fire extinguishers will be limited in the near future by even stricter environmental laws.

Fire extinguishers should be placed in several locations. Fire hoses should not be located inside the store (risk of leaks), but in the corridor nearby. It is advisable to limit the power of the water jet by installing a special diffusing spray head. Be aware that water can be the cause of great damage to textiles. Of the available portable fire extinguishers, the type that sprays a carbon dioxide 'snow' is the most suitable for extinguishing small fires in a textile collection; those that use powder or foam are less suitable as it is very difficult to remove the residues from textiles afterwards. The store should be fitted with burglar and fire alarms which alert the local police and fire brigade. Last but not least, the atmosphere in a store may be conditioned at low levels of oxygen.

Low oxygen atmosphere

The possibility of implementing a low oxygen atmosphere in museum and archival stores is currently being investigated. The idea is to reduce the level of oxygen in the air to a level where fire cannot propagate, thus limiting the risk of an outbreak of fire. To achieve this for a storage facility, special air-conditioning equipment will have to be installed. There are several benefits.

Maintaining an entire store at a low oxygen level of 15 to 17% will reduce biological activity and assist in the control of museum pests. By reducing the oxygen in the air, the degradation of materials by oxidation is reduced. Further research is necessary to establish how different materials will survive in a low-oxygen (i.e. nitrogen) atmosphere. It is known, for example, that organic dyes fade more slowly in low oxygen levels. Although the durability of many pigments is found to increase in a nitrogen atmosphere, a small minority fade more rapidly in the absence of oxygen (Maekawa 1998: 9). Additional benefits include the impossibility of an outbreak of fire so that a sprinkler system is no longer necessary, excluding any risk of water damage. Moreover, an oxygen level of 15 to 17 % is still sufficient for humans to breathe without the use of oxygen masks (Burg 2003).

6.1.3 Quarantine

It is necessary to provide a special, isolated quarantine room near the storage facilities in which objects coming into the museum from outside can be inspected for insects and fungi. In order to ensure that there is no active infestation, the objects should remain in quarantine for two to six weeks. The RH and temperature inside the quarantine room should be similar to those in the storage area. Contaminated objects should be sealed to avoid infesting other objects in quarantine, and should be treated as soon as possible (see section 5.4). The quarantine room can also be used for isolating suspect objects from the store.

6.2 Storage systems and materials

6.2.1 Suitable systems

The store will have to be equipped with a storage system suitable for a textile collection. Not only the system but also the materials from which it is made should be chosen carefully. Cupboards are more or less static storage systems that are closed by means of sliding, rolling or common doors. They have the advantage of being dust-free on the inside, provided that the doors close properly. Objects stored within cupboards are protected against mechanical damage such as that caused by accidental nudging. One of the disadvantages, however, is that cupboards are fixed and therefore inflexible. If cupboards are used for storing costumes they should be at least 70 cm deep.

More flexible is the high-density storage system (also known as compact storage) in which (movable) cupboards are placed on rails, allowing them to be packed together or rolled apart at any point. The system makes efficient use of the available space. The objects inside remain dust-free provided the cupboards are always packed together after use. It is very important to keep the space surrounding the cupboards clean; rolling the cupboards creates air movements capable of whirling around any dust present. There are some other disadvantages: the lack of air movement between the tightly packed cupboards may lead to the formation of uncontrollable microclimates, which could be beneficial for insects and fungi. These can also spread more easily through a collection when high-density storage is used. Objects stored within these cupboards should be secured in order to withstand any shock and vibration when the cupboards are rolled.

Drawers are useful storage units in which smaller items and flat textiles can be stored. Objects stored in drawers are dust-free provided the drawers close properly. The objects should be secured inside the drawer to withstand any shock and vibration caused by opening and closing the drawer. It is a known phenomenon that greater care is used in opening a drawer – as one is not familiar with the contents – than in closing it. The advantage of removable drawers is that they can be used as a means of transportation.

Racks with shelving are flexible storage systems built up from standard units; their flexibility also allows for future adjustments to be made. The disadvantage is that racks are open so that objects are not protected from dust. This problem can be solved fairly easily, for example:

- A roller blind can be fixed to the top of the rack. There will however be gaps along the sides and bottom which will allow the ingress of dust; this can be reduced by leading the sides of the roller blind through U-shaped profiles. The action of rolling up the blind is somewhat uncontrolled

with the risk that objects behind it might get damaged.
- Venetian blinds also provide incomplete dust exclusion but they do have the advantage that the objects behind are protected against damage caused by bumping.
- By far the most economical – and probably the most practical – solution is to make special curtains or dustcovers. Curtains can be hung from curtain rails or fixed to the top of the rack with a hook and loop fastener (see section 9.2.7). In the case of rails, an extra strip of fabric should be used to cover the top, preventing dust from whirling down through the gap between rails and rack. In order to reduce the amount of dust that can enter from the sides and bottom, the curtains can be fixed to the rack with a hook and loop fastener. Attach the hard hook part to the rack and the soft loop part to the curtain in order to prevent damage should the curtain move and accidentally touch an object stored behind.

Curtains or dustcovers can be made from different types of material. If made from fabric, unbleached, densely woven cotton (calico) is the most suitable. It is fairly inexpensive and has the advantage of being an organic material itself, which means it will help to buffer changes in RH. The material should be washed before use (at a temperature of at least 60 °C), so that any finish present is removed, but also to avoid any shrinkage in the future.

In well-controlled climates, synthetic non-wovens such as polypropylene or polyethylene fabric (e.g. Tyvek) can be used (see section 9.2.7). These materials are inert, lightweight, sturdy and easy to work with as they do not fray. The advantage is that they are water-repellent and at the same time allow for air movement and exchange of water vapour through miniscule pores in the material. They should not however be used in unstable climates, as moisture regulation is somewhat delayed, resulting in an increased risk of fungal growth. Due to their electro-static nature they attract dust and other particles in dry dusty environments.

Sliding doors are another more expensive option. Doors attached by hinges are only useful if the doors can be opened by 180 degrees.

For the storage of rolled textiles, storage systems from the furnishing industry (e.g. carpet racks) are often used. It is important that rolled textiles can hang freely in order to avoid the textiles being crushed by their own weight or that of the roll. In most systems, a strong, rigid tube is placed inside the roll and subsequently positioned in the rack. Be aware that a rolled textile should not be able to unroll by itself; this can be prevented by using tubes with a square or triangular section inside the rolls, which are positioned, in pre-formed notches in the racks. Another solution is to cover and secure the rolled textiles by means of tapes (for rolling textiles refer to section 6.3.1).

Wire netting racks, commonly used for the storage of paintings, are less suitable for the storage of textiles. Textiles often have raised or loose elements, which can easily get caught in the wire netting, resulting in mechanical damage. Wire netting racks should only be used for the storage of framed textiles such as samplers.

Figure 74 Object stored in dust and lightproof, acid-free cardboard boxes (photo courtesy Erfgoedhuis Zuid-Holland).

Figure 75 Storage of rolled textiles (photo courtesy Erfgoedhuis Zuid-Holland).

6.2.2 Suitable materials

General requirements
Stores are closed spaces, often with inadequate ventilation. It is therefore important to be familiar with the risks involved in using certain types of materials for storage. Some materials can emit harmful gases that may attack the objects in store. Some of the most common harmful gases and vapours are listed below (Hallebeek 1987, 1993):

- *Formaldehyde* combines with oxygen and moisture, which is present in the air or on the surface of objects, to make formic acid (HCOOH), one of the stronger organic acids. It can be released by: wood and wood products (plywood, chipboard, etc.); paints and coatings; formica, masonite and fibreglass; paper and cardboard; textiles with formaldehyde finishes (see section 1.7); plastics such as polyester, formaldehyde resins, insulation foam and some types of polyurethane foam.
- *Acetic acid* is an organic acid which is less aggressive than formic acid in solution, but more aggressive in the form of vapour, when it affects lead. It can be released by: wood; polyvinyl acetate adhesives or plastic; polyester; non-vulcanised rubber; sticky tape (Sellotape/Scotch tape).
- Gases containing *sulphur* such as sulphur dioxide and hydrogen sulphide (H_2S) – the latter smelling strongly of rotten eggs – corrode metal and tarnish silver. They are also thought to reduce the tensile strength of textiles. They can be released by: vulcanised rubber; paint; wool; felt; parchment; leather; animal glue made from bones; polysulphide adhesives and plastics.
- *Nitrogen oxides* (NO, NO_2) are transformed in the air into aggressive acids. They are emitted by: cellulose nitrate adhesive; imitation leather.
- *Ammonia* (NH_3), a gas that forms a base (alkali), is mainly released naturally by organic materials as they age.

A list of some of the most common materials used within stores is given below.

Wood
Wood and wood products are traditionally used to make cupboards, racks and shelving. They are relatively inexpensive and easy to process. Their great advantage is their hygroscopic nature, providing a natural buffer in a climate in which the relative humidity is constantly changing. This is one of the reasons why the use of wood is often advised in poorly conditioned storage areas. A disadvantage is that the wood itself responds to changes in climatic conditions by warping, resulting in problems opening and closing drawers and cupboards.

Wood and wood products are one of the most significant sources of formic acid and acetic acid. Oak and spruce are acid woods with an average pH of 3 to 4; birch and pine have an average pH of 5 to 6. The pH value of wood is not an indication of the total amount of acid present; it only indicates the percentage of free formic acid and acetic acid. Once these have evaporated, which happens over a number of years depending upon the temperature and relative humidity, wood still releases acetic acid mainly from the acetyl groups, which are bound to cellulose. Even the least acid wood types will still release enough acid, at any stage, to corrode metal. Mahogany, meranti, birch and pine are types of wood with low levels of free acid.

The effect of acid vapours on textiles may not be noticed for some time (on metal the effect can be observed more rapidly) but subtle changes will take place. This is illustrated by the example of the linen tablecloths and napkins from Petronella Oortman's dolls' house in the Rijksmuseum in Amsterdam. The table linen was stored, as in normal life, folded, either in the linen press or in cupboards made from oak. During the conservation treatment of the textile contents of the dolls' house, it was observed that those areas of the linen cloth that had been in direct contact with wood over a long period of time were more severely yellowed than areas that were folded inside. Upon unfolding the tablecloth and napkins the differences in yellowing could be clearly seen. After conservation, these linen cloths were replaced in the linen press and cupboards, but in order to protect them from the acid emitted by the wood, barrier foils (see section 9.2.4) were placed between the textile and the wood.

Examples of materials containing wood are: plywood, chipboard, medium density fibreboard (MDF) and hardboard. In contrast to solid wood – which, depending upon the type of wood, emits a lot of acetic acid and small amounts of formaldehyde – these types of wood products will release small amounts of acetic acid and a lot of formaldehyde. Plywood is composed of several thin layers of wood pressed together using adhesives. Chipboard, MDF and hardboard are made from wood particles and fibres which are glued together and pressed into sheets. They are sometimes laminated with sheets of formica. The adhesives used are a major source of formaldehyde.

Three types of adhesives used are: ureaformaldehyde, melamineformaldehyde and phenolformaldehyde. The latter is the most stable and therefore the least harmful in a museum environment. Medite ZF (zero formaldehyde), specially designed for museum purposes, has a much lower formaldehyde emission than the standard MDF products due to the use of a formaldehyde-free binding agent, but the acetic acid emission is nonetheless high. When using wood or products containing wood, it is important to be aware of the disadvantages of these materials and how they can be reduced.

Coatings
When using wood in the museum store it is advisable to use the least acid wood types such as birch and pine. Of the wood products, waterfast glued plywood (for marine or exterior use) made from pine is suitable as it has a very low emission of acid vapours compared to ordinary plywood and MDF.

In order to reduce the emission of harmful vapours from wood and wood products, they can be varnished or painted. But varnishes and paints may themselves sometimes give off harmful products. A study carried out at the British Museum showed that the tested liquid coatings, polyurethane varnishes and the vinyl emulsion paint all reduced the emission of acid vapours under normal circumstances. In a higher RH, however, they seemed to have hardly any effect and sometimes even had a negative effect on the acid emission (Thickett 1998). Better results were achieved by covering the entire surface of the wood or wood product with (self-adhesive) barrier foils such as Melinex (polyester/polyethylene terephthalate PET), Moistop (polyester/aluminium/polyethylene film) and Marvelseal 360A (polypropylene/polyethylene/aluminium/polyethylene) (see section 9.2.4). It should be pointed out that the emission of harmful gases from the wood continues underneath the barrier layer; any damage or degradation of the layer may result in release of the acids. Unfortunately, comparative studies into the effect of paints and varnishes on wood and wood products do not all draw the same conclusions.

Varnishes and resins
Latex paints can be used depending upon their components. Any latex paint should first be tested. In general they should not be used near silver objects because the components containing sulphur in the paints will tarnish the silver. The following can be used in museum stores:

- Vinyl-acrylic paints
- Butadiene-styrene paints
- Acrylic emulsion paints
- Two-component epoxy paints
- Polyurethane emulsion paints
- Latex-polyurethane paints

The following are not suitable for museum purposes:

- Oil paints
- Oil-modified polyurethane paints
- One-component polyurethane varnishes
- Alkyd paints
- Epoxy-ester paints
- Aluminium paints
- Silicone paints
- Most of the one-component varnish types

Never place an object directly onto wood or wood products – even the less acidic wood types will cause damage over time although the process will be slower than with the more acidic types. Place a barrier foil between the object and the wood, such as Melinex or acid-free card (the latter should be replaced regularly as it in turn degrades more quickly as a result of the acidity of the wood). It is preferred practice to have a white or light-coloured layer underneath objects to enable any new damage – such as fibre loss or possible insect activity – to be noticed more easily. Tyvek (polyethylene fabric) may be used but it must be realised that it will not prevent harmful emission from the wood; after all, one of its properties is that it can 'breathe' through tiny pores in the material.

Metal
Metal is used increasingly in museum stores. Its greatest advantage is that, provided it is well finished, it will not give off harmful products. It requires less maintenance than wood and is not affected by insects. Metal does not warp with changes in RH so drawers continue to run smoothly and cupboards open easily. Metal is not hygroscopic, however, and therefore provides no buffer against fluctuating RH. This also poses a risk: in abrupt climatic changes with sufficiently high levels of absolute humidity, condensation may form on the metal when the temperature of the metal surface reaches dewpoint.

It is advisable to avoid direct contact between textiles and metal surfaces, even though they are inert. The risk of condensation and unwanted chemical reactions can be avoided by placing (acid-free) cardboard between objects and the metal shelf, or packing objects in (acid-free) cardboard boxes (see Fig. 74). These materials can also act as a buffer in the event of climate changes (see below).

Metal can be enamelled, i.e. coated with a vitreous powder which, when heated in an oven, fuses to the metal surface, creating a hard and continuous protective layer. Another technique for providing metal with a continuous protective layer is to give the particles of the finishing product an electrical charge before spraying onto the metal (Craddock 1994: 133). Galvanised steel can be used in storage under museum conditions. Aluminium should be anodised so that it has an inert surface.

Cardboard
One of the great advantages of using cardboard in storage is its buffering quality in changing climatic conditions; a disadvantage is that most of the modern 'common' cardboards are made from recycled material in which waste products such as inks and metal particles are present. The use of special acid-free (lignin-free) cardboard made from 100% cellulose material with a neutral pH is therefore recommended. Eventually this cardboard will acidify due both to natural degradation and the absorption of harmful acid substances from the air. Another option is to use acid-free buffered cardboard, which has an inbuilt alkaline reserve of calcium carbonate; this neutralises acids and keeps the cardboard acid-free for a longer period of time. The level of acidity can easily be tested with a pH pen but never use this pen on museum objects! Random checks should be made regularly so that a collection maintenance programme can be set up to replace all boxes with new ones.

As stated above, preference should be given to acid-free (buffered) cardboard boxes. If these are not an option due to financial restraints or availability, ordinary boxes could be used with some adaptation. They must be completely covered on the inside with a barrier foil (see section 9.2.4), or with layers of acid-free tissue paper, in order to prevent impurities from the cardboard from affecting the objects stored inside. Note that the use of barrier foils is expensive and negates the buffering qualities of the cardboard in changing climatic conditions.

Textiles made from vegetable (cellulose) fibres should be stored in an acid-free environment, as acid degradation products accelerate the natural degradation of this material. For textiles made from animal fibres, however, a slightly acidic environment (pH 5–6) is not harmful. For example, shoes made from leather could be stored in ordinary shoeboxes. Leather is slightly acidic due to its tanning process therefore a mildly acidic environment will not harm the leather. The shoes should preferably be wrapped in tissue paper in order to avoid direct contact.

Special cardboard boxes for museum storage are available in standard sizes. Depending upon the supplier, they can be purchased flat or ready-made in three-dimensional form. The flat boxes can be constructed without the use of adhesive or tapes. Ready-made boxes are often stapled or stitched; test to ensure that any metal present is rust-free before using them for storage.

It is advisable to use standard sizes and to adapt cupboards and racks to fit these sizes optimally, but there will always be objects that do not fit into standard-sized boxes. Tailor-made boxes can be made from sheets of (acid-free) cardboard or inert synthetic materials such as polypropylene or polyethylene (see section 9.2.1). Synthetic corrugated sheet material is extremely useful. The sheets are made up from two layers of plastic connected by rows of parallel ridges, creating channels. The material is lightweight and fairly rigid. By simply cutting one layer of the plastic alongside or perpendicular to these ridges, the sheet can be bent and folded into a three-dimensional shape. The heat from a hairdryer or electric paint stripper can be used to mould plastics into a shape, which becomes permanent once the material has cooled down (Schlichting 1994). One of the main disadvantages of using this type of sheet material is that only a few adhesives and tapes will adhere permanently to the plastic. Hot-melt glues applied with a hot-glue gun can be used but mechanical fastenings are preferred. Boxes can be stitched together using strong upholstery needles and cotton button thread. Cotton tapes can be attached to parts of the box, so that, for example, one side can be opened in order to gain access to an object more easily.

6.2.3 Access to and use of storage facilities

Access to storage areas should be controlled and limited to a few authorised members of staff only, including the storekeeper, the curator of the collection and the conservators. Other museum personnel and visitors should only be allowed to enter the stores when accompanied by an authorised person. Limiting the number of people who can enter storage areas makes it easier to observe storage procedures and to reduce mistakes in location registration. Removing objects or returning objects to the wrong location can seriously disrupt the location registration system and basically represents the loss of that object. It is advisable to record anyone entering the store either by manually logging visitors in a logbook or using a computerised system (see section 11.5.2).

All those who are given permission to enter the store should be aware of the institution's procedures, i.e. they should register any objects leaving, entering or being replaced or relocated in the store in order to maintain an up-to-date location registration. They should also be instructed in the code of conduct for handling objects. Authorised staff should be aware of the disaster plan and should know what to do in case of an emergency (see section 12.3).

There are occasions when collections in store should be made available for study and research purposes. In this case, unambiguous rules should be drawn up in order to regulate proper use of the facilities and to limit any risk of damage to objects. A proper working space should be provided where researchers can examine collection items. Such a space should preferably be adjacent rather than inside the store. It should have similar climatic conditions to the storage areas so that objects being moved from storage to the working space are not exposed to climatic changes.

No plants or flowers can be permitted inside storage areas and the consumption of food and smoking must be forbidden. Packaging and exhibition materials should not be stored inside museum stores: they represent a fire risk and utilise expensive space. Large stocks may result in superfluous old and unusable material taking up valuable storage space. These materials should be stored elsewhere, preferably in a conditioned space – packaging materials will deteriorate more quickly when stored in uncontrolled environments – and should be discarded when they are no longer fit for use. It is good practice to disinfest materials (see section 5.4) used for packing, storage and exhibition prior to use within the collection.

6.2.4 Objects in storage

In general, materials used in cupboards, racks, shelves, drawers, etc. should be inert and should not accelerate the natural degradation of textiles. All packaging material in direct contact with textiles should preferably be acid-free (see section 6.2.2) or inert. If materials are to be used whose potentially harmful properties are unknown they should first be tested (see section 9.1).

Textile objects should be stored dust-free as textiles retain dust. It is therefore necessary to pack objects individually or store them in boxes. Cupboards and/or racks should be covered with doors, curtains, etc. in order to reduce dust deposition on the objects stored inside.

Objects in store should be inspected for insects and fungi by random checks. A visual inspection should be made every time a cupboard, drawer or box is opened. Because some parts of the collection might be accessed less frequently it is advisable to carry out a random check at least once a year, preferably in spring or early summer, i.e. the time when insects are most active. Objects that are known to be ultra sensitive to insects, such as wool, fur and feathers and 'dirty' objects, should be examined with extra care. Insects are shy therefore pay particular attention to dark and undisturbed areas such as inside pockets, under collars, in seams, etc.

In the event that the larvae of insects are found, direct action should be taken (see section 5.4). Alarm bells should ring if empty cocoons or shed skins are discovered (though these could be old remains from a previous infestation). Objects on which these are found should be isolated from the rest of the collection, placed in quarantine and examined regularly for the next few weeks to establish whether or not the infestation is still active, and which insects are present.

The storage space should be organised and user-friendly; sufficient space should be allowed between cupboards for objects to be removed easily. As a general guide, the space between cupboards should be at least one metre. Secure steps should be provided so that objects stored at higher levels can be reached safely.

Objects should not be placed directly on the floor but in cupboards, racks or on planking/pallets at least 15 cm above floor level – this avoids direct contact with the colder surface of the floor (where RH levels are usually higher), makes cleaning the store easier, and protects the objects from minor flooding.

The accession number of an object should be clearly visible on any packaging (box, cover, etc.). Photographs of the objects can be attached to the packaging in order to aid identification and retrieval. In the case of an object placed in open storage (i.e. not wrapped or packed), its accession number should be easily visible on a label without having to handle the object. Chip technology has been developed which allows the minimisation of the handling of objects and reduces the possibility of mistakes. In addition, objects should have their accession numbers directly attached; in the case of textiles they are usually sewn in (see section 11.5).

6.2.5 Location of collection(s) in museum buildings

It is common museum practice to store collections in different storage areas based on provenance. This is not logical from the preservation point of view as different materials require differing climatic conditions. In a textile store, further division is necessary, since textile objects come in a variety of shapes and sizes and are often made from several different materials. Large museums can allocate particular spaces for the storage of costumes, tapestries, flags and banners etc., but in small museums it is often not feasible to store different parts of the textile collection separately. In these cases, the available space should be divided so that similar objects can be placed together, i.e. all costumes together, all accessories together, rolled textiles together, flat textiles (often in boxes) together and so on.

Sometimes the textile collection represents only a small part of a museum's collection and a separate store is not available. If this is the case the textiles should be stored together with the works of art on paper or paintings, which require similar climatic conditions.

In ethnographic collections, less stringent divisions can be made on the basis of the materials used in objects, as combinations of different materials in one object are fairly common. The division of space is often based on the provenance of the sub-collections and a further distinction is made on the basis of object type, shape and size. It is still preferable to create special storage conditions for certain materials. At the ethnographic museum in Rotterdam (the Wereldmuseum) the stores are divided on the basis of geographic provenance with the exception of all textiles, paper and coins from these collections, which are stored separately in dedicated storage areas. The textile store is located in the area with the most stable climatic conditions.

6.3 Storage of textiles

'Textiles' can be divided into groups of objects that require a similar type of storage as follows:

- Large and/or long two-dimensional textiles such as tapestries, lengths of fabric, ribbons, etc.;
- Smaller two-dimensional textiles such as (archaeological) fragments and fabric samples;
- Flat textiles with pile such as knotted carpets and velvet;
- Flat, composite objects such as flags/banners and framed textiles;
- Three-dimensional textiles such as costumes, etc.;
- Three-dimensional objects with a combination of different materials such as accessories, toys and upholstered furniture.

6.3.1 Large and/or long two-dimensional textiles

Textiles in this group include, among others, tapestries, carpets (without pile), lengths of fabric such as saris and cashmere shawls, long (lace) ribbons, simple flags without lining or decoration, etc. In general, it is preferable, both for economic (space) and safety reasons, to roll these objects.

General guidelines for rolling textiles
Rolling textiles should only be carried out by staff with the necessary knowledge and patience. Textiles are often not completely straight and smooth. They can be distorted or deformed by uneven tensions in the fabric; this is often clearly seen in oriental carpets made by nomadic tribes (both with and without pile). These deformations are caused by the fact that the loom had to be dismantled and reassembled every time the tribe moved on, as a result of which the warps were tensioned differently. Distortions can also be formed during the object's use or in exhibition by the uneven stretching of fabric. Some objects are constructed in different layers; tapestries usually have a lining and flags have a pole sleeve.

Unfortunately, the rolling of textiles is often perceived as an easy job to be assigned to unskilled staff. Textiles can be severely damaged if they are not rolled correctly – uneven tensions in the fabric and rolled-in or fixed pleats or creases can break over time. It is therefore advisable to seek guidance and instruction from a textile conservator. To roll a tapestry correctly can take several hours and involve several people.

First it should be established whether or not an object from this group can be rolled without causing damage; this will be determined by the condition and construction of the object. The textile should not have any sharp creases or crumpling as these will be crushed when rolled. If such is the case, the object should first be treated by a textile conservator in order to relax the fabric. The presence of holes, tears and slits makes the rolling more difficult, but not impossible.

The rolling of large textiles is a job for at least two people. Fabrics with a width of more than 1 m cannot be safely rolled by one person. In order to roll large textiles, such as tapestries, on average one person is required per metre width. The object should be lying flat before starting to roll but with large textiles this is often not possible. The entire width of a textile should lie flat and straight; the length can be arranged in loose concertinas (Fig. 76).

As it is often not possible to obtain tables of similar height, the rolling of large textiles may be done on the floor. First clean the floor and place a clean sheet, long and wide pieces of acid-free tissue paper, polyethylene or polypropylene fabric on the floor. Rolling large textiles on the floor is often easier as it provides a better overview of the process.

Tubes

It is important to choose tubes of the correct diameter for rolling. Using a tube with too small a diameter will create unnecessary tension in the fabric; too large a tube will make the process more difficult. As a guide, the diameter should be at least 100 (preferably 200) times the thickness of the fabric, i.e. a tube of at least 25 cm diameter, but preferably 50 cm, is necessary to roll a tapestry with a thickness of 2.5 mm (Graaf 1974).

Textiles decorated with embroideries or applications of paint layers can sometimes be rolled depending upon the flexibility of the different layers and the condition of the object. If the textile is in good condition and the decorations are capable of following the curve of the roll, the object can be rolled. A tube with a large diameter, at least 200 times the thickness of the fabric, should be used to avoid too much tension on the decorative layers.

The length of the tube should be greater than the broadest part of the textile to be rolled; allow for at least 10 cm handling edge on either side.

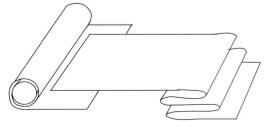

Figure 76 The rolling of large, flat textiles.

Acid-free cardboard tubes are preferred. If these are not available, ordinary cardboard tubes can be used provided they are wrapped in a barrier foil (see section 9.2.4) to prevent impurities and harmful products from the cardboard affecting the textile. Heavy tapestries and carpets require more sturdy tubes. e.g. the grey drainage pipes, traditionally made from PVC (polyvinyl chloride) and nowadays from polyethylene due to environmental issues. They have a smooth surface, which makes rolling more difficult, but by pulling a cotton stockinette over the tubes a slightly rougher surface is created.

Woven fabrics are usually rolled in the direction of the warp. Tapestries are therefore rolled from the side (see section 1.5.4). It is sometimes easier to roll extremely long pieces of (lace) ribbon onto two tubes, rolling from either end of the ribbon towards the centre, in order to distribute the abundance of material.

The question that often arises (and which cannot be answered easily) is: which side should be uppermost when rolling? When rolling a textile, two different tensions occur; the outside of the rolled textile is stretched, whereas the inside is compressed. Before rolling flat textiles, determine which side of the object can better withstand stretching or compression. Both tensions will be reduced by increasing the diameter of the roll. Textiles composed of one layer and without decorations – such as embroidery and applications – should, in principle, be rolled with the proper side inwards for protection. Textiles with printed and painted decorations can only be rolled if the pigment particles are properly adhered to the ground layer and if the paint layers are flexible enough. Always use a tube with a large diameter (25 cm or more). In those instances where the paint layer is intact and flexible, it may be better to roll with it facing outwards. If the paint layer is flaky or when pigment powder can be observed, it is best not to roll; if this is unavoidable, roll the object with the decorated side inwards. Sometimes an object is painted on both sides; this type of textile is better not rolled. With printed textiles, the pigments or dyes are usually more embedded in the textile, so the textile can be rolled with the decorated side facing inwards.

Textiles composed of several layers – those with linings and textiles with decorations such as embroidery and flexible applications – are usually rolled with the decorated side facing outwards. In the case of a lined object, the lining, which is against the roll, will be compressed and might even crease depending upon the extra allowance of fabric, which was added to the lining. These types of deformations are often unavoidable, but should never appear on the outside of the object.

From which end should an object be rolled? This also depends on the condition and the construction of the object. It is best to roll the object from the end which is least damaged. Thickenings in the fabric, such as pole sleeves in flags, should finish up on the outside of the roll so that they cannot be crushed or cause irregular tension.

During rolling, a form of interleaving should be applied to separate the layers of the rolled object. A layer of acid-free tissue paper for example will prevent the layers of textile from clinging to each other, thereby causing damage when the textile is unrolled. Textiles with surface decorations like sequins or beads should always have this form of interleaving to keep the decorations from catching on the subsequent layers above it. It also prevents the transfer of loose particles such as pigments, fibres, dirt and/or stains to other parts of the object. When rolling large pieces of textile, a roll of acid-free tissue paper is most useful. For smaller sizes and long, narrow strips of fabric or ribbons, sheets of acid-free tissue paper can be used. Pre-washed, unbleached and undyed cotton (calico) can be used as an interleaving layer when rolling heavy carpets or tapestries.

The interleaving layer is usually placed on top of the object if the object is smooth and straight. When rolling damaged or deformed objects, it is better to place the object on top of this layer so that the object is visible during the rolling process. The edge or end from which the object is to be rolled should be placed between two layers of tissue paper in order to prevent it being deformed or creased at the start of the rolling. A fringed edge can be rolled with greater ease in this way (Fig. 77). Ensure that sufficient tissue paper is left at the end to go at least once around the rolled object, thereby completely covering it.

During rolling, equal tension should be applied. When more than one person is helping, it is important to watch each other's tension and speed. The correct tension for rolling textiles is a matter of intuition and experience and cannot be described clearly. It may be that an object is deformed to such an extent that it cannot be rolled straight. Such deformations are best dealt with by locally placing a thicker interleaving layer in between (e.g. an extra sheet of acid-free tissue paper). In the case of thicker fabrics such as tapestries, these irregularities can be evened out using a more springy and voluminous material such as polyester wadding (see section 9.2.7).

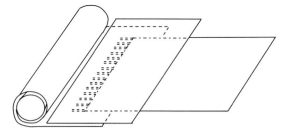

Figure 77 Rolling a textile with a fringed edge using an interleaving layer.

The rolled object should finally be wrapped in order to protect it from dust and handling. Some museums choose not to do this in order to maintain visual access to the objects. In this case, the rolled textiles should be stored in dust-free drawers (Fig. 78). Otherwise, large rolls of textile can be wrapped in densely woven cotton fabric. Lay a piece of fabric, wider than the object and long enough to fit at least one and a half times around it, under the roll, and roll it around the rolled object. This cover can be closed by means of cotton tapes (approximately 3 to 5 cm wide) and/or with hook and loop fasteners. Stitch a long strip of the soft (loop) side to one end of the cotton tape and stitch another smaller piece of the hard (hook) side to the other end of the same cotton tape, so that the tape can be used to close different widths of rolls. In this way, the tapes can also be adjusted to the right tension.

Smaller and less heavy rolls can be covered with acid-free tissue paper and tied with narrower cotton tape (approximately 1 cm wide) to the correct tension. The tapes should not press into the textile but should not be so loose that the textile can unroll. All materials used should be pre-washed, unbleached and undyed.

A rolled textile should not be set down on a flat surface as its own weight and that of the tube may crush the textile – the ends of the rolls should be raised on blocks or pads so that the rolled textile does not touch the surface. The force of gravity will still compress the textile at the top of the roll; for this reason it is advisable to turn a rolled textile occasionally.

6.3.2 Small two-dimensional textiles

Boxes
Small two-dimensional textiles such as (archaeological) fragments, fabric samples, samplers,

handkerchiefs, etc. can often be stored in boxes. Cardboard boxes of preservation quality are available in several standard sizes. As mentioned previously, it is advisable to choose standard sizes and to adapt cupboards and racks to fit these sizes optimally (see section 6.2.2). Avoid packing boxes of textiles too full as the layers at the bottom will be crushed; full boxes may also be too heavy to handle. Textiles packed in boxes should be separated from each other by a layer of acid-free tissue paper. Heavier pieces and those in good condition should be packed at the bottom; lightweight and vulnerable textiles should be placed on top. If boxes are too large for the objects they can be filled with padding material in order to prevent the contents shifting when the boxes are handled. If polyester wadding is used, it should be wrapped in acid-free tissue paper to prevent it from clinging to the objects.

If the textile is larger than the box, first consider whether it would be better to store it rolled. If not, and if a special tailor-made box is also not an option, the object may be folded to fit the box provided the folds are sufficiently supported using rolls of acid-free tissue paper, polyester wadding or 'stuffers' (Fig. 79). The latter can be made from cotton stockinette filled with a voluminous material such as polyester wadding or cotton wool. Lightweight acid-free tubes, with a small diameter (approximately 5 to 10 cm) and extending beyond the edge of the object, can also be placed in the fold line. This simplifies handling of the textile as it can be picked up by the tube. When folding textiles, acid-free tissue paper should always be placed between the layers. Perpendicular fold lines should be avoided.

Small pieces of textile can also be stored inside drawers. The number of layers should be limited and acid-free tissue paper should be placed in between textiles. There are several different ways to ensure easier access to and handling of fragments. For example, fragments can be placed on rigid boards covered with flannel (to provide a certain amount of friction) (see section 8.5). To increase efficient storage of a large group of fragments, these boards can be stacked inside drawers; to prevent the textiles from being crushed, separators should be placed between the boards (Fig. 80).

Extremely fragile textiles, e.g. archaeological fragments, require extra care. There are several different ways of storing fragile textiles; the choice of method depends on the condition, size and the use to which the collection is put. The chosen method should ensure that fragile objects

Figure 78 A drawer with rolled textiles (collection Wereldmuseum Rotterdam).

Figure 79 Schematic side view of a textile folded inside a box.

Figure 80 A collection of textile fragments stored on rigid boards, covered with flannel and stacked inside a drawer (collection Wereldmuseum Rotterdam).

Figure 81 An archaeological textile fragment stored in a special storage system which allows study of the fragment on both sides without having to touch the object (photo courtesy R. Lugtigheid).

can be handled without the need to touch them. A study collection should be stored in such a way that it can be easily researched without having to handle the objects. Fragile textile fragments can be placed on fabric-covered, acid-free cardboard (see section 8.5). When both sides of a fragment need to be accessible for research, it may be sandwiched between semi-transparent conservation grade fabric (such as silk crepeline, Tetex or nylon net) (see section 9.2.7) and fixed into a subframe (Fig. 81). In this case it is strongly recommended that the advice of a textile conservator be sought as the wrong application of a good solution could cause irreversible damage.

6.3.3 Flat textiles with pile

This group of textiles, which includes knotted carpets and velvet, is particularly vulnerable due to its pile. Larger items, such as carpets, are usually rolled for storage (following the general guidelines described in section 6.3.1). Textiles with pile are best rolled with the pile inwards and in the direction of the grain, providing that the ground weave is in good condition. The pile will be kept upright in this way and is therefore better protected. Pile fabrics with fragile or brittle ground weaves should be rolled with the pile facing outwards in order to prevent the ground weave from splitting due to stretching. If the size of pile fabrics permits, they are best stored flat (e.g. in boxes or drawers). They should not be stacked, as this will crush the pile.

6.3.4 Flat, composite objects

Flat, composite objects such as flags, banners, thangkas and framed textiles (e.g. framed samplers) are stored, depending upon their condition, either hung or laid flat. The choice of storage system depends upon the quantity, the overall condition of the objects and the available space. Preference should be given to flat storage; flags and especially banners are often decorated with heavy, thick appliqué of cardboard and metal threads. They usually have heavy fringes and tassels. If possible, do not place these on top of each other as they can cause damage to the fabric. When hanging, the forces of gravity create continuous stress on the object, resulting in mechanical damage (see section 2.4.2). Cupboards with drawers are a good solution for the storage of small flags and banners. Ideally, one drawer should contain only one layer of textile. Unfortunately this is a luxury that is often not achievable due to lack of space. Depending on the height of the drawer and the condition of the objects, several (but usually no more than three) can be placed on top of one another, separated by layers of acid-free tissue paper.

Vulnerable objects should be placed on rigid boards (see Ch. 9) by which they can be lifted from a drawer. Try to avoid the possibility of the contents shifting when the drawer is opened and closed. In order to provide a proper view of all the objects stored in a drawer, it should be capable of being opened completely; otherwise an object that has become crumpled at the back during the opening and closing of a drawer may go unnoticed.

Sometimes it is not possible to provide ideal storage because of lack of space or funds. Flat, composite objects, such as banners in good condition, can be stored by hanging. The tension in these objects caused by the forces of gravity can be reduced somewhat by attaching pre-washed, unbleached and undyed cotton tapes to the bottom of the banner and/or its tassels. These tapes can then be attached to the hanging mechanism (usually a pole) so that the weight of these elements is no longer being carried by the object itself. It is recommended that each hanging object should have a dustcover to protect it from dust and any damage caused by rubbing against another object. There are disadvantages to storing objects in dustcovers however; the cost aspect and the fact that the object is obscured from sight so that its condition cannot easily be assessed. Damage can be caused to the objects if dustcovers are removed unprofessionally. When these types of textile are stored in dust-proof cupboards, a single layer of acid-free tissue paper, polyethylene or polypropylene fabric can be placed between the objects in order to protect them from abrasion.

6.3.5 Three-dimensional textiles

This group includes costumes, traditional dress, uniforms, ecclesiastical garments, and ethnographic costumes such as kimonos, etc. These objects are often difficult to handle due to their shape, size and weight and their storage requires special attention. Both hanging and flat storage have their advantages and disadvantages. Objects in good condition can be hung provided their weight is not too great. The forces of gravity will always result in permanent stress on hanging objects, subsequently causing strain and stretching in the textile (methods to relieve these tensions will be discussed later). Objects in poor condition, for example: costumes of weighted silk; dresses made from flimsy, fragile lace or silk organza with heavy embroidery (such as some dresses from the 'Roaring Twenties') and clothing with slits, tears and holes (especially on the shoulders) are better preserved by being stored flat. The disadvantage of flat storage for three-dimensional textiles is that there is usually no drawer or box large enough to house the object without having to fold it.

Hanging storage
Every costume item should have a special hanger, adapted to fully support the shoulders and distribute the weight of the hanging object over a wider surface area. Such a hanger is not easily found but can be made by adapting an existing coat hanger. A standard plastic coat hanger can be used as a base. These are available in a number of standard sizes (26, 33, 38, 40, 42, 44/45 cm). The plastic should be a chemically stable type such as polyethylene or polypropylene, and should not contain any plasticiser. Be aware that some manufacturers sell coat hangers made from recycled plastic – these should be avoided as the types of plastic used will not be known. When in doubt, arrange for a sample of the material to be analysed. Wooden hangers can be used provided that the wood is varnished. Coat hangers made from metal wire can sometimes be useful as they can be bent to the desired shape before being padded and covered. Wrap the metal in barrier foil before covering it to prevent the migration of any corrosion products through the padding and covering. This type of hanger is not strong enough, and therefore not suitable, for heavy garments.

The size of the basic hanger should be smaller than the shoulder width of the costume as it will become larger when padded out. Polyester wadding or cotton wool can be used as a padding material. The hanger should be shaped to give optimum support to the shoulder area. The padded hanger is next covered with pre-washed, unbleached and undyed fabric. Depending upon the type of costume to be hung from the hanger, the cover can be made from towelling, a densely woven, smoother (cotton) fabric or stockinette. A somewhat coarse surface such as towelling or stockinette is more suitable for hanging heavier garments as it provides a certain friction which prevents the object from sliding off the hanger. Such a surface could, however, damage fragile, flimsy and vulnerable textiles. In these cases it is better to choose a smoother fabric.

The great advantage of tubular stockinette is that it requires less stitching as it only needs to be sewn at either end.

Uniforms and costumes with stand-up collars require extra support around the neck to prevent the collar from sagging during storage. In some instances, the weight of the costume is simply too great and will cause too much stress on the shoulders. In order to relieve some of this tension, tapes of pre-washed, unbleached and undyed cotton can be stitched to the waistband of the costume using a very fine needle and thin but sturdy, undyed cotton thread. Stitching should only be carried out in undamaged areas and preferably where the construction of the object is strengthened (e.g. in the waistband seam, side seams, etc.). The tapes can then be tied around the hanger so that the weight of the skirts no longer has to be carried by the costume itself.

Trousers and skirts can be hung from coat hangers with similar tapes stitched to strategic points in the waistband. There is no need to cover the coat hanger in this case as it is not in direct contact with the object (provided it is made from inert material). Trousers can be hung over a special trouser hanger if the condition of the textile and the cut of the trousers allow. Use a polyethylene or polypropylene trouser hanger and pad it with something like the insulation material used for central heating pipes. This foam should either be inert or be covered with barrier foil in order to prevent off-gassing. A final cover of stockinette completes the trouser hanger.

Ecclesiastical garments such as chasubles and dalmatics often have a slant on the shoulder line and, in addition, are richly decorated and heavy. It may be very difficult to find a suitable commercial hanger for these types of objects, but one can be made from a wooden coat hanger. Rounded shoulders are created by placing acid-free cardboard rollers over the hanger. Another method is to pad a fibreglass lath with polyester wadding and cover it with stockinette. A hanging device is then fixed to the centre of the lath. The fibreglass lath should have sufficient elasticity to allow it to bend under the weight of the object, thereby attaining the rounded shape. The lath should not, however, be too flexible; otherwise it will not provide any support.

Some costumes have an easy cut with the sleeves set in straight lines, such as kimonos and some ecclesiastical garments. These can be hung from a tube, preferably one made from acid-free cardboard or covered with a barrier foil (to prevent

Figure 82 Children's costumes on padded coat hangers (photo courtesy Erfgoedhuis Zuid-Holland, collection Zuiderzee Museum, Enkhuizen).

harmful off-gassing) and stockinette (to provide a somewhat coarser surface). The tube can then be hung by a hook attached at its centre or from a pole stuck through the tube and suspended in a rack.

In hanging storage, costumes should be separated by dustcovers in order to prevent the shoulders or other parts from rubbing against each other and thereby causing mechanical damage. Dustcovers can be made from pre-washed, densely woven, unbleached and undyed (cotton) fabric of a lightweight, but sturdy quality. Polypropylene and polyethylene non-woven fabrics can also be used. Cotton is flexible, soft and strong but can become fluffy over time. It is hygroscopic and therefore has a buffering quality in fluctuating RH. Synthetic non-wovens are easier to process as they do not unravel; they can be washed to make them softer and more supple. The synthetic fibres do not have any buffering qualities as they are non-hygroscopic. Tiny pores in the material will however allow for the migration of moisture.

Flat storage
Drawers and boxes can also be used for the storage of three-dimensional textiles. Flat storage is sometimes preferable to hanging, especially when objects are in poor condition. Unfortunately, drawers and boxes are rarely large enough to accommodate an entire costume without it having to be folded. When using boxes, a minimum height is necessary (approximately 30 cm) in order to avoid the crushing of a folded object. If at all possible, the box should be slightly wider than the width of the costume's shoulders.

The sleeves, any pre-shaped bust, folds and pleats should be padded before packing the costume using acid-free tissue paper (crumpled to make the paper softer and more voluminous) or polyester wadding. Prior to this it must be decided at which points the costume is to be folded; this is usually at the shoulders and at the waist. Every fold line must be supported. An interleaving layer (acid-free tissue paper) should be placed between all layers of fabric as the object is folded in order to prevent any parts clinging to or rubbing against each other. The sleeves should be folded first, across the bust at the height of the shoulders. The skirt should be spread out as much as possible. The extra width in the skirt should next be folded inwards so that the folded skirt fits in the width of the box. The upper body of the costume is then folded over the skirt at the waist. In some instances, the skirt will have to be folded once again across the length in order to fit the costume into the box. It is all too clear that undesirable folds are unavoidable when costumes are stored in boxes.

Pre-shaped costumes and accessories
Some costumes have a specific three-dimensional shape which is obtained by pressed folds and pleats, e.g. starched or otherwise stiffened costume parts such as caps, bonnets and aprons. These types of costume often play an important role in traditional dress and the way in which these parts are assembled into a complete costume is unique to a specific region. Such costume elements are also found in ethnographic collections; for example, *angissas*, which are folded and starched headscarves from Surinam (Fig. 83).

In the past, these objects were often disassembled, de-starched/unstiffened and stored flat in order to save space. For exhibitions, they had to be reassembled and finished by experienced individuals from the region of origin. Unfortunately this expertise is dying out worldwide and has already disappeared in many European regions. For this reason it is important to record on film the process of finishing these elements and the assembling of the entire traditional costume. The re-stiffening and finishing of textile is an aggressive process which often involves water, a stiffening agent such as starch, and heat; none of which are beneficial to historic textiles. It will, therefore, be necessary for museums to keep some representative examples of these types of costume in pre-shaped form and store others in an unfolded condition to maximise use of space. Pre-shaped objects such as caps and bonnets should be stored safely on special supports made to fit their particular shape (see section 6.3.6).

Figure 83 An *angissa*, a folded scarf from Surinam, which has been stiffened with tapioca and folded into a fan shape (photo courtesy Wereldmuseum, Rotterdam).

6.3.6 Three-dimensional objects

The difference between this group and that mentioned above is that the objects in this category are made from a combination of different materials together with textiles (e.g. fans) in which paper, textile, bone, ivory and metal may be used. Other objects in this group are costume accessories such as gloves, shoes, hats, bags, umbrellas and parasols; dolls, teddy bears and sample books also fall into this category. Many of the objects in ethnographic collections belong to this group, for example; masks, headdresses, fans, thrones, parasols and upholstered furniture. As a general rule, the safe storage of these objects often requires individual supports which release stress on the objects and give general support to their shape. If at all possible, the supports should be constructed in such a way as to allow the objects to be handled by the supports – this minimises direct contact and therefore reduces potential damage.

Shoes, gloves, bags and hats
These objects are similar in that they derive a certain three-dimensional shape from their construction. This shape is best preserved when fully supported by a specially made mount. When time and funds are limited, mounts made from crumpled and shaped acid-free tissue paper may be acceptable for a short period, but they will slowly be compressed under the weight of an object and will in time lose their supporting properties. The paper itself will also degrade and need to be replaced. Ideally both time and funds should be made available to provide more durable supports for these objects, which should then be stored dust-free, for example, in boxes.

Hats can be supported on specially shaped blocks of polyethylene foam (e.g. ethafoam), which is available in sheets of various densities. It can be cut easily with a sharp knife. In order to achieve the correct height, several layers may be required. They can be fixed using hot-melt glue or cocktail sticks stuck in between the layers. The basic form of the foam should be slightly smaller than the object to be supported; the material is rather hard and rough and should be padded with soft wadding and covered with a pre-washed, undyed and unbleached fabric. Cotton stockinette is suitable as it can be stretched over the support in order to minimise pleats. The fabric cover can be attached by pushing it into small cuts made in the bottom of the foam support, thereby eliminating the need for adhesive or stitching. The finished support should raise the hat from the surface on which it stands.

Another method is to use commercially available foam heads, preferably made from inert plastics (see section 9.2.8), which can serve as a basic shape. Before using these, obtain information about the types of plastic used. These ready-made heads should be adapted/altered to fit the object; which might involve removing or adding material to achieve the correct shape. Less inert plastics should be covered with a barrier foil to prevent any harmful off-gassing reaching the object. Then they should be padded to create a softer surface and covered with fabric.

Supports can also be created from acid-free card, cut and bent into shape (often easier if it is slightly wetted-out). This requires some skill and the supports are not as durable as those made from inert foams (Fig. 84). Large, flat hats with wide brims, such as Frisian or German sunhats (Fig. 85), should be stored flat, as the crown of the hat is not rounded enough to balance safely on a head. Not only the crown, but also the brim should be supported.

Soft hats can be filled with pads made from cotton stockinette filled with soft padding. Stiff hats, with fairly rigid shapes, can be supported in storage on pillows filled with small round polystyrene beads. If the pillowcase (made from, for example, cotton jersey) is approximately 40% full, the contents can be manipulated so that the pillow takes on the shape of the object. This is a more efficient method, as this standard support material can be used to fit a variety of objects.

Hats should preferably be stored dust-free, for example, in boxes. Custom-made boxes may be necessary as standard-sized boxes will not accommodate the often awkward shapes and sizes (see section 6.2.2).

A hat complete with its original hat box has extra significance for a museum (Fig. 86). These boxes are usually made from cardboard, wood or metal but unfortunately they are not suitable for safe storage. The hat should be stored in new conservation-grade packaging. The original box should, of course, be preserved, but kept with other objects made from similar materials.

Shoes can rarely be supported by one rigid support shape as too much tension would be imposed on the object during insertion and removal of the support. A rigid support in two or three parts may solve this problem; a separate support for the toes and the ball of the foot, one for the ankle and, if necessary, one for the instep. These supports can be made from plastic foam, covered with wadding and a smooth fabric such as silk jersey (in order to reduce friction when inserting the support). The separate support parts can be linked by pieces of cotton tape, so that even the toe support can be removed easily. Soft shoes can be filled with pads made from silk jersey filled with soft padding.

Shoes should preferably be stored dust-free, for example in boxes. Often, special boxes will have to be made. It is advisable to fix the shoes to a board and to construct a box with one fold-down side, so that board and shoes can slide out easily for handling (see section 6.2.2).

Gloves and bags often require softer supports. They can be filled with pads which form the general shape of the object. As these pads can be compressed, they will adapt to the shape of the object and accommodate small irregularities. The pads can be filled with quality cotton wool, polyester wadding or small polystyrene beads. These types of objects should preferably be stored dust-free, for example, in boxes. Several objects may fit into one box, side by side – avoid stacking objects as their three-dimensional shape may get crushed. Drawers are also useful, but make sure that objects are separated from each other so that they cannot become entangled. Also, ensure that the objects are fixed so that they cannot move about when the box is being handled or the drawer is being opened and closed.

Fans

Traditionally, fans are stored folded, and often in their original box, as this saves space. However, depending on their condition, the unfolding and folding of fans causes stress on, and abrasion of, the material, which can lead to unnecessary mechanical damage. It is therefore recommended that fans which have intact ribs and leaf should

Figure 84 An example of a head support made from acid-free cardboard bent into shape (collection Rotterdams Historisch Museum).

Figure 85 A Frisian straw sun hat with a small crown but large brim, properly supported on a specially made support (collection Rotterdams Historisch Museum).

Figure 86 An example of a hat stored in its original box which is unsuitable for long-term storage (a bicorn hat in a tin box) (photo courtesy Erfgoedhuis Zuid-Holland).

be stored unfolded. In order to support the open fan evenly, a special tailor-made support is necessary, which follows the shape and gradient of the fan. Such a support can be made from layers of acid-free card or inert foam (Daalen and Lingbeek 1999: 21–33) cut and stacked to follow the correct shape and gradient. The support may have to be padded to give it a softer surface and finally covered with fabric. A note on the storage of open fans: in the event of unstable climatic conditions, this could lead to unwanted distortion, as the ribs of the fan may warp in response to changes in relative humidity.

Fans in poor condition, i.e. damaged leaf, broken or missing ribs, should generally be stored closed. Such fans should not be handled since this would cause even more damage. Fans should be stored in dust-free drawers or boxes. It is important to make sure that they are separated from each other and fixed within the drawer or box in order to minimise movement. Figure 87 shows a drawer in which the fans have each been given a special box tray; this allows for handling and prevents abrasion.

Umbrellas and parasols
If the construction of an umbrella or parasol is intact, and the condition of the textile part is reasonably good, then it is best to store these types of objects upright, either hanging from the tip or by fixing the handle in a support. Any original bands used to fix the fabric in place should be released so that the textile can hang without any tension or sharp creases forming. In order to prevent dust from settling on the objects, special dustcovers can be used. These are also useful in avoiding damage that may be caused by abrasion and handling, especially when an umbrella or parasol is placed in storage between similar objects. They can otherwise easily hook into each other.

Umbrellas and parasols in poor condition, either with a broken handle or ribs or with damaged textile parts, should be stored laying flat in boxes. In order to reduce stress on the folds in the textile, they should be lightly padded. If the handle is still stable, it is advisable to raise the object by placing small blocks of inert material underneath the handle and the tip, thus reducing pressure on the textile.

Dolls and teddy bears
Dolls, teddy bears and similar objects are best kept in boxes. Depending upon their condition, they may be stored upright or laid flat; an upright position ensures that there is no pressure on any clothing or plush. The doll or figure can be placed in a safety harness made from cotton tape positioned around the waist and closed with a hook and loop fastener. Straps attached to this are then used to hang the object inside the box (Fig. 88). A stand can be made to support the object around its waist or just under the arms (it is unavoidable that some clothing or plush will be compressed at the point of contact). If an object is unstable, i.e. it has broken parts, it is better to lay it flat, preferably on a soft pad.

Figure 87 Fans stored unfolded in special box trays placed inside a drawer (collection Rotterdams Historisch Museum).

Figure 88 A doll stored in a box using a safety harness made from cotton tape positioned around the waist and closed with a hook and loop fastener (photo courtesy A. Groeneveld, collection Zuiderzee Museum, Enkhuizen).

Upholstered furniture
Upholstered furniture (chairs, couches etc.), can often be placed on racks in storage. Each piece should be protected with a dustcover, ideally one which resembles its shape (for identification) but slightly larger for ease of removal (Fig. 89). Dustcovers can be made from pre-washed, undyed and unbleached fabric or from inert polyethylene or polypropylene non-wovens (see section 9.2.7).

Objects made from or with plastics
Some three-dimensional objects may be made from (or with) plastics, such as plastic dolls, bags, hats and even costumes. Plastics were used with increas-

Figure 89 Upholstered chair protected from dust with a tailor-made dust cover (photo courtesy Erfgoedhuis Zuid-Holland).

ing frequency throughout the 20th century and today they are found in abundance. Plastics are polymers with a high molecular weight, which in pure form are often hard and brittle. Industry uses several methods to make plastics more flexible:

- By adding small quantities (approximately 2 to 3%) of a substance with a high boiling point (e.g. dibutylphthalate). These molecules work their way between the polymer chains and act as a lubricant, as a result of which the macromolecules can move more easily in relation to each other. Such a substance is called a plasticiser.
- By copolymerisation with a monomer that would create a soft polymer when polymerised on its own. Such plastics are termed 'internally plasticised'.

The first group of plastics present a risk in museum collections as the plasticiser evaporates over a period of time, making the plastic sticky at first and then hard and brittle. Plastics in the second group are more stable and will retain their flexibility.

Since plastics can emit harmful products (e.g. hydrochloric acid or nitric acid) upon degradation, it is advisable to separate any plastics present in a collection from textiles. For example, a plastic doll should be undressed if the plastic is suspected of presenting potential problems in the future. The clothing may be kept in the same box, provided it is separated from the plastic components and the box is adequately ventilated. It would be safer, however, to separate the textiles completely from the object and store them elsewhere. A plastic doll that has already become sticky can be placed on a piece of silicone release paper or Teflon to prevent it from sticking to its box. If objects are dismantled and stored separately, this should be well documented. It is known that cellulose nitrate (used in old film material and early plastics), can spontaneously combust at temperatures above 41 °C (depending upon its state of degradation). Special fire precautions should be observed with this material.

Any plastics that have become sticky (or have droplets on their surfaces) should be analysed in order to determine whether they represent a risk to the rest of the collection. Objects that are known, or are suspected, to have been made from unstable plastics should also be monitored. Some practical tools are available to help with monitoring and provide an early warning system (Matsumura 2002).

Research into the safe storage of unstable plastics is being carried out worldwide. Some of the findings suggest that storing plastics without oxygen, at lower temperatures and/or using active carbon as a trap for released gases (see section 9.2.8) may help to solve the problems. An oxygen-free environment is created by packing the object into a special plastic bag in which the concentration of oxygen is reduced either by flushing it with nitrogen or by adding oxygen scavengers such as Ageless (see sections 5.4.1 and 9.2.8). Research carried out at the Netherlands Institute for Cultural Heritage (Instituut Collectie Nederland 2003b) showed that bags made from laminated plastics are suitable.

Rubber

Objects made from rubber need special attention. Both natural and synthetic rubber are used e.g. in shoes (soles) and as a water-repellent layer on modern rain clothing. Rubber turns hard and brown upon degradation and sometimes becomes sticky. Research has shown that the degradation processes can be retarded by storing rubber in an anoxic (without oxygen) environment (see above) and at lower temperatures.

7

Transportation

The movement of objects from one location to another can be classified as either *internal transport* within the same building, i.e. to and from the exhibition space, the photography department, conservation studio or storage or *external transport*, the movement of objects to outside facilities such as an external store, conservation studio or other museums and institutions (on loan). In order to avoid damage to objects, it is important to plan and prepare both internal and external transport with great care. Greater care is normally taken with the transportation of loans. It is in the museum's interest that objects sent on loan are professionally transported and are returned in the same condition in which they left. Insurance companies dictate increasingly strict conditions for the quality of loan transport. It is commonplace for the expenses incurred in transport and packing to be included in the budget for an exhibition (usually the borrowing museum's responsibility). In general, less attention is paid to the movements of objects unrelated to loans or in cases where the expenses are borne by the lender.

The transportation of textile appears to be simple – indeed, the transportation of glass or ceramics is more daunting to most of us. Textiles are flexible and therefore absorb energy better. This does not mean, however, that textiles are less vulnerable – they are usually much more sensitive to friction, pulling and folding.

To pack an object properly for transportation, it is necessary to be familiar with the object, the route and the means of transport to be used. The following eight-step approach (developed by Helicon Conservation Support b.v. as a teaching tool used in training courses dealing with art packaging and transport) covers all of these aspects:

1. Determining the object's fragility.
2. Risk assessment of the route.
3. Optimising object and/or route.
4. Determining the necessary protection and designing the packaging.
5. Packing the object.
6. Transporting/couriering.
7. Unpacking and checking the object.
8. Evaluation.

In fact, it is recommended that these steps, in particular 1 to 3, should be adopted whenever an object is handled.

7.1 Determining the object's fragility

An object's fragility is determined by assessing its sensitivities. It is necessary to have an understanding of how the object is constructed, the material(s) from which it is made and its condition. Aspects to consider are:

- Where is the object's centre of gravity? This is the point at which the mass of an object is concentrated and the pull of gravity will have to be compensated for before an object can be moved, however small the displacement. An object with a low centre of gravity has most of its weight close to the ground. This provides the object with greater stability and decreases the risk of damage when it is moved. Handling such an object from the top (by pushing or pulling) will, however, cause localised stresses that might result in damage. An object with a high centre of gravity is inclined to be unstable, especially when the object is moved. An object with loose parts needs extra attention because each part has its own centre of gravity. The best way to lift an object is to hold it just below its centre of gravity. This will prevent the object from breaking and reduces the risk of tilting. For example, a chair: the centre of gravity of a chair is often in the seat, towards the back. Therefore, a chair is best lifted by its seat. If it is lifted by its back, the forces of gravity may pull the chair apart. A robust chair can withstand these forces but a chair with a weak construction might be damaged or even fall apart.

- How many parts does the object have? Parts are not always easy to recognise. For example, a stump-work box may have several loose drawers and they in turn might possess contents. Components which are part of the construction and give the object stability should be used to handle, support or secure an object. Decorative parts make the object look attractive – e.g. the tassels and fringes of a banner – but are more susceptible to damage and, therefore, should not be used for handling, supporting or securing the object. Parts that become loose during transport can cause a lot of damage.
- Construction: how are the different parts of an object connected? The construction of an object provides information about its stability and sturdiness. Some constructions are intended to come apart; others are permanently fixed. Detachable connections may have lost their inherent friction and become unstable. Fixed connections, i.e. by means of stitching (seams) or adhesive, may still be in good condition or may have come (partly) undone. Sometimes it is safer to take a detachable object apart and handle all parts separately (the location of each part should be documented). Each part must then be regarded as an object in itself.
- From what material(s) is the object made? What techniques and processes have been used in manufacturing?
- Are there any finishes? Finishes can be applied for protection, and/or to change the appearance of the material. A finish can make an object more sensitive, e.g. a waterproof layer of linseed oil on a 19th-century fisherman's linen shirt. Over time, the oil hardens and becomes brittle, increasing the sensitivity of the object and accelerating the degradation of the linen.
- Is the object damaged? Existing damage, old repairs and even modern conservation treatments can influence the stability of the object and its reactions to the environment. An example of this is when a textile is treated with a thermoplastic adhesive. Maintaining the correct temperature is extremely important as this material responds to changes in temperature (see section 1.1.2).

Each object has its own sensitivities and responds differently to external forces and environmental changes. Problems often arise when objects are being handled since human intervention is required either directly (e.g. lifting by hand) or indirectly (e.g. driving a forklift truck). Proper planning and attention during handling are vital.

During the handling process, several types of external mechanical forces (or transport) may occur:

- Friction between the object and its packaging materials or between parts of the object itself. This force can be helpful when objects need to be stabilised during transportation, but applied incorrectly it can be harmful.
- Pressure, if equally distributed over a large area, will not necessarily cause damage – this depends upon the object's surface, its strength, construction and the direction of the force in relation to the surface. Pressure concentrated on one small area, however, leads to damage and must therefore be avoided. Be aware that an object may be exposed to pressure due to its own weight. If an object is hollow this pressure can cause it to collapse. Providing a proper support may overcome this problem. If an object is made of mixed media, the pressure caused by the weight of one material can affect the other material(s).
- Shock: the impact of shocks is often underestimated. Shocks can be caused by many different events: a packed object being dropped; a truck driving over a bump in the road or when performing an emergency stop. A shock is an energy impulse that happens suddenly and the effects are direct and intense. The damage it causes depends upon the amount of energy released by the shock and the absorption of this energy by the object. In general, textiles are capable of absorbing shocks. Complications set in when an

object is made from several different materials, as these materials will all react differently to the energy impulse of a shock.
- Vibration: another external force experienced during transportation is vibration. The major difference between shock and vibration is that the latter is ongoing. Vibration consists of a constant series of impulses, and a material must continually respond to this energy input. The intensity of these impulses is often low, but the duration is long. The main risk from vibration is the triggering of resonance, which occurs when the vibration has the same frequency as the characteristic frequency of the object. The energy impulse is then amplified by the reaction of the object. Resonance causes materials to become 'tired' and ultimately results in damage.

When determining the fragility of an object, it is necessary to take into consideration how the object will react to the above-mentioned forces. In addition, external forces, environmental factors (RH, temperature, pollutants, etc.) must be considered (see Ch. 3) when analysing the sensitivities of an object.

7.2 Risk analysis of the transportation route

Before an object is moved – either internally or externally – the route of its journey has to be examined and assessed. Objects transported internally are exposed to different risks from those transported externally the greatest of these being negligence and carelessness. An object that has to be moved should always be accompanied by at least two people and should never be left out of sight. The move should flow naturally from origin to destination and should be completed without interruption – if an object is temporarily put down and left unattended, there is an immediate risk of damage or theft. The following aspects should be considered.

Accessibility of the point of departure
This refers to the exhibition space, storage facilities, conservation studio, etc. It is important to check whether the object can be retrieved, where it can be packed (if necessary) and which route has to be taken to reach the destination. A physical check of the internal route should be carried out prior to moving an object. Doors, passageways and lifts should be measured. An object's dimensions are usually smaller than the packing in which it travels!

Accessibility of the destination
This may be a known location within the same institution. If an object is sent out on loan, however, the host institution may be unfamiliar. It is therefore necessary to confer with the host institution about the accessibility of the building and the intended location of the object within it. The dimensions of the packed object and the route it will travel to reach its final destination should be double-checked. A suitable location for receipt, unpacking and (temporary) storage should be arranged and communicated prior to the move. Regulations regarding acclimatisation should also be discussed between the parties involved.

Risk analysis and planning
Proper risk analysis and planning should be carried out before any action is taken. All subsequent communication between those involved needs to be clear and precise. Some lenders are very specific about the conditions they require for their objects – this may not coincide with the general installation planning.

Necessary resources
Often the easiest way to transport an object through a building is to carry it by hand (stairs and other obstacles can be negotiated easily when walking). Shocks and vibrations are therefore almost entirely absorbed by the person carrying the object. Unfortunately, accidents do happen that are harmful both to the object and its carrier. If an object has to be carried by hand, always ensure that the carrier is accompanied by another person who can survey the handling, notice hazards or problems and open doors.

Trolleys, racks and carts
A variety of trolleys, racks and carts is available for internal transportation. Attention should be paid to the loading capacity of the device (the springs) and its wheels. Springs only work optimally for a predefined weight band. If the load is more or less than that of the band, the springs will not offer any protection and the shocks and vibrations will be passed directly to the object the device is carrying. To overcome this problem, rigid springs can be used that, for example, operate optimally with a load of 40 kg. In order to reach optimal absorption, the weight of any object lighter than 40 kg should be supplemented using loose weights. Wheels are important too: solid wheels will pass on shocks and vibrations. If devices with solid wheels are to be used, the object must be packed before trans-

portation. This packaging should cater for shock and vibration absorption. Wheels with inflatable tyres can absorb part of the shock and vibration and therefore offer more protection than solid wheels. The tyres should be well maintained and properly inflated. It is recommended that devices with wheels of vulcanised rubber be used, as these absorb shocks and vibrations to a certain extent and have the added advantage that they do not deflate.

7.2.1 Means of external transportation

The means of transportation used depends upon the route and destination. There are three main options: truck, plane or ship. Trains are rarely used because too many factors are unverifiable.

Trucks
Trucks can be used for both national and international transport. Although ordinary removal companies can be used, it is advisable to employ a company which specialises in transporting museum objects. The staff will be more familiar with the specific demands of art transportation as well as the associated administrative tasks, and they often have a packing department experienced in custom-making crates and packaging for objects. The trucks of these specialist companies have to meet certain standards. Art transporters sometimes make use of climate-controlled trucks. These climate systems, however, are standardised. If only one small crate is put into the cargo hold, the climate will be unstable. If a larger load is transported, the climate will become more stable as less air has to be conditioned. The volume of the load helps to keep the climate stable. It should be noted that when loading and unloading takes place in open air, this artificial climate cannot be maintained and will be lost; also, short journeys do not allow sufficient time for this preferred climate to be reached.

Trucks produce vibrations with a frequency of between 1 and 200 Hz. This means that all those materials that have their characteristic frequency within this range are at risk of creating resonance. This can be prevented – either by adapting the object, or by using a package that prevents the vibrations from reaching the object within this frequency.

The main advantage of using trucks for the transportation of museum objects is that they can be monitored at all times. It is advisable to have a member of staff on board the truck to supervise all stages of the move. More advanced international companies can make use of satellite-tracking devices, allowing the progress of the truck to be followed.

Planes
Planes are used for longer distances. If an object is transported by air, its packaging should take into account large changes in climatic conditions that will occur. It is vital that this type of transport is accompanied. An object packed in a crate becomes 'cargo' and is often handled accordingly in the race to load cargo into the correct plane as quickly as possible. Special stickers with warning signs should be clearly placed on the crate and airport personnel need to be made aware of the fragile freight. Useful stickers are:

- *Direction of flight*: i.e., the direction in which the crate should be facing in order to protect the object from forces caused by the acceleration and deceleration of the plane. Placing the crate lengthwise in the flight direction will minimise the absorption of these forces. As the crate may be travelling in all directions on conveyer belts en route to the plane, it is likely that shocks in other (perpendicular) directions will occur. The packaging should protect the object from these uncontrolled movements.
- *Fragile*.
- *Protect from all elements*: the time between leaving the truck and entering the plane can be potentially harmful. This sign indicates that the crate should not be exposed to the elements, for example, left outside in the rain or extreme heat. As there is no guarantee that this request will actually be implemented, the packaging should protect the object from these potential hazards.
- *This side up:* this label is useful for pallet construction. It can furthermore be specified in the paperwork which accompanies the crate.

As it is difficult to check whether these demands have actually been met, it is important to use a crate that can withstand the worst-case scenario.

The vibrations produced by planes are of a frequency of approximately 100 to 1000 Hz. During movement on the ground, lower frequencies also occur, caused by friction between the tyres and the tarmac.

A small object can be packed in a box or suitcase and taken on board the plane as hand luggage. It is best to reserve a seat for the object so that it can be strapped to the chair. The seat will then absorb the shock and vibrations. Furthermore the object can be kept under constant observation. The temperature on board a flight is reasonably stable although the RH is very low. It must be noted that luggage carried by hand can potentially be exposed to more shocks on the move towards the plane than cargo, but this method speeds up the process of checking in and out.

Ships

If time is not an issue, or if the size or weight of the crate is too great even for transport by plane, transportation by ship can be considered. The objects are put into large containers which are hoisted on board. No guarantee can be given about the storage of a container so an upper deck location has to be considered when designing the packing. A ferry may offer an alternative since the truck containing the object(s) is driven onto the boat with the advantage that it does not have to be unloaded. The truck's engine must be switched off while on board thereby cutting off its climate-control system (it may be possible to reserve an electric connection to the truck on the ferry).

The issue of surveillance arises when objects are packed in large containers as they cannot be monitored. This is also a problem with a truck on a ferry as all passengers must leave the vehicle deck before departure. Therefore it is important that the doors of the truck are securely locked and fitted with an alarm system. The courier should carry out periodic checks.

Vibrations produced by ships have a frequency of approximately 1 to 100 Hz. During loading, large shocks can be expected.

7.3 Optimising the object and/or route

After thoroughly examining the object in step 1, it may become clear that the object needs to be 'optimised'. Examples are the mounting of a fragile two-dimensional textile onto a fabric-covered board or the preparation of a support for a hat. It is important to consider the long-term possibilities when deciding upon an adjustment rather than using a temporary solution to immediate dilemmas. It is good practice to try to find a multipurpose solution in order to make the handling of the object easier for all scenarios and to minimise contact in the future.

Optimising the route should also be considered. Step 2 may have indicated several obstacles that can be found both inside and outside the building – from a doorstep to a gravel path. There is often more than one solution. If a crate has to be transported across a gravel path, one option is to carry it by hand provided it isn't too heavy. Another option is to put shock-absorbing materials inside the crate; this would involve higher material costs. A third solution would be to place a metal driving sheet on the path, which solves all the problems at once. In some cases the solution may mean taking an alternative route.

7.4 Determining the necessary protection and designing the packaging

Based on the outcome of steps 1 to 3, a decision should be made on how the object is to be packed. Before actually packing the object, the method that will provide the required protection should be determined and the necessary protection and packaging materials selected. Too often, an object is packed using the materials at hand without considering the special needs of that object.

For example, what would be the best way to move a travelling costume exhibition with costumes displayed on purpose-made mannequins from one venue to the next? One solution is to completely dismantle the exhibition every time it moves on to the next location. The costumes and accessories are disassembled, packed into acid-free boxes and re-mounted every time the exhibition changes location. This may sound like a familiar scenario but there are several drawbacks. The mounting and dismantling of the costumes involves a considerable amount of handling and time. It may not be possible to guarantee that a textile conservator is present each time a display is dismantled or erected. Each time the costumes are dismantled the items have to be checked against a list to ensure that nothing has gone astray. The packing in boxes may cause unwanted creases in the fabric of the costumes, which would then have to be relaxed every time the costumes are mounted.

Another solution might be to move the dressed mannequins in specially made crates. The packaging material would be more expensive, but this would be a one-off investment that would pay for itself by the reduction of labour. Within the crate, excessive movements of the costume should be restrained. This can be done by fixing the mannequin at its base, thereby avoiding any contact between the object and the crate. If necessary, the costume can be wrapped in a suitable cloth or thin polyethylene foam (e.g. Ibicel, see section 9.2.2) to hold it together. If the material of the costume is sensitive to friction, there should be as little contact as possible between the packaging material and the fabric.

Detachable or loose accessories such as bags, shoes and hats should be packed separately. The supports made for their display are best used to support their three-dimensional shapes during transportation.

7.5 Packing the object

Finally, the object has to be packed using the method and materials selected in steps 1 to 4. A special area or space – clean, sufficiently spacious and free from clutter – should be dedicated to the packing. All necessary materials and tools should be within reach.

When handling objects, always consider personal safety as well as the safety of the object. Wearing an apron or other working clothes protects both the object and personal clothing. A decision has to be made as to whether gloves are to be worn and if so, what type would be most appropriate. If necessary, respiratory protection should be worn: P2 protection when working with fine dust; P3 protection when working with fungally infected objects or if there may be old pesticide residues present. For suitable packaging materials and safety protection, see Chapter 9.

It is advisable to document the condition of the object before packing it. A condition report and/or photographs of the object should accompany any external transport. It is also wise to include directions for unpacking the object as the recipient of the package may not be familiar with it.

7.6 Transporting/couriering

A member of staff should accompany internal moves at all times but external moves may require the supervision of a courier. All the paperwork, including insurance arrangements, should be prepared ready for external transports. As the object will be out of sight at some point (i.e. in the truck, the cargo area of an airport, etc.) data loggers can be incorporated inside the packaging in order to monitor conditions during transit. Data loggers are specific: some log the environmental conditions (RH and temperature) while others monitor shocks and vibrations. In order to enable interpretation of the data, a logbook should be kept during transportation, noting times of loading, unloading, special events, etc. A data logger will only show you what *has* happened – it cannot prevent incidents from happening.

7.7 Unpacking and checking the object

If possible, the object should be unpacked in the presence of a member of staff or an appointed courier. This is particularly important for objects that are sent out on loan. The condition of the object should be checked against a previously made condition report and any new damage recorded. Data loggers, if used during transport, should be downloaded and the data interpreted. A special area or space should be dedicated to the unpacking of objects. A quarantine area is most suitable. All packaging material should be kept.

7.8 Evaluate and improve approach

An evaluation should be made in order to learn from mistakes. If an object has to be transported several times, an evaluation should take place after each move to determine whether improvements to working standards are required.

8

Textiles on display

Exhibitions of textiles can attract large numbers of visitors. For this reason some museums have an exhibition space dedicated to temporary textile exhibitions. Textiles may be exhibited in a thematic exhibition, or as part of a (semi-)permanent exhibition or as an integral part of an historic setting, such as an interior. Each type of exhibition imposes specific demands for the environmental conditions and the maintenance of the textiles exhibited. It raises the issues of whether or not to exhibit textiles in showcases and the ways in which different categories of objects e.g. two- and three-dimensional textiles, can be exhibited.

8.1 Temporary exhibitions

In this type of exhibition, textiles are put on display for a predetermined, relatively short period of time. The design of the exhibition may be based around the objects on show. It is important that a textile conservator is involved from the start, liaising with the curator, designer and exhibition installers to ensure that no damage is caused to objects by the exhibition methods or the materials used.

Before a decision is taken as to which objects should be exhibited, it is necessary to assess and document their condition (see section 12.2.1). Condition reports provide a reference for the inspection and maintenance programme. Any new damage should be recorded, and, if necessary, stabilised. In principle, it is advisable to display textiles in showcases (see section 8.3.6). Unstable objects should perhaps be excluded, or conserved before being exhibited. It should be established whether or not special supports will have to be made in order to exhibit the objects safely. Each object has specific requirements which should be met during the exhibition. These requirements should be made clear at an early stage so that the curator, the designer and the conservator can take them into consideration. Points to consider include the method of exhibiting (e.g. in a showcase or in an open space, flat, hanging, on a mount, etc.), lighting and environmental conditions. Once the exhibition is finished, the objects should be moved to the quarantine area. Their condition should once again be reassessed and compared to the earlier condition reports. The objects should be surface-cleaned to remove any dust present. If there are no signs of problems such as insect activity they can be returned to storage.

8.2 Textiles as part of a (semi-)permanent exhibition

Textiles usually play a role in (semi-)permanent exhibitions – indeed, textile objects are excellent 'illustration' material. They feature in our everyday lives and are therefore easily recognisable – we wear clothing, live in upholstered interiors and our choice of textiles can say a lot about who, or what, we are. A domestic setting, however humble or opulent, is incomplete without the necessary household textiles. A display which describes the textile industry or the applied arts of a region will not be complete without examples of the textiles produced in the area.

Any textile object in a (semi-)permanent exhibition should be rotated, i.e. it should be replaced by a similar object after a certain period of time in order to limit the amount of damage the object suffers during exhibition. The collecting policy of a museum should address these requirements.

The length of display time can be established with reference to the condition of the object and the environment in which it is to be displayed (e.g. lighting (see Ch. 4), climatic conditions (see Ch. 3), dust levels etc.). If there is daylight in the exhibition area, the total exposure time will have to take account of the extra hours that light is incident on the display outside the exhibition's opening hours. As discussed in Chapter 4, this type of situation should be avoided if possible. When deciding how long an object will be on display, the potentially harmful operations of mounting and dismounting should also be taken into consideration.

In an open exhibition, i.e. when an object is displayed outside a showcase, the exposure time for textiles should be reduced even further, as light, dust, climatic changes in the room and the possibility of the public touching the object will have a greater impact. Textiles on open exhibition should be checked more often for signs of insects, fungi or any new damage which may occur. Dust deposition is one of the biggest problems for textiles that are on open display. It has been discovered by monitoring dust deposition in various open displays, that the dust levels on the objects are reduced by distancing the audience from the objects by more than one metre (Lloyd 2002). Depending upon the environmental conditions, the condition of the objects and the number of visitors, objects on open display should be inspected regularly (at least once every three months) and carefully dusted or otherwise treated when appropriate (see section 10.4.1).

8.3 Textiles in interiors

Textiles are an inseparable part of any (historic) interior – curtains, bedding, carpets, tapestries, and upholstered furniture – and will therefore be on permanent display in historic houses, castles and palaces. It is important to ensure that the environmental conditions are as optimal as possible for the preservation of these objects (*National Trust Manual* *of Housekeeping* 2005). A maintenance plan is vital, defining the different tasks and their frequency, and indicating who is responsible for their implementation. This plan should be revised whenever necessary, for example, when practical experience has shown that certain tasks that need to be undertaken can be performed more or less frequently. Those responsible for carrying out maintenance tasks (staff, often assisted by volunteers) should be given the appropriate training on a regular basis so that they remain involved and alert to any potential problems. Some of the issues the maintenance plan needs to address are:

- Lighting (see Ch. 4 and section 8.3.1): which lights should be on during opening hours and at what level? When should curtains or shutters be closed? What type of artificial lighting is used and who is responsible for replacing broken lamps? Are UV filters on the windows and artificial lights necessary and if so how often should they be replaced?
- Environment (see Ch. 3 and section 8.3.2): who is responsible for monitoring RH and temperature? How are these monitored? Which rooms should be equipped with local air-conditioning units, such as (de-)humidifiers? Who is responsible for their maintenance? Which doors can be left open and which should be kept closed in order to maintain a stable climate while simultaneously allowing sufficient air circulation?
- Cleaning: how are the levels of dust deposition monitored and when should appropriate action be taken? What methods can be used to remove dust (see section 10.4.1)?
- Visitors: what size of group is allowed? How often does routing need to be changed? How should certain objects be protected from human interference, i.e. visitors (see section 8.3.3)? What type of events should be allowed?

8.3.1 Light

Curtains, carpets and upholstered furniture should be protected from direct sunlight by blocking the windows. Sometimes, however, a compromise will have to be found since the public needs light to be able to view a room properly. If diffused daylight is allowed to enter the room, for example, by means of semi-transparent curtains, the windows should be fitted with UV filters (see section 4.3.3). To help the public adjust to low light levels, the background lighting throughout the building should be kept uniform and at a low level (see section 4.1.3). This could be achieved, for example, by the use of minimal background lighting with additional (spot) lights, triggered by sensors that only operate when visitors are present.

8.3.2 Environment

Maintaining a constant climate in historic buildings can be fairly complicated, especially when there are large numbers of visitors. The installation of an air-conditioning system is often not an option for historic buildings for obvious reasons and may not even be necessary – many were built in such a way that seasonal changes have a delayed effect on the indoor climate. Medieval castles with their thick walls are a good example of this. Each situation is different, however, and should be addressed accordingly (see Ch. 3 for several methods to achieve acceptable environmental conditions).

8.3.3 Abrasion

The presence of people in historic interiors tends to be detrimental to textiles, e.g. the public may have to walk through rooms across original carpets. Unfortunately, there is no one solution that will prevent any damage to carpets unless they are removed from display and put into storage, which is often not desirable. One way of at least avoiding abrasion from visitors' feet is by partially rolling a carpet so that the visitors' route no longer crosses it. This may be difficult to achieve, especially when an interior is filled with furniture. Another option is to cover the original carpet with a runner (drugget). By placing a thick, soft layer between the original carpet and such a runner, the abrasion from visitors' feet can be somewhat reduced, but not totally avoided. It is advisable to change the routing now and again so that the abrasion is more uniform over the entire carpet, although it could be argued that it is preferable to restrict the damage to only one area. In some historic interiors, the public are given soft, padded slippers to wear over their shoes to protect floors and carpets. The collection keeper should make an informed choice as to which method should be implemented in a particular historic setting.

Carpets should also be protected from the strong indents caused by furniture. This can be achieved by positioning Perspex dishes under the legs of the furniture, which will spread the weight over a slightly wider area of the carpet. It is advisable to reposition furniture on carpets regularly.

Historic interiors often contain upholstered furniture. In order to prevent the public from sitting on or touching this type of furniture, it is important to create a (psychological) barrier between objects and visitors. This can be done by placing the objects away from the visitors' route, for example, behind a physical barrier, or on a platform, slightly raised from the ground. Tying a rope or ribbon across the seat may also be effective, but if tied too tightly it can cause damage to the object.

Curtains, wall-hangings, draperies and tapestries suffer from the public's attention in different ways. It is a known fact that people are tempted to touch textiles, especially when they already show signs of degradation. This inadvertently results in more damage. Unintentional contact with shoulders, elbows and bags also results in abrasion. In some interiors, specially-made Perspex shields are placed around curtains and in front of tapestries and wall-hangings to protect them from contact. This somewhat conspicuous solution offers appropriate protection. To reduce the risk of damage, the public can be requested to leave bags, backpacks, umbrellas, etc. in a cloakroom.

Inspection and maintenance
It is strongly recommended that the textiles in a historic setting are checked annually by a textile conservator; the condition of the textiles should be monitored and documented. Where necessary, appropriate first aid treatment should be carried out. It is also important to remove dust regularly (see section 10.4.1). Special maintenance contracts can be arranged with an external textile conservation specialist if an in-house textile conservator is not employed.

8.3.4 Replicas

Furnishings such as curtains in historic interiors are sometimes in such poor condition that conservation would not be able to recover the original effect of the object. In this instance, it is worth considering replacing the original with a replica. One of the advantages of this is that original colour schemes can be used which will present a clearer picture to the public of the original intention of the interior decoration. The original can be stored and safeguarded for posterity and future research. It is a mistake to imagine that replicas are a cheap option. The fabric for a proper replica will have to be specially woven, dyed, printed, etc. by specialists to match the original in colour, design, texture and lustre.

8.3.5 Seasonal closure

Some historic houses, castles, and regional museums have seasonal closures, usually during the winter period (*National Trust Manual of Housekeeping* 2005). In preparation for this period, the objects on display have to be prepared for closure or 'put to bed'. The climatic conditions inside the building should be kept constant throughout such a period. RH levels should be maintained by the use of (de-)humidifiers, the environmental conditions should be monitored and the local air-conditioning units maintained. The temperature can be lowered in order to reduce costs provided that the RH is maintained at a constant acceptable level. The advantage of lower temperature is that insects will become inactive and degradation processes will slow down. In temperate climates, the temperature should not drop below 12 to 15 °C, as seasonal changes would otherwise become too drastic. Seasonal changes in autumn and spring should be gradual so that objects have the opportunity to adapt to their new conditions. The risk of burst water pipes due to frost should be avoided at all times.

During this period of closure, all windows should be shut and daylight excluded. Artificial light should only be used when needed by the staff. The objects should be surface-cleaned so that they are dust-free (see section 10.4.1) and either wrapped or covered. Fragile objects that are relatively easy to move, can be placed in storage. Loose, small objects may be wrapped in tissue paper and packed in boxes. Mounted and framed textiles, such as embroideries in glass frames, should be removed from the walls (especially outside walls) and placed in boxes. These objects may otherwise suffer from uncontrolled changes in the microclimate inside the frame, which may lead to condensation. If this is not possible, a small distance between the framed object and the wall must be created to allow air to circulate. This can be achieved by attaching, for example, small pieces of cork to the back of the frame.

Loose, two-dimensional textiles, such as tablecloths and carpets, should, where possible, be rolled and stored away.

Curtains, which are usually held to one side by cords and tassels, should be released so that their folds and creases can relax. If possible, heavy curtains should also be removed and stored, either rolled or folded in boxes (see sections 6.3.1 and 6.3.2) in order to relieve stresses on the material caused by the forces of gravity. This may well be a hazardous operation however; the use of ladders or scaffolding may create the risk of damage, not only to the curtains, but also to the historic interior. If this risk is thought to be too great, then the stresses on the material caused by the forces of gravity can be relieved by draping the curtains in an S-shape over a roller, suspended approximately halfway up the curtain's length. Some of the weight of the curtain is thus distributed.

State beds with canopies should, in an ideal situation, be protected from dust by some form of tent construction although in practice this may not always be possible. It is advisable, as an alternative, to install an extra curtain rail or similar construction around the bed, from which lightweight, densely woven cotton fabric can be hung during the closure period. On 17th-century European paintings of interiors, it can be seen that this practice was not uncommon at the time. Bed sheets and covers should be removed wherever possible or otherwise covered with a lightweight smooth fabric (to avoid abrasion). Other pieces of upholstered furniture such as chairs, and lampshades, should be protected with dustcovers (see Fig. 89). Quality dustcovers are made from a lightweight, smooth material, and should be larger than the object. This not only allows air movement and the exchange of moisture but also helps to avoid abrasion by friction when the covers are removed. Cotton materials can be suitable but sometimes are not sufficiently smooth – this problem can be overcome by lining them with smooth silk. The advantage of using natural hygroscopic materials is that they can act as a buffer in changing environmental conditions. Synthetic non-woven materials, such as polypropylene or polyethylene fabric, can also be used. These materials are inert, lightweight, sturdy and easy to work with as they do not fray. An added advantage is that they are water-repellent while at the same time allow for air movement and exchange of water vapour through miniscule pores in the material. They should, however, not be used in unstable climates, as moisture regulation is somewhat delayed, resulting in an increased risk of fungal growth. Due to their electrostatic nature they attract dust and other particles in dry dusty environments.

8.3.6 Showcases or open display?

Showcases are recommended for exhibiting textiles in a temporary or (semi-)permanent display. Apart from the fact that they protect the exhibited objects from being touched by the public, theft or vandalism, they also create a barrier for insects and dust. Showcases may not be used in historic interiors for aesthetic reasons, however in some historic houses in the UK, special large-scale showcases have been made to protect state beds and rare upholstered chairs (e.g. at Knole in Kent and Ham House in Surrey, both National Trust properties).

The question of whether or not objects should be on open display depends on the type of material, the condition of the object, and the length of the exhibition and the amount of damage that is considered acceptable. Objects in poor condition belong in showcases. Textiles attract and hold dust particles from the air. Thin and open-weave fabrics such as mousseline and textiles with a fluffy surface such as velvet should therefore be housed in a dust-free environment. Textiles from which dust particles are more easily removed without damage may be placed on open display for a restricted period of time provided there is sufficient distance between the object and the public (or a barrier put in place) to protect them from being touched.

Some museums use showcases that are open at the top. These provide a certain amount of protection to exhibited objects as they are protected both from being touched and from draughts. There is, however, no protection from dust and fluctuating climatic conditions. If a museum has already taken the decision to display textiles behind glass, there is no reason other than cost-cutting for using these open-top showcases. Such showcases should be covered or, if this is not possible, made more dustproof. Stretching a gauze-like synthetic material such as Tetex (see section 9.2.7), in the right colour over the top will be barely visible but, because it is electrostatic, it will attract and hold the dust.

The level of dust deposition on objects on open display – as well as on those inside showcases – can be monitored by placing a small piece of dark-coloured paper in a discreet position on which any dust will be clearly visible.

Climatic conditions and light also play an important role in the decision whether or not to display objects in open space or in a showcase.

8.3.7 Climatic conditions and showcases

There are several types of display cases but they all intentionally create a microclimate. The simplest showcases are not airtight and therefore allow air circulation, but fluctuations in temperature and RH in the display area have a delayed effect on the microclimate inside the showcase. At the other end of the scale are the completely airtight showcases made from conservation-grade materials. These have additional buffering materials or are fitted with special air-conditioning units in order to maintain a constant RH. Conditioned display cases can provide the solution when exhibiting fragile objects in exhibition areas which do not have a constant climate. Climate control can be provided by using buffering materials such as conditioned silica gel, Art Sorb, Pro Sorb (see section 9.2.8) or even cotton wool, inside the base of the case (exchange of moisture takes place through holes in the base of the case). These materials can also be added inside the support mounts made for individual objects.

Objects which are extremely sensitive to oxidation, e.g. early plastics and rubber, can be displayed in an oxygen-free atmosphere. This can be achieved in airtight display cases flushed with an inert gas such as nitrogen. Oxygen absorbers, such as Ageless, can be placed inside to remove any oxygen that seeps into the showcase. The RH inside the showcase must be maintained at 30–50%. The smaller the showcase, the easier it is for this environment to be created and maintained.

The use of appropriate conservation-grade materials in the building of showcases is vitally important, especially for airtight cases in which the concentration of harmful gases can reach unacceptable levels. Research has shown that unsafe materials are still used too often (Grzywacz and Metro 1992), often resulting in a concentration of organic acids far greater inside the display case than outside in the exhibition room (Eremin and Wilthew 1998: 15). The acids originated from the wood, MDF, chipboard, varnishes and lacquers used to build the showcases. Levels of acetic acid, formaldehyde and formic acid inside a showcase can be reduced by placing active carbon cloth inside.

It is strongly recommended that all the materials to be used in an exhibition should first be tested. Samples can be analysed by a specialist laboratory or by carrying out the 'Oddy test', a simple test which can be undertaken without the necessity for too much specialised equipment (see section 9.1). Enough time should be allowed to carry out these tests; results may take between two and four weeks. It is more efficient to use materials that have been tested previously. It is important to be aware that manufacturers can change the composition of products without notification.

In some instances, the objects themselves are the source of pollutant gases, one such example being the early plastics (see section 6.3.6).

8.3.8 Light and showcases

Lighting the objects in a showcase is a fairly complex matter and several aspects should be taken into account (see Ch. 4):

- The light source should not emit infrared (IR) radiation. If IR radiation enters the showcase, the temperature inside will rise and the RH will consequently drop. This change will harm the exhibited objects.
- Ultraviolet (UV) radiation from the light source should be filtered out.
- The position of the light source (inside or outside the showcase) and the method of lighting are very important.
- The public should not experience any discomfort, such as glare, from the lighting.

The light source is best placed outside a showcase even though it may be difficult to avoid disturbing reflections. Another acceptable method would be to place the light source inside a special compartment at the top of the showcase. This compartment should be well ventilated so that heated air can escape. By passing light through milky glass, an even, diffused light can be created inside a display case. It should be noted that the light levels at the top of the showcase will be higher than at the bottom.

A third possibility is to use fibre optics. Fibre optics (made from glass fibres or synthetic material) is not a light source as such but a medium for transporting light over distances (see section 4.6.1 and Fig. 50).

8.4 Exhibiting textiles

The lighting should comply with the general requirements described in Chapter 4, i.e. UV radiation should be excluded and IR radiation should be reduced as much as possible. The lighting level, and the time of exposure, should not amount to more than the preset maximum lux-hours, appropriate for the light sensitivity of the object (see sections 4.1.3, 4.8 and Table 13). The environmental conditions should be as constant as possible, with a RH of between 45 and 55%. Always maintain RH levels below 65% to reduce the potential for fungal growth and above 35% to prevent desiccation and shrinkage of organic materials. Slow changes as a result of the changing seasons are acceptable. Fluctuations that occur repeatedly over a period of a few hours and a few days are potentially damaging and should be avoided (see section 3.1.2). A compromise should be found for the temperature; a low temperature is optimal for the preservation of textiles but the public's comfort also has to be taken into account. A temperature of between 18 and 20 °C is a good compromise (see section 3.1.1).

Potentially hazardous materials should not be used in the construction of the exhibition. The composition of all paints, lacquers, plastics, wood types, upholstery fabrics, fillers, etc. should be assessed beforehand and, where necessary, tested for the possible emission of harmful substances (see section 9.1). If there is a requirement that the materials used should be fireproof, establish whether or not the fire retardants are harmful to the objects being exhibited. One method of making upholstery fabrics fire retardant (carried out by specialist companies) is to treat them with salts, but these are known to corrode metal when it comes into contact with a treated fabric (see section 1.7).

Each textile object requires a different method of display – the different types of textiles are described in section 6.3.

8.4.1 Large and/or long two-dimensional textiles

Large pieces of flat textile are usually displayed vertically for practical reasons even though their original position may have been horizontal, as in the case of large carpets. The available exhibition space is used more efficiently and the public can view the entire object at a glance. Stresses created by the forces of gravity – especially for large and heavy objects – must, however, be considered. Vertically exhibited textiles should be in good condition or given an appropriate support by a textile conservator. They should also have a suitable hanging mechanism. One method of slightly reducing the stress in vertically displayed textiles is to support them on a slanted surface.

Large textiles are often displayed in open spaces as they are unlikely to fit into showcases. They should be given a lining of lightweight, densely woven fabric to protect them from dust and abrasion from the wall.

Two-dimensional textiles can be hung in a number of different ways, but one of the most common methods is to use a hook and loop fastener.

This has several advantages. The bond between the hook and loop components is extremely strong and capable of carrying large weights, so the weight of the object can be distributed evenly. Hook and loop fasteners can also be used to mount textiles under a slight tension, i.e. when wall-hangings are mounted. In this case, all sides of the textile are fixed by a hook and loop fastener to the wall. During exhibition, the tension can, where necessary, be fairly easily adjusted by carefully loosening the bond between the hook and loop sides, readjusting the tension and pressing the two sides together again. Great care must be used when removing an object attached with hook and loop fasteners. The textile should never be pulled; a tool, such as a ruler or round-edged flat stick, should be used to separate the hook from the loop side. Another great advantage of a hook and loop fastener is that, in case of an emergency, the textile can be released by pulling it away from the wall.

Method for attaching hook and loop fasteners to textile objects (Fig. 90)

There are several different types of hook and loop fasteners, but the self-adhesive type should never be used in close contact with textile objects (see section 9.2.7). The loop (soft) side is first given a lining. It is recommended that the strip of loop side is machine-stitched to pre-washed cotton twill tape, slightly wider than the width of the strip; the twill tape is then hand-stitched to the reverse of the object. In this way, hand-stitching through the tough loop side is avoided and the stitches are also protected from damage when the hook and loop sides are pressed together and pulled apart.

Stitching should penetrate through the object so that its weight is evenly spread. It is advisable to involve a textile conservator in this task as the choice of materials, the type of stitching and the tension with which it is applied are all matters for expert judgement. The hook (hard) side is then attached to the exhibition support. When using wood, one of the least acidic types should be selected (see section 6.2.2). The hook side can be fixed to the wood using rust-proof staples rather than adhesives, as these may emit harmful gases. The adhesive bond could also be adversely affected by the weight of the object and fail. When hanging large textiles such as tapestries, it is advisable to use a batten onto which the hook side is fixed. By using a pulley system, the batten can be lowered to the floor, allowing the textile to be fixed in a more convenient position. Afterwards, the textile can be raised to the required level.

Another method for hanging large textiles utilises a pole sleeve fixed to the textile or incorporated into the lining. A pole can be inserted into the sleeve from which the textile can be suspended. The round or preferably flat pole should be as small in diameter as possible: if the pole is too large this can cause distortions at the top of the textile when pushed through the sleeve and while hanging.

The use of curtain rings, or tabs, should be avoided as these do not provide an even distribution of weight; original rings or tabs, of course, should not be removed. The weight of the object can be relieved a little by using hook and loop fasteners attached to the top reverse side of a curtain. This will give the appearance of the curtain hanging by its original hanging system. It is even possible to maintain the original curves at the top of the curtain when the hooked side of the fastener is attached to a pre-shaped wavy/curved aluminium strip or similar material.

Large pieces of lightweight two-dimensional textiles, such as saris and cashmere shawls, can be hung by means of magnetic strips (of the rare earth type). The textile is positioned on a metal (iron) strip (which can be pre-shaped) and held in place using a (flexible) magnetic strip. In order to separate the textile object from the metal and the magnetic strip, pieces of fabric – preferably soft and fluffy material such as cotton flannel, which provides a useful friction – must be placed in between. The metal and the magnetic strip can also be covered with fabric prior to use. This method of hanging should only be used on textiles in good condition.

Occasionally it will be sufficient to show only part of a long, two-dimensional textile. In this case,

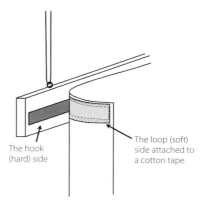

Figure 90 Diagram showing the hanging system for large flat textiles using hook and loop fasteners.

the textile can be rolled on a tube; the tube can then be fixed in the exhibition and part of the textile can be displayed by unrolling it.

A textile conservator should always be involved when hanging large and heavy textiles such as tapestries as the correct application of linings and hanging systems require professional knowledge.

8.4.2 Small two-dimensional textiles

Small two-dimensional textiles, such as (archaeological) fragments and fabric samples, can be displayed flat. The surface with which the textile is in contact should not harm the object. It is always good practice to use an inert barrier between the textile and the surface on which it is lying. These textiles can also be positioned on padded, fabric-covered, rigid boards (see section 8.5.2), which may be displayed at an angle of 45 degrees. In most cases, the object does not have to be pinned or stitched in place, particularly if the board is covered with fabric of a slightly rough texture, such as brushed cotton, which provides a useful friction. It is important to ensure that this material does not shed fibres onto the object.

When the textile is to be exhibited at an angle greater than 45 degrees, it should be mounted onto the supporting board by stitching. The mounting of textile objects using conservation stitching techniques should be carried out by a textile conservator. Expert judgement is required to determine the correct tension, suitable stitch type and appropriate materials to be used. Textiles should preferably be mounted under similar climatic conditions (in particular, RH) to those present in the exhibition space.

The advantage of stitch-mounting textiles on a rigid board is that a glass or Perspex cover can be placed over them allowing them to be displayed, dust-free, outside showcases. Mounted textiles can also be framed. It is important to allow enough space between the object and the glass or Perspex to avoid the textile being crushed. For short-term display it is sometimes sufficient to just pin the object in place using entomological pins. In section 8.5, some methods for making a padded, fabric-covered board are discussed.

Archaeological textile fragments should be displayed horizontally. If they are in good condition, displaying them on a padded, fabric-covered board placed at a slight angle may also be acceptable. By far the best method is to display archaeological fragments in their storage supports so that handling is minimised (see section 6.3.2). More often than not, archaeological material is too fragile to be hung, even if it has already been conserved, so archaeological textiles should always be provided with an adequate support. Some institutions, for example, the Abegg Stiftung in Switzerland and the Metropolitan Museum of Art in New York, have experience in mounting extremely fragile textiles, such as archaeological fragments, in pressure mounts. This uses the principle of the fragile textile being pressed into a soft, padded support by a sheet of glass or Perspex (Fig. 91) thereby providing full and even support. As there is only a tiny amount of air present inside the pressure mount, climatic changes will have little effect on the mounted textile. This technique sounds easy, but requires a lot of experience to be carried out correctly. As yet, very little scientific research has been undertaken regarding the long-term effects of pressure mounts (Windsor 2002). There is the possibility, due to the nature of the glass being fluid and the Perspex being electrostatic that, over time, the pressure-mounted textile might adhere to this layer, potentially making this a non-reversible method of mounting. When some archaeological fragments from the National Museum of Kuwait (which were pressure-mounted in the 1980s in the US) were inspected, no damage could be detected by visual examination with both the naked eye and stereomicroscope; the fibres did not appear to have been compressed by the Perspex mount.

Figure 91 Example of an archaeological textile fragment that is pressure-mounted in Perspex and protected by a separate Perspex cover, which is being lifted in the photo (photo courtesy Textile Conservation Centre, University of Southampton, objects from the collection of the Al-Sabah Collection of Islamic Art, Kuwait).

Sometimes artefacts, e.g. accessories, are placed on top of textiles in order to enliven their exhibition. This is not ideal for the preservation of the textile but by taking a few precautions it is possible to avoid damage to the textile. Note that heavy objects, such as candlesticks and boxes, should never be placed on top of historic textiles as their weight will cause damage to the textile over a period of time. Lightweight objects may be placed on top of textiles.

If the 'setting' is placed inside a showcase, it is often possible to hang the object just above the textile (e.g. using invisible nylon fishing line) so that it appears to be resting on the textile. If the textile is in good condition, the object may be placed on top of it, providing that the textile does not have any fragile decorations, such as embroidery or sequins. To protect the textile from the object to be placed on top of it, cut a piece of fairly stiff barrier foil (e.g. Melinex) in the same shape but slightly larger than the object, and place this between the object and the textile. Take care to avoid sharp edges and corners in the Melinex as these may cut the textile.

8.4.3 Flat textiles with pile

Depending upon their condition, flat textiles with pile, such as knotted carpets and velvet, can be exhibited in any of the ways described above. Be aware that these textiles, especially carpets, may be very heavy. Never place any objects on top of the pile as this will crush it. It may not be possible to follow this rule for pile carpets in historic interiors, in which case the damage caused by furniture can be minimised by placing Perspex dishes underneath the legs in order to distribute the weight of the furniture more evenly. Where possible, it is best to exhibit textiles with pile in a dust-free environment as they attract and bind dust easily.

8.4.4 Flat, composite objects

Objects in this group include flags, banners and mounted textiles such as framed samplers. For these objects, a vertical or slanted presentation is often required for aesthetic reasons.

Flags and banners in good condition may be hung from their original pole provided this is still strong. There should be no localised tensions or distortion in the textile while hanging. The pole, usually painted or gilded wood, can be suspended by nylon fishing line and protected from the possibility of being cut by the line by a piece of soft felt or brushed cotton. Fishing line may also be used to hold the flag or banner in place when it is positioned on a sloping board. The line may be stitched around the pole through pre-made holes in the board and tied to the back.

Large flags and pennants in good condition may be hung in exhibition so that they still appear to have their flying characteristics. This can be achieved by guiding the object over several tubes of acid-free card or Perspex that are suspended in the air at slightly different heights (Fig. 92). The tubes should be covered with a fabric that provides appropriate friction to prevent the object from sliding off. Another method to consider is the use of magnetic strips as described in section 8.4.1.

Flat, composite objects in poor condition may have to be fully supported in order to be displayed safely. The conserved object can be stitched to a padded, fabric-covered board. If the original pole for the object is still extant, it may have to be accommodated in a pre-shaped dent in the board, which is necessary to reduce stresses in the textile. If, however, the original pole is missing, a hollow tube of Perspex, with a diameter slightly smaller than the pole sleeve, may be a safe solution (Fig. 93).

Textiles mounted on their original frames, such as embroideries and room or fire screens, require extra attention while on display. It is fairly rare to find textiles still in their original mounts and most present a conservation dilemma: the original (wooden) frame, the (rusty) nails, and the applied tension are harmful to the textile, resulting in damage such as splitting, rust stains and discoloration. Conservation options are best assessed together with a textile conservator. In extreme

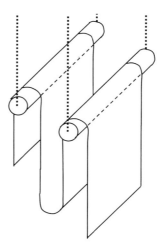

Figure 92 Diagram showing how to display a flag emulating its flying characteristics.

cases, the original frame may have to be removed and stored separately from the textile, but not before the method of mounting has been thoroughly documented. If a mounted textile is still in reasonable condition, there is no reason to remove it from its original frame.

Extra care should be taken to ensure stable climatic conditions when exhibiting textiles mounted on frames; fluctuations in RH and temperature will affect the textile and the mounting materials differently, thereby creating tension. Vibrations should be kept to a minimum as the tensioned textile will respond to this by resonating like a drum. It may still appear to be intact, but can split unexpectedly. The object should be placed in a dust-free environment, as the removal of dust from such a tensioned surface is risky. In other words, when on display, these objects belong in showcases.

8.4.5 Three-dimensional textiles

To help the public fully appreciate and understand a costume's shape and function, it is best to display it three-dimensionally, although there are exceptions. Ethnographic costumes, for example, sarongs, are sometimes displayed as two-dimensional pieces of textile, thereby focusing on their design. In this case, the use of images (photographs/video) may illustrate how the costume was worn.

The preparation of a costume exhibition involves a significant amount of time and attention. Knowledge of costume history and a technical knowledge of dressmaking is necessary in order to present a historic costume correctly. Additional images – such as original fashion pictures, paintings and photographs – are very helpful in recreating the era being represented. Creativity and ingenuity are also required as resources are often limited.

Dummies
Special dummies are available for displaying historic costumes. The dummies in the Kyoto Costume Institute in Japan, for example, were specifically designed for museum purposes (they were developed in conjunction with the Costume Institute of the Metropolitan Museum of Art). There are four models in this set, each one available in two different sizes (small and medium). The available models are: 18th century, Empire, 19th century and Belle Époque (Fig. 94). Unfortunately they are not available in children's sizes, men's sizes or in 20th-century silhouette. The dummies are easy to use

Figure 93 A gilded silk 16th-century banner mounted on a padded, fabric-covered board. The missing pole is replaced with a Perspex pole (photo courtesy ICAT textielrestauratie b.v., collection Frans Halsmuseum, Haarlem).

as the waistline and hips can be adjusted and the heads, arms, and legs are detachable. These dummies are fairly expensive but are a good investment in the long term.

Fashion dummies used in high street shops are not suitable for displaying historic costumes. They are usually fixed in an exaggerated position and have immovable arms and heads. They are also too big. In the past, humans were smaller and their proportions different. Dummies originating from the 1950s and 1960s are sometimes better proportioned and may still be available in clothes shops. Stylised dummies, such as the 'old-fashioned' tailor's dummy, i.e. a stuffed torso on a wooden stand, may be more suitable. Modern dummies for children's clothes may also be useful. Some foam rubber dummies were found to be suitable for temporary displays. These foam dummies have heads and limbs, which may be necessary for the display of ethnographic or

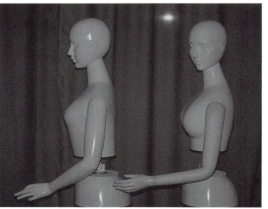

Figure 94 Two dummies suitable for different periods of fashion (photo courtesy Rijksmuseum, Amsterdam, costume dummies from the Kyoto Costume Institute).

traditional costumes where veils, headdresses and jewellery are equally as important as the costume. The material from which the dummies are made must be tested before use as it may contain plasticisers; these can migrate out over time and create liquid droplets on the surface of the plastic.

Making a suitable dummy
Modern fashion dummies, although not useful for displaying historic costumes, can serve as a basic shape from which suitable dummies may be cast. A fashion dummy that will fit a given historic costume has to be smaller than the costume and have roughly the same proportions. It should be without arms as the cast is only made from the torso. Children's dummies often fit these requirements.

The base dummy must first be covered with a barrier foil in order to prevent the costume from making direct contact with it during the initial fitting. Smooth silk stockinette is useful as it creates a surface which will not abrade the costume. In addition, the elasticity of the stockinette allows for local padding, which helps to adapt the basic shape. After fitting the costume onto the dummy base, extra padding can be positioned underneath the stockinette in order to create the correct silhouette and proper support for the costume. Polyester wadding may be used as a padding material. Do not pad the basic shape too much as this can be done at a later stage after the cast dummy has been made. During this initial phase it is extremely important to work effectively and efficiently, so that handling of the costume is minimised and risk of damage to the textile reduced.

Once the dummy base has been modified to the correct proportions and silhouette, it serves as a mould from which the new dummy will be cast. In order to protect the dummy, it is first wrapped in a barrier foil. Next, it is covered with a casting material, which is usually applied wet; for example, gummed paper tape, buckram or papier mâché. Experience has shown that it is best to work from the shoulders downwards. Depending on the weight of the costume, more than one layer may have to be added. When using buckram, the layers can be added one after the other, but when using gummed paper tape, each layer should first be allowed to dry before applying the next one. The final layer should be left to dry for at least 24 hours. The cast can then be cut along its sides and removed from the base. The two halves can be joined using the same casting material.

In order to make the new dummy sturdier, a rigid disk of inert material (for example, polyethylene foam) can be inserted at the waist. This can also serve as a base into which the dummy's stand can be secured. If necessary, the dummy can be cut away to the costume's neckline making it almost invisible inside the costume. The sharp cut edge should be smoothed and finished off using appropriate conservation-grade tape. With lightweight costumes a stand may not be necessary; the mounted costumes can be hung using nylon fishing line attached to the dummy.

Buckram and paper tape are sensitive to moisture so dummies made from these materials must be varnished in order to make them more durable. It is important to remember that although the material costs of these dummies are not high, creating the correct shape is very labour intensive.

Another way to make a dummy is to cut disks of rigid and inert material (polyethylene foam) and stack them to create a support. The dimensions and silhouette of the costume should be recorded and then cut out from a sheet of foam. The foam disks are then stacked on top of each other and fixed with a hot-melt glue gun. This durable and solid shape is more suitable for heavier costumes (Larouche 1997; Willman 1997: 173; Brum and White 2002).

Both these types of dummy must then be finished off. The form is given a softer surface by covering it with a thin layer of polyester wadding. Following this, the shape is covered with stockinette (a simple white cotton T-shirt may suffice). Where necessary, some local padding may be added underneath the covering fabric.

The last suggested method is to use transparent polycarbonate, which is available in several thicknesses. This flexible sheet material can be easily cut and bent into shape. By applying heat, the bent shape created can be made permanent. Torso supports can be constructed by cutting the pattern of the costume from this material. The correct shape is obtained when the pattern parts are pieced together using adhesive or stitching. The support can be used as it is, because the material is transparent. It can also be covered with fabric to make it slightly softer and provide some friction in order to support and hold the costume in place.

Undergarments are extremely important in obtaining the correct silhouette for a historic costume; particularly corsets, crinolines, paniers and petticoats. Original undergarments should not be used as they will be subjected to unnecessary tension – and will not be seen by the public. Replicas should be used wherever possible. For example, a nylon net petticoat can create the effect of a wide bulging skirt instead of the original crinoline. Undergarments may be duplicated using unbleached cotton. Modern stays of flexible carbon or glass fibre can be used in replica corsets instead of traditional baleen.

If arms and legs are to be used, these can be made from tubular stockinette, such as bandages or support hose that can be stuffed to the appropriate thickness and firmness. The limbs can be fixed in a bent position by placing stiff electric cable inside the padding, which can then be bent into shape. The limbs can be attached to the torso by means of hook and loop fasteners or ribbons.

Some of the garments in ethnographic collections have a T-shape, such as kimonos. These can be displayed using the same method employed for storage, i.e. by putting a covered tube through the arms and then hanging the roll in the display.

If a head is required on a dummy, the hairstyle or an artistic impression of it should also be considered (Burnham 1999: 8). In some costume exhibitions, the 'problem' of the heads can be solved in an artistic way. Cooperation between the designer, curator and textile conservator often results in exciting displays (Fig. 95).

Facial expressions, hairstyles and ethnographic features may be requested to support the message of an exhibition; however, they can also be a distraction. An exact facsimile of a person is rarely required; a well-designed impression usually suffices to help the public visualise a certain person or ethnic group. A good example of this was the exhibition of the costumes of Queen Victoria, 'From Queen to Empress: Victorian Dress 1837–1877', held at the Museum of London in 1998. In order to display the different phases of her life, three types of dummies were made: one for her childhood, one for her adolescence and one to show the costumes from her later years. The dummies were given simple heads with minimal facial expressions based on existing portraits of the queen – only the nose and soft outlines of her eyes and mouth were shown. The result immediately evoked an association with Victoria.

In a similar exhibition in the Netherlands of the costumes of Queen Wilhelmina (1880–1962), held at the Royal Palace Het Loo in 1998–1999, the costumes were displayed on tailor-made dummies without heads or hands. The image of the queen was evoked here by means of photographic and film material, which, together with a recognisable posture of the torsos, readily recalled the queen's image (Fig. 96).

Figure 95 An example of a costume exhibition in which the costumes are mounted onto dummies. The cooperation between the designer, curator and textile conservator has resulted in an artistic solution to the so-called 'head problem' (photo courtesy Rijksmuseum, Amsterdam).

8.4.6 Three-dimensional objects

It may be the curator's wish to display not only the costume, but also the matching accessories. In traditional costumes for example, the headdress is often extremely important in creating the complete picture. Other accessories, such as handbags, fans, umbrellas and jewellery, may also be added to the display. If the dummy is made without hands to hold the accessory, it may be fixed with nylon fishing line to the arm or even to the ceiling, provided this does not cause any damage to the object. An illusion of a complete outfit is often sufficient to create the appropriate image (Fig. 97).

Supports for hats can be tailor-made by simply following the method for dummy-making, i.e. casting them from existing hat moulds into buckram, gummed paper tape, papier mâché, etc. (see section 8.4.5). Commercially available plastic heads can also be used, providing the plastic is inert (see section 9.2.8). Whichever supports are chosen they should be padded and covered with fabric. These solid-type supports do not always fit comfortably with the aesthetic of an exhibition; as long as the basic mount of the hat provides sufficient support, artistic and 'open' supports may also be used. For the exhibition 'Chapeau, Chapeaux' in the Rijksmuseum, Amsterdam (30 October 1997–29 March 1998) hat supports were made from black electric cable which was bent into the correct shape. Fragile or floppy hats were given an inner support made from buckram (Fig. 98)

Figure 96 An example showing how the costumes of the Dutch Queen Wilhelmina were displayed on tailor-made dummies without heads or hands. The image of the queen was evoked by additional items such as her portrait, photographs and film (photo courtesy R. Mulder, Paleis Het Loo, Apeldoorn).

Some pieces of headgear can be supported on 'invisible' supports made from Perspex, polycarbonate or buckram. These can then be hung at the appropriate height above a costume, thus dispensing with the need for the dummy to have a head. It should, however, be possible to pass a thin nylon fishing line through existing holes in the headgear. In straw hats, small holes are already present because of the construction, but in a felt hat this may not be the case. Polyethylene foam can also be used for constructing supports. A stand can be attached to the back of the showcase onto which this support can be fixed in such a way that the hat appears to float.

Objects made from a combination of materials, including fans, umbrellas and dolls, must be displayed in constant climatic conditions. Different materials respond in different ways to changes in RH and temperature. Each material has its own requirements: metal, for example, should be kept

Figure 97 An example of an imaginative display of Dutch traditional costume (photo courtesy K. Steltenpool, collection Zuiderzee Museum Enkhuizen).

Figure 98 An example of an artistic hat support made from black electric cable which was bent into the correct shape (photo courtesy Rijksmuseum, Amsterdam).

at a low RH in order to prevent corrosion. Organic materials, however, require a slightly higher RH, otherwise they become brittle and more vulnerable. A compromise needs to be found for suitable environmental conditions for composite objects.

Using display cases in exhibitions helps to achieve a more stable climate for their contents. Another great advantage of the use of display cases is that they can be made dust-free reducing the need to remove dust. This is particularly important for more complex objects. Different materials retain dust in different ways so an object may appear to be dirtier in some parts than others, e.g. a fan made from a leaf of bobbin lace with bone ribs – the ribs can be cleaned to a greater extent than the lace.

In order to display three-dimensional objects safely, tailor-made supports are necessary. The materials used should be inert, preferably acid-free, and the mounts should support the object adequately. Perspex is often used as a display material; and because it can be bent into many different shapes, it is also transparent and therefore barely noticeable. Working with Perspex, however, requires both experience and specialised tools. Polycarbonate, which is also transparent, can be made into supports more easily and polyethylene foam can be shaped by cutting it with a sharp knife. Other possibilities for supports include buckram, papier mâché, gummed paper tape and acid-free card (see section 8.4.5).

Shoes, gloves and bags usually require some stuffing in order to maintain their correct shape. For short-term exhibitions they can be stuffed with polyester wadding or crumpled acid-free tissue paper. Heavier objects, or objects that will be on display for a longer period of time, may require a more rigid support, for example, one made from polyethylene foam, padded and covered with fabric. This will prevent the stuffing from collapsing over a period of time as can happen with acid-free tissue paper.

In order to exhibit fans safely, tailor-made supports are necessary. It is important to fully support the leaf of the fan and its ribs. The mount should also follow the gradient of the fan. Perspex is often used for making fan supports as its transparent nature does not interfere with the full appreciation of a fan. Sometimes an adaptable basic support may be useful: the round shape that supports the fan leaf can be positioned at different angles by fixing it into preformed grooves in its base.

Dolls, teddy bears and similar objects in stable condition are often displayed upright. The stand should support the object around its waist or just under its arms (like a harness). Unfortunately, it is unavoidable that some clothing or plush will be compressed at the point of the support. Unstable objects should be laid flat, preferably on a soft pad (see section 6.3.6).

When displaying upholstered furniture, it is important to protect it from the public by ensuring that it is not used for seating (see section 8.3.3).

8.5 Appendix

8.5.1 Materials for making a padded, fabric-covered board

The board material (see section 9.2.1)
Acid-free card can be used for smaller size boards, but it is not rigid enough for larger ones. Laminating several layers together using polyvinyl acetate glue or double-sided tape (conservation quality) will make a board which is not only more rigid but also heavier.

Foam board, covered on either side with acid-free card (e.g. Kapaline or Centerfoam) is more suitable for larger sizes as it is lighter and more rigid than acid-free card. The disadvantage of this material is that it is easily dented and the foam layer has been known to degrade and crumble over time.

Inert sheet material may also be used. Polyethylene corrugated sheets (e.g. Correx) are more suitable for smaller sizes as larger pieces might bend. To reduce the flexibility of corrugated sheets, two or three layers can be stuck together using double-sided tape. The direction of the channels in the sheets should be placed at right angles to each other in order to increase rigidity.

Aluminium honeycomb sheets (e.g. Hexlite) are extremely rigid and can be used for larger sizes. The material is also lightweight and very strong. These materials are more expensive but are more durable than those mentioned above.

Wood and products made from wood (see section 6.2.2) can also be used for larger sizes. Sheets of marine plywood or acid-free card can be mounted on a wooden frame to create the appropriate dimensions. When using wood or wood products, a barrier layer should be added in order to prevent harmful gases from migrating onto the mounted textile. To overcome this potential problem, special aluminium foil (for example Moistop or Marvelseal) or other barrier layers such as Melinex can be used. Be aware that a lot of time and effort can be spent on upgrading 'cheap' materials – it might be more cost effective to invest in more durable materials even if they are more expensive.

The padding
Several materials can be used to create a soft surface such as polyester wadding or brushed cotton fabric (see section 9.2.2).

The fabric cover
The choice of fabric to cover the board depends upon the desired effect. Sometimes a slightly rough surface may be needed to create friction between the object and its support. Avoid the use of open weave or elastic fabrics as these are difficult to process. Always use washed materials (to ensure that any finish has been removed) and make sure that the dye is tested beforehand for fastness to washing. Dyed textiles whose colour bleeds in water should not be used. The composition of the material should also be known. It is good practice not to mix protein fibres with cellulose fibre textiles and vice versa.

8.5.2 Instructions for making a padded, fabric-covered board

Three different techniques are presented for fixing the padding and the fabric cover to the board: using conservation-grade adhesive tape (double and single-sided), needle and thread or a combination of the two.

Adhesive tape
Only use tested, conservation-grade double and single-sided tapes such as Gudy-O, Filmoplast and Tyvek tape (see section 9.2.3). The padding is first fixed to the front of the board using double-sided tape along its edges. The fabric cover is then tensioned keeping the grain straight (the warp or weft of the textile is lined up parallel with the edge of the board) over the board and folded onto the reverse side. This process can be carried out using pins which are positioned, working from the centre of each side towards the corners, thereby stretching the fabric. On its reverse side, fix the fabric to the board with double-sided tape or polyvinyl acetate adhesive (wood glue or bookbinder's glue), and finish the edges off with, for example, Tyvek tape (Fig. 99). This is a quick and simple way of making a fabric-covered board but the strength of the tapes should not be relied upon for long-term exhibitions. Extra security can be obtained by stitching the corners of the fabric cover at the back.

Adhesive tape or adhesive and stitching
Polyester wadding cannot be used as padding when this method is used. A soft woven fabric such as brushed cotton is more suitable. This layer is stretched onto the board and folded at the back,

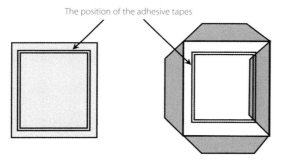

Figure 99 Board covered with padding (light grey) and fabric (dark grey) cover using conservation-grade adhesive tapes (obverse on left, reverse on right).

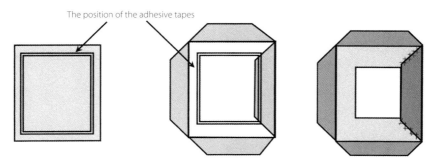

Figure 100 Board covered with padding (light grey) and fabric (dark grey) cover using conservation-grade adhesive tapes and stitching (obverse on left, reverse on right).

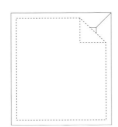

Figure 101 Board covered with padding and fabric cover using stitching (reverse side).

fabric cover is then fixed to the padding fabric using blanket stitch. The corners of the fabric are secured by stitching (Fig. 100).

Stitching
First, the padding is positioned and folded onto the back of the board, where it is then cut short along the edges of the board. Next, the fabric cover is tensioned over the board and folded to the back. The fabric can now be stitched at the corners. A second piece of fabric cover, slightly larger than the board, is then tensioned over the back, where it is stitched with folded edges to the previously applied fabric cover. This is the most time-consuming method but it does ensure that the tension in the fabric cover is maintained for a longer period of time (Fig. 101).

where it is fixed using double-sided tape or polyvinyl acetate adhesive (wood glue or bookbinder's glue). The cut edges of the fabric may be finished with Tyvek tape. Next, the fabric cover is tensioned over the board and folded to the back, where it is cut slightly shorter than the padding fabric. The

9

Materials for conservation

When adopting a commercially available product for conservation purposes, it is important to remember that commercial products change frequently – new products come onto the market while others are discontinued. It is therefore necessary to ask for the product information sheet for any new product(s) you intend to use and, when in doubt, to have it checked by a conservation scientist. And remember, manufacturers can change the composition of products without notification.

9.1 Research

In order to establish whether or not a material emits any harmful gases a test should be carried out. One such test is the so-called 'Oddy test', named after the former Keeper of the Department of Conservation at the British Museum. It is a non-specific test, which means that it does not analyse exactly which gases are emitted from the test material or in what concentration, but only indicates whether or not any harmful gases are released.

The following description of the test is based on an adaptation of the Oddy test by the former Central Research Laboratory for Objects of Art and Science in Amsterdam (now called the Netherlands Institute for Cultural Heritage) (Hallebeek 1987).

Fill a 100 ml glass tube with distilled water to a level of 3 cm. Next, place a wad of cotton wool (pharmaceutical quality) just above the water level, so that it does not get wet. A sample of the material to be tested is placed on top of the cotton wool, for example: wood chips, a few drops of adhesive, a piece of plastic or a piece of fabric used in exhibition. If it is necessary to test a liquid, this should first be sampled onto a piece of new filter paper (laboratory quality). Another wad of cotton wool is then placed just above the sample, and a piece of metal foil is placed on top of this. This foil must be completely clean and should be thoroughly degreased with ethanol or acetone. The metal foil can be lead (to indicate weak organic acids, such as acetic acid and formic acid), copper, bronze or brass (to indicate strong acidic vapours and chlorine compounds), silver (to indicate gases containing sulphur) and copper or aluminium (to indicate alkaline vapours such as ammonia). Lead is often used as it reacts more quickly than copper, bronze or brass. Finally, the tube is sealed. Do not use rubber as this will affect the test.

The water creates a high RH inside the tube, as a result of which degradation reactions are accelerated. It is recommended that the test be carried out at a moderate temperature of up to 60 °C in a laboratory oven. This will accelerate reactions even further. Any harmful gases emitted by the material will then migrate through the cotton wool and finally reach the metal. If the surface of the metal foil appears to have changed in texture or colour within two weeks at 60 °C or up to four weeks at room temperature, it can be concluded that the material is unsafe to use. Make sure that a control test is always carried out at the same time. This consists of a test tube filled with the same contents as described above but without the material sample. This will show how the metal reacts to the conditions in the tube without the presence of the material to be tested.

Another simplified version of the Oddy test: a sample of the material to be tested is placed in a small 20 ml glass beaker. Three pieces of metal foil, i.e. copper, lead and silver, are folded over the edge of the beaker. The small beaker is placed in a larger beaker of approximately 80 ml, containing approximately 2 ml of distilled water. The larger beaker is then sealed (Bamberger 1999). Others showed that a consistent method must be used in order to achieve reproducible results (Robinet and Thickett 2003; Green and Thickett 1995).

9.2 Products

The following list describes products that have been used with textiles. It should be noted that some materials still used frequently are unsuitable. Product names and availability might differ from country to country (see section 6.2.2 for a discussion of materials suitable for use in the safe storage of textiles) (*Syllabus* 2002; McGregor 1994; Tetreault and Williams 1992).

9.2.1 Sheet materials for making supports

- Acid-free card: this is lignin-free, high quality cardboard which is available in different colours. Use only the white variety (or those with water-fast colours) for storage to avoid the risk of colour transfer to the objects. As is the case for other acid-free paper products (e.g. acid-free tissue paper) the acidity of the card will increase over time. The acidity can be tested using a pH pen. If used near objects made from vegetable materials; the cardboard should be replaced when the pH value drops below 6. If used near objects made from animal material, the cardboard should be replaced when the pH value drops below 5. Acid-free cardboard may be 'buffered', i.e. it has an alkaline reserve which delays the acidification of the material considerably. This material should not be used near proteinaceous textiles as the buffering agent can cause the textile to degrade due to the high alkalinity it produces. These materials are expensive. Note that in literature the term 'buffering quality' is often used in relation to wood and paper. In these instances, it refers to the hygroscopic nature of the material which will level out climatic changes.
- Aerolam: see Hexlite.
- Artfoam: see Kapaline.
- Cellite: see Hexlite.
- Centerfoam or Museum Centerfoam: this is a lightweight, fairly rigid type of sheet material consisting of two layers of acid-free card with a layer of polystyrene foam in between. It is less durable than Kapaline. The foam inside is not inert and will therefore degrade and crumble over time (after approximately six years depending upon climatic conditions).
- Correx: this is a synthetic corrugated board which consists of approximately 90% polypropylene and 10% polyethylene. There are several thicknesses, from 2 mm to 15 mm. The sheets are made from two layers of plastic connected by rows of parallel ridges, thus creating channels. The material is lightweight and fairly rigid. By simply cutting one layer of the plastic parallel, or perpendicular, to these ridges, the sheet can be bent and folded into a three-dimensional shape. The heat from a hairdryer or electric paint stripper can be used to mould plastics into a shape which is permanent once it has cooled down (Schlichting 1994).
- Foamboard: see Kapaline.
- Hexlite (also referred to as Aerolam, Cellite Fibre, Cellite Aluminium): this is an extremely rigid, unbreakable, lightweight board that derives from the aviation industry. One type consists of two layers of fibreglass with aluminium honeycomb in between. Another form of this material that may be used is made of two layers of aluminium, again with aluminium honeycomb in between. It is extremely good for making supporting boards for the exhibition of large two-dimensional textiles. It is however expensive and difficult to process.
- Honeycomb cardboard: this type of cardboard is made up of two layers of thin cardboard with honeycomb cardboard in between. It is rigid and strong and is also available in an acid-free state.
- Kapa: see Kapaline.
- Kapaline (also known as foamboard, artfoam and kapa): this is a lightweight, rigid sheet material. It consists of two layers of acid-free card with a layer of polyurethane foam in between. It is comparable to Centerfoam but is more durable. It can easily be made into supports, boxes, etc. and is often used as a backing board for paintings. The disadvantage, however, is that the foam will

turn yellow at the cut edges and crumble over time.
- Polycarbonate: this material is transparent, unbreakable and filters out UV; it is often used in museums and historic houses as secondary glazing. It is also available in thin sheets, which are flexible and can easily be cut and bent into shape to create supports for three-dimensional objects. The bent shape can be made permanent by heating. For example, torso supports can be constructed by cutting the pattern of the costume from this material. By piecing the pattern parts together, using adhesive or by stitching, the correct shape is obtained.
- Museum Centerfoam: see Centerfoam.

9.2.2 Materials used in making supports

- Buckram: see Etamine.
- Ebicel: see Ibicel.
- Etamine (also referred to as buckram): this is a starched cotton fabric. When wet it becomes soft and sticky allowing it to be moulded around any shape. Upon drying it becomes hard. It is suitable for making supports for the exhibition of three-dimensional textiles, e.g. costumes. It remains water-sensitive once it is dry.
- Ethafoam (also referred to as Itef, Nopafoam): this is an inert polyethylene open-cell foam, which is available in several densities, thicknesses and colours. Only white and black have been found to be safe for use in museums, and overall the white variety is preferred. It is an ideal material for making hard, solid supports as it is easy to cut and process. It has a rough surface however, and needs to be finished with a soft padding and/or cover. It is low weight, has good shock-absorbing properties and is resistant to water and chemicals.
- Ibicel (also referred to as Ebicel or Multifoam): a thin layer of polyethylene foam. It is suitable for covering metal shelves in storage and is also used as packaging material.
- Itef: see Ethafoam.
- Kubicel: see Plastazote.
- Multifoam: see Ibicel.
- Nopafoam: see Ethafoam.
- Perspex (also known as Plexiglas): a polymethylmethacrylate (PMMA) inert, transparent plastic that is available in all thicknesses and sizes. With some experience, and the right tools, supports can be made from Perspex for fans, hats, etc. It is used more often in exhibition than in storage.

One disadvantage however, is that Perspex has an electrostatic charge.
- Plastazote (also referred to as Kubicel): this is an inert polyethylene closed-cell foam which has a softer surface than an open-cell foam and is therefore more suitable for storing fragile textiles such as archaeological material.
- Plexiglas: see Perspex.
- Polyester wadding (Fibrefill): this is a non-woven material which can be manufactured in three different ways where the fibres can be: glued together using adhesive; melted together using heat or tangled using needles (needle punch). Ideally, it is safer to use the needle punch variety and avoid those containing adhesives.
- Polyurethane foam: soft foam with good shock absorbing and insulation properties. It should only be used in short-term packaging and should not be used in direct contact with the object. It does not provide support to objects as it crumbles over time. It is available in sheets (grey foam) or as a liquid compressed in spray cans. The latter form expands upon spraying and solidifies around shapes or in moulds (used to create dummies).

9.2.3 Adhesives and tapes

There are several different types of adhesives and tapes available. They need to be handled with appropriate precaution and care. The use of these materials on objects should always be checked first with a textile conservator.

- Acrylic adhesives (e.g. superglue): these do not emit harmful substances but should never be used on objects as they are irreversible. They can be used to make boxes, etc.
- Epoxy glue (e.g. Araldite): the two components are mixed together to make strong and durable connections in supports or packaging. It should not be used close to objects.
- Filmoplast (produced by Neschen): this is an acid-free paper tape that should not be used on objects. However, it is safe to use in making boxes, supports, etc.
- Gudy (produced by Neschen): this is a double-sided tape that is safe to use near objects.
- Gummed paper tape: this can be coated with polyvinyl alcohol, polyvinyl acetate adhesive or a mixture of both, which can be made sticky by wetting. It is available acid-free and is suitable for making boxes, supports, dummies, etc.

- Masking tape: this should only be used on the outside of packaging.
- Gluton: this adhesive is safe to use near objects. It is a starch-derived, water-based adhesive and does not contain any harmful solvents.
- Polyurethane: these glues are acid-free but irreversible. Do not use them on objects.
- Polyvinyl acetate (PVAc): these types of adhesives (wood glue and bookbinder's glue), emit acetic acid while drying. Once dry, these adhesives emit only a small amount of harmful substances. They can be used to make boxes, supports, etc. but are not used in display cases.
- Polyvinyl chloride tape (PVC): this is used in the packaging industry. It is a very strong, brown plastic tape, but should only be used on the outside of the packaging. It loses its strength after approximately one year and leaves traces behind that cannot be removed. Never use polyvinyl chloride tape on objects.
- Tyvek (polyethylene) tape: this is a strong, water-repellent tape suitable for finishing off cut edges of fabric on fabric-covered boards or for making boxes.

The following types of adhesives and tapes should never be used:

- Polyester glues: these are known to emit acetic acid.
- Polysulphide glues: these glues are not suitable as they contain sulphur, emit acids and are inflammable and toxic.
- Sellotape: a transparent tape which was unfortunately used frequently in the past directly onto objects to repair damage. It loses its strength easily and the transparent plastic layer of the tape is released over time. The adhesive migrates into the object where it yellows and often remains sticky. This residue is difficult to remove.
- Rubber cement glue: is irreversible and may previously have been used for the restoration of tapestries.

9.2.4 Barrier foils

- Clingfilm: this is made from polyethylene without a plasticiser. It is safe to use when isolating unsuitable materials making them more suitable for use near textiles. An example of its use is the wrapping of metal or wooden coat hangers before padding them.
- Marvelseal 360A: a polypropylene/polyethylene/aluminium/polyethylene barrier film that is suitable to seal wood and wood products to prevent the release of harmful gases. Once applied, the surface must not be punctured or damaged as this will allow the harmful gases to leak out and reach the textile.
- Melinex (also referred to as Mylar): a transparent polyester/polyethylene terephthalate (PET) plastic foil without plasticisers is available in several thicknesses. Although an inert material, it allows vapours to pass. As a result, it cannot completely stop harmful gases from wood and acid cardboard from migrating. It has an electrostatic charge that sometimes makes it difficult to handle. Sleeves made from Melinex are commercially available for the storage of smaller objects and photographs.
- Moistop: a polyester/aluminium/polyethylene barrier film, it can be used in a similar way to Marvelseal.
- Mylar: see Melinex.

9.2.5 Packaging material

- Acid-free tissue paper: a lignin-free, high-quality paper made from cotton, flax or purified wood fibres. Extremely useful for packing textiles for storage and used as interleaving when rolling textiles. The degree of acidity increases over time and consequently the paper will turn yellow as the material degrades. Acid-free tissue paper should be replaced regularly (approximately every five years depending upon the environmental conditions and the material with which it is in contact). The pH value of the paper can be tested using a pH pen. If used with objects made from vegetable materials, the paper should be replaced when the pH value drops below 6; if used with objects made from animal material, the paper should be replaced when the pH value drops below 5. Buffered acid-free paper is available, but this is not recommended for use with textiles.
- Bubble wrap: a polyethylene plastic composed of one or two layers of plastic with air pockets either on top or in between. It can be used as a packaging material for objects in transit, but should never be in direct contact with the objects. If using single-layer wrap the air pockets should always be on the outside in order to prevent damage to the objects if they burst. Bubble wrap is also available with the air pockets enclosed between a layer of plastic and a thin

layer of polyethylene foam (Ibicel). This type of material is more durable and safer to use when in contact with objects. Bubble wrap has limited shock-absorbing qualities and works only if the bubbles are intact.
- Ethafoam: see section 9.2.2.
- Polyester wadding: see section 9.2.2.
- Ibicel: see section 9.2.2.
- Itef: see section 9.2.2.
- Multifoam: see section 9.2.2.
- Nopafoam: see section 9.2.2.
- Plastazote: see section 9.2.2.

9.2.6 Personal safety

Gloves
Several types of gloves are available for the handling of museum objects. Gloves serve two purposes: first, they protect the object from the sweat and grease from hands; secondly, they protect humans from any contamination by the objects, which are often dirty and soiled or could contain pesticide residues. The disadvantage of many gloves is that they reduce the sense of touch – this is potentially dangerous when handling objects. Gloves may also have a slightly rough surface to which fibres from the objects can cling easily. It may therefore be better in some instances to handle textiles with bare hands provided they are clean and dry.

- Cotton gloves: these are commonly used in museum environments for handling objects in general, but are less suitable for handling textiles. They have a rough surface to which textiles cling and, as a result, fibres are transferred. Some types can be washed – these are the more expensive types with a proper cut – while others lose their shape in washing and become difficult to use. Some cotton gloves have small raised dots on the palm to provide better grip. These dots are made from nitrile foam, polyvinyl chloride (PVC) or latex. The latter contains sulphur, which is known to cause damage to some materials such as silver. All of these materials have been found to give off harmful substances such as plasticisers and should not be used.
- Latex gloves: these are tight fitting and provide a better grip than cotton gloves. They should be used only once and thrown away after use. Gloves with talc powder inside (to reduce sweating), should not be used as this powder may contaminate textile objects during handling. It should be noted that some people are allergic to these gloves and they should not be used to handle silver.
- Vinyl gloves: also tight fitting, they provide a better grip than cotton gloves and are preferable to latex. Gloves with powder inside should not be used (see above).
- Nitrile gloves: again, these are tight fitting and provide a better grip than cotton gloves. These types of gloves are also preferable to latex and can be used when handling some chemicals. Please refer to the information sheet provided with chemicals in order to establish the suitability of these gloves for this purpose. Not all nitrile gloves are safe to use as some are produced with polymer slip coating and others have been chlorinated.

Masks
- Respirator masks: these are divided into dust, gas and vapour respirators (semi-facial and full facial). When working with fine dust, P2 quality suffices; for fungi and old pesticide residues a P3 quality is required. The P indicating coding is labelled on the packaging and on the mask itself. Not all masks are disposable; some have filters inside that should be changed. Disposable respirators should be discarded after use and never reused.

9.2.7 Fabrics, non-wovens and fabric tapes

- Aplix: see hook and loop fastener.
- Cotton: this is a relatively cheap material that is available in different structures (woven, knitted, etc.), and densities. Any cotton fabric used should be unbleached, preferably undyed (or otherwise with proper dye fastness), and of a good quality. Before application, it should be washed thoroughly in water heated to at least 60 °C to remove finishes and to avoid future shrinkage. The cotton fabric used for making duvets is very suitable as it is densely woven, lightweight and often available in larger widths.
- Hook and loop fasteners (also known as Velcro, Aplix): these are made from nylon and are available in a variety of colours. The hook side is rough and the loop side soft. When pressed together, the two sides form a very strong mechanical bond which can be broken by tearing the strips apart. The backs of the tapes are coated with polyurethane or an acrylic substance (or a combination of the two) in order to secure the loops and hooks. Research has shown that

the acrylic coating is more stable and this type should therefore be used for museum purposes. The self-adhesive type should not be used near museum objects as the adhesive present can be harmful and fails after a period of time. As a precaution, hook and loop fasteners attached to textile objects should be replaced every 15 to 20 years (Leath and Brooks 1998).
- Non-woven interfacing (e.g. Vilene): this is a non-woven polyester fabric. Non-wovens in which the fibres are melted together using heat are safe to use.
- Nylon net: this is extensively used in textile conservation. It can be dyed to match the colour of the object. In addition, it can be used to make supports for costumes, for example, in petticoats.
- Polypropylene non-woven fabric (also referred to as PP fabric): this is water-repellent but at the same time allows for air circulation and the exchange of water vapour through miniscule pores in the material. It should not be used in unstable climates, however, as it delays moisture regulation, which could result in an increased risk of fungal growth. It is cheaper than Tyvek but not as durable.
- Silk crepeline: a gauze-like, transparent fabric which is used in textile conservation. It can be dyed to match the colour of the object.
- Tetex (previously known as Stabiltex): a gauze-like fabric made from polyethyleneterephthalate, it is used in textile conservation and is available in several colours.
- Tubular bandage: a tubular knitted cotton tricot that is suitable for covering coat hangers and rolls. It can also be stuffed with soft padding materials to create supports for objects. Medical tubular bandage does not have to be washed prior to use.
- Tyvek: this is a polyethylene non-woven fabric (see above). It is available both with and without an anti-static layer; the former should not be used as it is not inert and is known to corrode metals.
- Velcro: see hook and loop fasteners.

9.2.8 Other materials

- Active carbon (as powder or in cloth): this is capable of purifying air and water by binding organic pollutants to itself. It can be used in storage or in display to improve air quality. Filters in air-conditioning systems also contain active carbon. It can absorb pollutants up to a certain maximum level, after which it releases them back into the air. It should be replaced before it becomes saturated.
- Ageless Eye: a small indicator tablet that can be used to indicate the level of oxygen in a sealed oxygen-free environment. It turns pink when the oxygen level is below 0.1% and purple when the oxygen level is above 0.5%. Adjusting to the low oxygen level may take several hours, but the tablets turn purple within five minutes when the oxygen levels pass 0.5%. Ageless Eye is relatively cheap but has a restricted shelflife of up to six months (when stored in a refrigerator in a bag containing an oxygen absorber).
- Art Sorb (see also Pro Sorb): a passive buffer composed of 90% silica gel (SiO_2) and lithium chloride (LiCl), which can be used to condition sealed spaces (i.e. microclimates). It buffers the RH inside a microclimate by absorbing or releasing moisture when the RH of the microclimate differs from the one at which it was conditioned. It is available in beads, sheets and cassettes and can be regenerated. Lithium chloride is a corrosive substance for many metals and Art Sorb should therefore not be in direct contact with objects.
- Desi Pak: desiccant clay (bentonite) in sturdy, dustproof paper or non-woven bags; ideal for drying Art Sorb or Pro Sorb cassettes or beads. Between 0% and 40% RH, one 35 g bag absorbs 6 g of water. This drying agent can be regenerated by heating the bags in an oven at 110 to 130 °C.
- Japanese paper: available in a wide range of paper types and thicknesses, it is a material long used in paper conservation. It has been used increasingly in textile conservation as it is extremely versatile. It is also used for numbering textile objects (see section 11.5.3).
- Nylon fishing line: an almost invisible and extremely strong line that is suitable for use in storage and display. It is fairly sharp and precautions should be taken if it is used with objects to prevent it from causing damage.
- Oxygen absorbers or oxygen scavengers (Ageless, RP System, FreshPax): the most commonly used oxygen absorber is Ageless-Z (Mitsubishi Gas Company), which was developed for the food industry. The permeable plastic sachets are filled with fine iron oxide powder, potassium or sodium chloride, and a zeolite. It can be used to create an oxygen-free environment in a sealed volume. Ageless-Z reacts with oxy-

gen most rapidly at 75% RH, but the reaction is still significant even at 45%. One sachet of Ageless Z-1000 can absorb 1000 ml of oxygen, the amount present in approximately 5 litres of air. The number of packages necessary to create a low-oxygen atmosphere can be calculated from the volume of the sealed object in its bag. The reaction between scavenger and oxygen produces heat and moisture. The contact between sachet and object must, therefore, be avoided. As the bags contain some organic material, their buffering capacity is usually enough to counteract moisture production. RP System (Mitsubishi Gas Company) is an alternative scavenger developed for preserving metals and electronic parts. FreshPax (Multisorb Technologies) is comparable to Ageless, developed to protect packaged food, pharmaceuticals and other products against loss of quality.

- PH pen: used to measure the acidity of a material. The material being tested is marked with this pen; the colour change of the ink, which depends on the acidity of the material, is compared to a reference scale. Never use this pen on museum objects!
- Pro Sorb (see also Art Sorb): this is a silica gel suited to stabilise RH inside museum display cases and storage cabinets. It has an exceptional adsorption capacity within the 40 to 60% RH range. Pro Sorb is able to maintain a stable RH within narrow margins by its ability to both absorb and desorb water vapour; it is supplied preconditioned to the desired humidity level. With a longer lifespan than other silica gels, it consists of 97% silicon oxide (SiO_2) and 3% aluminium oxide (Al_2O_3). It contains no lithium chloride. Reconditioning to their original RH value can be done easily by weight within the first 1–2 years. After a longer period of time, due to the slow degradation shown by all types of silica gel, conditioning must be checked with a calibrated hygrometer.
- Plastics: in general, plastics that are safe to use near textile objects are polyethylene, polypropylene, polycarbonate, polystyrene, acrylics, polytetrafluorethylene (Teflon), polyester and polyethyleneterephthalate (Scott Williams 1997: 95).
- Silica gel: a passive buffer that can be used to condition sealed spaces (i.e. microclimates). It buffers the RH inside a given microclimate by absorbing or releasing moisture when the RH of the microclimate differs from the one at which it was conditioned. Conventional silica gels are quite useful in the range between 0% and 40% RH as well as above 75%. In the intermediate region, 40 to 75% RH, Art Sorb and Pro Sorb are far superior – their buffering capacity is up to five times higher than the capacity of conventional silica gels. Silica gel can be regenerated many times at temperatures between 130 and 150 °C. Orange silica gel is sold in beads of 2 to 5 mm. This product is replacing the indicating 'blue gel' currently presumed to cause cancer. Depending on its moisture content, orange silica gel changes its colour from yellow to red. It can be blended with non-indicating silica gel, e.g. at a weight ratio of 1:9.
- Zip-lock bags: these are made from polyethylene and are available in different sizes. They are ideal for storing detached fragments. They are also used to store small objects, for example, jewellery and hair accessories. This should be done with great care; the bags can be perforated for long-term storage to avoid uncontrollable microclimates. They should not be used to store unstable plastic objects.

10
Conservation and restoration

10.1 The history of conservation

Restoration, repair, active and passive conservation, preventive conservation and preservation are just some of the terms used to describe the safekeeping of cultural property. In this chapter, an attempt is made to clarify this terminology and the role of the textile conservator in relation to that of the keepers of collections (i.e. collection manager, curator, storekeeper, etc.) – suggesting which tasks can be carried out by keepers and when they might have to call on the expertise of a conservator.

To clarify the above-mentioned terms it is helpful to look at the history of the safekeeping of our textile cultural heritage. Textiles have been kept for historic, artistic, economic, cultural, social, religious and emotional reasons. They are often passed on from one owner to another simply for economic or practical reasons. In the courts of Europe, series of tapestries were not only passed on through a family but could also change hands as valuable trophies of war. Some individual textiles have become world famous – the Bayeux tapestry and the Turin shroud for example; other textiles have been kept for emotional value such as a sampler made by a great-great-grandmother when she was a child. Ethnographic textiles were often acquired from the colonies of the time or from isolated communities within the home country as curious examples of different cultures.

Many textile objects have been treated with great care in order to preserve them for posterity. The meaning of the word 'care' has, however, changed over time. Historically, the treatment of damaged textiles was carried out with great skill, for example, the darning of holes and worn-out areas. Damaged areas were cut out and replaced. In general, the aim of the treatment was to repair the damage so that the object could be used again. Repair work was usually carried out at home, although professional craftsmen, such as tailors and tapestry weavers, were also involved in maintaining textile items. Fourteenth-century sources reveal that the maintenance work on tapestries was sometimes carried out by renowned tapestry ateliers. It is known from 15th-century records that the dukes of Burgundy brought their tapestries to the ateliers in Brussels for maintenance (Hefford 1971: 57). It can be deduced from the available sources that tapestries, which were in constant use, were cleaned and repaired every 20 to 30 years (Hutchison 1990: 10).

In the 19th century, this process changed, and maintenance work on textiles was increasingly carried out by antique dealers and amateurs. As a result of the Industrial Revolution, the services of professional craftsmen slowly disappeared and a new profession, that of the 'restorer', emerged. The restorer dealt mainly with the appearance of an object and aimed to return this to its original state. As a result, both traditional skill and craftsmanship were discarded. To restore tapestries, damaged areas were cut out and replaced with pieces of the same or a similar tapestry. When upholstered chairs were treated, the entire upholstery would often be replaced. Historic textiles were treated in such a way that they could be reused. Their shape and size could be adapted, especially if this meant a handsome profit for the art or antique trade. Considerable amounts of archaeological material excavated at the end of the 19th and the beginning of the 20th century was deliberately fragmented. For example, the decorative bands and emblems were cut from Coptic tunics as the remaining costume was not considered to be of any interest. Large Peruvian textiles were also cut into smaller pieces in order to sell them individually for greater financial gain.

During this period, scant attention was paid to the environmental conditions in which textiles were stored and displayed. There were no requirements for the durability of materials used in restoration. In the early part of the 20th century, restoration materials for textiles, such as yarn, were dyed with synthetic dyes, which at that time had very poor lightfastness. Restorations that were carried out with these materials faded and discoloured rapidly, and today this deterioration is clearly visible (Fig. 102).

The Second World War changed the attitude to preservation in Europe. In the Netherlands, many cultural treasures were removed from museums and stored in bunkers to protect them during the war. When they were retrieved during peacetime, many of them were in a deplorable state (not necessarily caused by the storage period), especially tapestries, flags and banners. Their condition was so poor that no available treatments were considered suitable and the search for more appropriate solutions was initiated. The post-war era also saw the emergence of a new ethic: the concept that any treatment should respect the historic and aesthetic integrity of an object. The term 'conservation' was coined in order to differentiate these new methods from the old idea of 'restoration'. It stated that treatment should be aimed at stabilising an object's condition and also included measures that could be taken to delay natural degradation. A conservation treatment was no longer aimed at just improving the appearance of an object – although the removal of harmful dirt, the rearrangement of loose or detached fragments, and the relaxation of unwanted creasing could make a textile more 'readable'. Any treatment carried out should be reversible.

In the 1950s and 1960s the Netherlands played an active role in the further development of textile conservation. This was stimulated by the generally poor condition of the country's textile cultural heritage. The following translated quote from 1955 clearly describes the difficult situation:

> Many museums [in the Netherlands], possess textile objects of historic and aesthetic value, which are severely damaged or weakened by all sorts of influences. These textiles are usually not displayed for fear of causing more damage. They are often placed in storage, where they are only accessible to those who study them. The

Figure 102 Detail of a 16th-century tapestry showing an old restoration carried out with synthetic dyes which have discoloured due to poor lightfastness (photo courtesy ICAT textielrestauratie b.v., collection Castle de Haar, Haarzuilens).

drawback is that only a few people can see them. Severely damaged pieces (where the mechanical strength of the fibres is diminished to such an extent that fragments are constantly being lost) suffer from even the most careful handling. In addition, many – especially small – museums do not have the space or funds available to create proper storage, as a result of which the preservation of the stored objects is even further endangered. (Sieders *et al.* 1955: 1)

In 1953, research into the development of new conservation methods for old, extremely fragile textiles, was initiated at the Laboratory for Textile Technique and Fibre Technology of the Technical University in Delft, the Netherlands. Initially, this project focused on the conservation of flags and banners, which were often made of silk and were usually in an extremely poor condition. The aim of this research was to develop modern conservation methods using synthetic polymers. This research project, in which the former Central Research Laboratory (now the Netherlands Institute for Cultural Heritage) was involved during the 1960s, led to the development of the use of synthetic adhesives in textile conservation (Boersma 1992).

In the 1980s, it proved necessary to further refine the term 'conservation' as there was an awareness that just 'conserving' an object was not sufficient. If a conserved object is placed in an unstable climate after treatment, all the conservation work may well be in vain. As a result, the terms 'active conservation' and 'passive conservation' were introduced. Active conservation indicates treatments that are carried out directly to the object, such as cleaning and supporting. Passive conservation is aimed not only at improving the environmental conditions for an object, i.e. stabilising RH and temperature, but also at the use of conservation-grade materials in storage and exhibition, etc.

10.2 Terminology

In the 1990s, international professional literature increasingly used the terms 'preservation' or 'preventive conservation' instead of 'passive conservation'. This shift in terminology coincided with a general tendency to spend more time and funds on the preservation conditions of entire collections and less on the conservation of individual objects. Diplomatically speaking, the term 'passive' was not well chosen as it seems to indicate negativity. This is not very helpful, especially when funds need to be raised! At the start of this new millennium it is time to define the terminology once more.

Restoration

This covers treatments, together with the preliminary research, which bring a damaged or partially lost object back to a predefined (original) condition. The aim of restoration is to return the object to such a state that its original function is reinstated, both aesthetically and structurally, for display or research purposes. Restoration can be at the expense of original material.

Conservation

This is the entire array of measures and treatments aimed at consolidating the object's condition as well as trying to avoid damage that may occur in the near future. The objective is to prevent unnecessary deterioration of an object so that it remains available for research or exhibition. Any treatment should respect the historic and artistic integrity of an object and should therefore be kept as minimal as possible. The appearance of an object might change after conservation for several reasons: the removal of harmful dirt and soiling, the rearrangement of loose or detached fragments or the relaxation of unwanted creasing. Damage can be masked using camouflaging techniques which do not directly intervene with the object. All treatments should be as reversible as possible. To differentiate conservation from preventive conservation, it is sometimes referred to as remedial conservation.

Preventive conservation

This includes those measures and treatments aimed at creating an optimum environment for storing and exhibiting objects, serving to avoid or delay the natural degradation of objects. These include climate control (temperature and relative humidity), light control, control of environmental pollution, pest management, prevention of fire and burglary and the use of appropriate materials in storage, transportation and display; as well as protection against vandalism, accidents, technical failures and disasters.

10.3 The textile conservator

A conservator is responsible for carrying out conservation treatments on objects and taking measures to preserve cultural heritage. In many countries, especially in northwest Europe, this person is still known as a restorer. In these countries, the word 'conservator' is used to describe the profession of a scientific researcher in a museum or the keeper of the collection – usually an (art) historian. In the UK the keeper or custodian is known as the curator. These different names for the same position can sometimes lead to confusion and misunderstanding.

10.3.1 Ethical code

A professional conservator should be aware of the ethical code of conservation. This internationally recognised code, established by professional organisations, the Institute of Conservation (ICON), formerly known as the United Kingdom Institute for Conservation (UKIC), the American Institute for Conservation (AIC) and De Vereniging Restauratoren Nederland, formerly known as VeRes in the Netherlands, provides the framework by which conservators can measure their methods and principles against generally accepted standards. Conservators are responsible for the objects they treat. This responsibility is expressed in respecting the integrity of the object. It is the responsibility of the conservator to try to preserve as much of the original material and information as possible. In the case of textile conservation, this means, for example, that original seams should not be undone unless this is absolutely necessary for the treatment – in which case, the original construction should be carefully documented. The ethical code requires that the conservator should keep up to date with the latest developments in conservation techniques.

In theory, any treatment should be carried out with due regard to the principle of reversibility. In practice this is not always achievable. For example, the wet cleaning of textiles is an irreversible process – fibres swell, dirt is removed and the textile is reshaped. The benefits of some treatments in the long-term preservation of an object might outweigh the argument for reversibility. Conservators should employ restraint in the extent of the treatments they carry out and should only carry out treatments that are necessary for the continued existence of an object. The person commissioning the work should not jeopardise necessary treatments by insisting on compromise.

10.3.2 Contracting out conservation work

In the Western world budget cuts are a way of life and many organisations have been forced to reduce the number of conservators in their employ. Collections are becoming more and more dependent upon self-employed conservators or conservation studios. Conservators often join together to form professional organisations with a code of practice, and some countries have a system of accreditation in place which aims to guarantee a certain level of professionalism.

Many conservators will charge a fee for making an estimate of the work to be carried out. In this event, the customer should receive a report that includes a description of the object and its condition, a well-founded proposal for conservation treatment and an estimate of the time and costs required to complete the work.

There may be difficulty of access in carrying out a condition inspection. The object may still be mounted (as is the case with wall-hangings), making it difficult to establish the exact condition of the textile. Part of the object may not be visible during inspection, e.g. objects with a lining. In other cases, tests will be necessary in order to choose the most suitable form of treatment. The conservator needs to make it clear in the conservation proposal that the treatment and/or the estimated hours of work may need to be adjusted to cover such eventualities.

If an estimate is not accepted within one year the conservator may suggest supplying a new estimate as it is quite possible that the condition of an unstable object may have deteriorated further during that time. The objectives for presentation after treatment are generally discussed in consultation with the client.

For large-scale projects, an estimate may be requested from more than one conservator or studio (a tender). This situation may result in the client accepting the lowest quote, regardless of whether the treatment is the most suitable for the object. It is therefore preferable to use a tendering system in which treatment proposals are submitted separately from their estimates and the selection based on the most suitable proposal. If the estimate for this proposal corresponds to the available budget, it should be accepted. If, however, this is not the case, then expert advice should be sought as to whether the estimate is realistic in relation to the proposal. If so, the available budget might have to be adjusted.

Before a conservator can begin an assignment, written acceptance of the treatment proposal and the estimate by the client is essential. The conservator will always start by photographing and documenting the object. The client can, of course, request copies of the photographs and documentation. During treatment, a conservator often takes further photographs, for example, when original constructions such as seams have to be undone in order to document a specific treatment. When the conservation work has been completed the conservator will submit a report that should include the following details:

- Registration number of the object
- Contact details of the client
- Contact details of the conservator
- Date of the treatment
- Description of the object
- Summary of previous checks and treatment reports (when applicable)
- The aim of the treatment
- Photographs of the object (when requested by the client)
- Any further documentation such as drawings and/or diagrams
- Treatment carried out (including the nature and extent of any alterations)
- Materials used and their composition
- Recommendations for handling the object and guidelines for preventive conservation
- Recommendations for periodic control (assessment appraisal)
- The number of hours worked and a specified costing.

10.4 Defining tasks

Various tasks may be carried out by the keeper of a textile collection, mainly preventive conservation work such as making boxes, covering coat hangers and preparing dustcovers. Other tasks which involve more handling of textiles, such as rolling (see section 6.3.1) and attaching registration numbers (see section 11.5.3) may also be carried out by the conservation assistant/collection management assistant but if there are any doubts, the advice of a textile conservator should be sought.

Conservation treatments – cleaning, supporting and camouflage of damage etc. – should be assigned to professional textile conservators. Some conservation treatments may also be carried out by trained conservation assistant/collection management assistants (under the supervision of a textile conservator), e.g. the removal of dust, attaching a hook and loop fastener to a flat textile or mounting a textile on a fabric-covered board. It should be noted that these conservation treatments may cause severe damage if not carried out correctly and, therefore, it is recommended that assistants should attend a course in the preservation of (historic) textiles in which these important points are discussed.

10.4.1 Mechanical cleaning of textiles

There are three methods for cleaning textiles: mechanical, chemical (using solvents) and wet cleaning (using water with or without detergent). The removal of dust is a mechanical treatment that may be carried out by the keepers of textile collections provided they have received proper training and are supervised by a textile conservator. Other cleaning treatments should always be left to the textile conservator. The reason for this is simple: serious damage can be caused to the objects if these treatments are not carried out correctly.

What is 'dust'? Dust can be described as unwanted matter that constantly precipitates from the air onto objects. It consists of sand particles, fibres, skin flakes, cobwebs, pollen, the remains of combustion (soot), etc. Being hygroscopic and often acidic, dust can damage textiles in many different ways. If moisture is absorbed from the air the harmful acids formed can cause chemical degradation. When dust particles are examined under a microscope, sharp edges can be observed. These small, sharp particles of dust cause mechanical damage to the textile as they move in between fibres and threads, a process which is accelerated when the textile is handled. Dusty textiles are more attractive to insects and provide sufficient nutrients for fungal growth (biological damage).

It is difficult to distinguish between dust and dirt. Dirt, even though it may be harmful to textiles, does not by definition have to be removed – in fact, it can be very important in the interpretation of an object. For example, a soldier's uniform worn during the First World War in the trenches tells a much more interesting story if it is still dirty. A camel bag from a nomadic tribe in the Middle East is more evocative when it still smells of greasy and unwashed wool. Therefore, an important question needs to be asked: if these types of objects are to be kept dust-free, does this risk removing some of the 'desirable' features?

The removal of dust and unwanted grime from textiles is not a simple task and the use of inappropriate techniques and tools can cause considerable and irreversible damage. A short description of different techniques used in mechanical cleaning is included in the appendix (see section 10.4.2).

In an ideal situation, dust should not be allowed to settle on objects but this, unfortunately, is not always possible, especially in historic interiors. There are various measures that can be employed to reduce the amount of dust reaching the objects. The use of airlocks and dust-trapping mats at the entrance of the building will reduce the amount of dirt from the streets brought in by visitors. Positioning the objects as far as possible from the public will also help to reduce dust levels (Lloyd 2002). Exhibition spaces must be easy to clean and this should be carried out regularly (the frequency depending upon the number of visitors).

The following textile objects should never be dusted by an unqualified person:

- Textiles that are tensioned on a frame: a mounted object may still look intact and stable, but the slightest touch may cause splits (see section 8.4.4).
- Painted and printed textiles whose paint layers or pigments have lost their bond with the textile: this includes textiles with gilding and the remains of wax (batik). Dusting this type of object may result in the removal of paint, pigment, gold or wax particles.
- Archaeological textiles: dusting archaeological textiles should not be necessary and can be avoided by keeping the textiles in a dust-free environment in storage and exhibition. Archaeological textiles should be handled as little as possible.
- Textiles in poor condition: these include embrittled textiles and those with a large number of holes.
- Textiles with a pile that is no longer securely fixed to the ground weave (the pile could easily be lost).
- Clothing and accessories made from plastic which has become sticky.
- Objects composed of different materials, e.g. fans should be cleaned by a conservator as each type of material requires a specialised treatment.

10.4.2 The removal of dust

There are several different methods of removing dust from textiles. The choice of treatment depends upon the vulnerability and the condition of the object to be cleaned. A mechanical cleaning treatment may be suitable, e.g. a vacuum cleaner with adjustable power – the lowest setting should create a suction that should just lift a piece of paper from the table. A number of small, easy-to-handle museum vacuum cleaners with low suction are commercially available. Useful nozzle attachments include a long and thin extension, a broad and flat extension and a soft bristle attachment. A set of different-sized brushes in a variety of stiffness and sizes is also useful. Brushes used for cosmetics and shaving are often suitable as they are voluminous and soft. To test the suitability of a brush, simply stroke it over the hand; if it feels soft and does not shed any hairs, then it can be used.

There are two basic principles of vacuum cleaning: the first with direct contact between the vacuum cleaner and textile; the second avoiding direct contact. Direct contact can only be used for cleaning sturdy textiles in good condition, e.g. carpets, upholstery and curtains. In order to avoid the textile being sucked into the vacuum cleaner, a semi-transparent barrier layer, of gauze or net fabric, should be placed over the textile. This layer will also reduce the friction between nozzle and textile. Plastic gauze, of the type used for making insect screens, is very useful. A nozzle with a broad and flat shape is preferred.

Pile carpets (in historic interiors) are best cleaned by rolling them with the upper side facing outwards during vacuum cleaning. In such a way, the pile is opened and the dirt can be removed more easily. Flat textiles (unpainted and without applications) may also be cleaned provided they are in good condition. These objects should be placed flat on a clean and smooth surface. A lower suction power, a finer mesh barrier layer and a smaller nozzle are preferred.

All three-dimensional textiles and objects should be surface-cleaned without any contact between the nozzle and the textile; the risk of the textile being damaged by the nozzle is too great. One of the most effective ways to remove dust is to stroke a suitable brush gently over the surface towards the nozzle of the vacuum cleaner held a few centimetres above the object. The suction power of the vacuum cleaner should be adjusted so that the textile is not lifted. A piece of gauze or net fabric in a neutral colour should be stretched across the nozzle. Dust and fibre material will accumulate on this piece of fabric enabling close attention to be paid to exactly what is being removed from the object. If too many fibres or other particles belonging to the object (such as paint particles) are being removed during treatment, it is wise to stop the cleaning. Using this method, dust and dirt collected on the barrier layer can also be collected for further examination or kept as proof of exactly what was removed.

11

Documentation

11.1 The documentary task: registration and documentation of a museum collection

Over a period of time every museum gathers information about a collection. Documenting the collection is an important part of the museum's role in order to make the collection, and the information connected with it, available to the museum staff and the public. Collection registration and documentation is the focal point at which different information comes together and is recorded, made accessible, adjusted and completed.

The method used for this task depends upon the requirements of a museum and the potential for making the collection accessible. All museums have one thing in common however: the need to record information according to well-defined rules. Collecting for a museum is part of a dynamic process. It is essential to define guidelines and set rules about collecting which establish when and how information about an object will be documented. The 'route of an object' in a collection should be defined. Information about an object is recorded at a number of stages early in the process. This chapter discusses what type of information should be recorded when an object:

- is acquisitioned;
- enters a collection as an incoming loan;
- leaves a collection as an outgoing loan;
- is numbered and documented;
- is checked for its condition;
- undergoes a conservation treatment;
- is moved.

It is important to make documentation one of the daily activities in a museum to ensure that an object can always be retrieved. This can be achieved by assigning the responsibility for the documentary task to a registrar or head of information management. Instructions and procedures relating to documentation should be put in writing and staff should be properly trained. Evaluation, adjustment and updating of the documentation system, and the staff responsible for it, are equally important.

11.2 Computerisation

Computers have become indispensable for museums wishing to improve access to information. To ensure effective and efficient computerisation, a museum must first set up an information plan to record why, where, what, when and by which means computerisation takes place. The computerisation of documentation in museums has increasingly tended towards the creation of entire collection information systems. Rapid technological developments and increasing standardisation have made it possible to integrate different types of documentation, such as those recorded in the 'route of an object', into one system. The great advantage of current software programs for museum documentation is that they are based on relational databases. 'A relational database is a database where all data available to the user is organised strictly as tables of data values, and where all database operations work on these tables' (Groff and Weinberg 1999: 54). In practice this means that data only has to be entered once, even though it may appear in different files. When specific data needs updating, this also only has to be done once as the entire database will automatically be updated, thus optimising data manipulation and retrieval. Current database programs can also contain text, image, and other (multi)media files. When choosing a collection registration system, check that it complies with the standardisation as set by SPECTRUM (Cowton 1997). If this is the case, the most appropriate program can be selected to provide information about the collection. It is a good idea to write a brief for the requirements of the institution and submit it to several suppliers.

If a straightforward catalogue is required to record which textile objects belong to the collection and who has the right of ownership, a simple software program listing the basic registration details may be sufficient. If this information is also to be used in the preparation of exhibitions, publications or educational activities, a more advanced software program should be sought, which may even include a link to information about maintenance facilities. With such an advanced program it is possible, for example, to plan the activities related to the organisation of exhibitions, to record loan administration and condition reports, and to export data to other programs such as a word processing program. Nowadays, it is even possible to provide public access to the information via the Internet; in this case, data output in HTML or XTML is required. If a library is available, it may be desirable to include its data in the system so that the relationship between the textile collection and the literature available is automatically created.

Computerised collection information systems can provide a wide range of possibilities. Their feasibility depends upon the implementation of the system and adherence to the rules governing the task of documentation within the organisation.

11.3 Objects entering the collection

The inclusion of a new object in a collection should be controlled by a procedure that aims to ensure that all information related to that object is recorded. At this point it is irrelevant whether the object is a potential purchase, a donation, a loan from outside, an object that needs to be identified or is required for a research project. Objects may enter an organisation in different ways: from a spontaneous gift left at the service counter in the museum to an object deliberately purchased at an auction by the curator. It has to be clear who is responsible for receiving and registering objects within the organisation. This may be the curator, but could equally well be someone from the collection department. Another member of staff must be authorised to act on his behalf when the appointed person is not available.

The incoming object has to be carefully unpacked in a separate area, ideally in the quarantine area. All packaging materials should be kept in case the object has to be returned. Next, the condition of the object must be checked, preferably in the presence of the provider. A check for the presence of fungi and harmful insects, such as moths and carpet beetles, is essential to avoid infesting the existing collection (see Ch. 5). After the condition check has been completed, the object will receive a unique reference number (not necessarily the registration or accession number which will be assigned later) attached to it on a loose label or pencilled on the outside of the temporary packaging material. Loose or detached parts should also be numbered and kept near the object to which they belong. In principle, all objects should be dealt with individually unless this is impossible due to the number of objects being offered at one time. For example, it is sufficient to give a box of fabric samples one reference number and make a note of the number of samples it contains.

11.3.1 Registration of objects entering a collection

Two types of forms can be used for registering objects entering the collection: a pre-numbered form of entry with a carbon copy (see section 11.6) or a register of incoming and outgoing objects with a 'delivery receipt' (in duplicate) (Berg 1998). In both cases, the transfer of the object is formalised when both parties sign the paperwork (i.e. before the provider leaves the building). The following data should be recorded:

- the reference number;
- the date of entry;
- the name and address of the owner (or the person acting on the owner's behalf);
- the reason for the transfer;
- if the object is to be returned in case of rejection;

- the date by which the object has to be returned (in the case of research, a loan or a donation that has not officially been accepted);
- the condition of the object;
- a short description of the object;
- as much contextual information as possible;
- the temporary location;
- the registration number (in the case of an acquisition or a loan from outside);
- the name of the receiver.

11.4 The sending out of objects

A museum is accountable for all objects that leave its premises. Objects may be sent out from the textile collection for a number of reasons such as: if a donation has not been accepted and is consequently returned to the owner, when an object is on loan or sent for conservation to an outside conservation studio. Official documentation should accompany any object or group of objects that leaves the premises, e.g. a copy of the loan agreement, the form of entry or the register of incoming and outgoing objects. In all cases, the receiver – who may be the owner – will have to sign the documentation upon delivery conforming to the agreements.

The transportation and insurance of the object(s) will have to be arranged according to predefined rules. When an object is to be transported to a foreign country, the necessary export licences and customs documentation will have to be arranged.

11.5 The acquisition of objects

Whether or not an object is added to a collection depends on the collection policy (see section 12.1) which expresses the objectives of the organisation. Most organisations try to strengthen their subcollections by acquiring new objects. For example, traditional costumes are an important subcollection for a regional museum that collects objects relating to local history. If the museum is offered items of clothing that already form part of the collection or which do not fall into this particular category of dress, these may well be rejected. An exception may be considered, however, if the object offered is comparable to that already in the collection but in much better condition. Alternatively an object may be accepted for educational purposes but not actually added to the collection – such an object should not be documented in the collection registration system.

The necessary steps that have to be taken in order to officially formalise the transfer of the object(s) in a legal document (once it has been decided that the object(s) complies with the collection policy) depends upon the method of acquisition:

- When an object is *purchased* it is important to keep the original receipts as well as all information related to any application for subsidies and grants.
- When an object is *donated* (i.e. during the owner's lifetime), the transfer documents have to be signed in order to make the agreement official. A special donation form can be used in which any possible conditions related to the definite transfer of ownership and the condition of the object are recorded. This is standard practice when a register of incoming and outgoing objects is used. A signed copy of the pre-numbered form of entry, on which the object is marked as a donation, can also be used for the official donation agreement.
- In the case of a *legacy* (i.e. something gifted in a will) it is important that it is accompanied by a legal document in which the wishes of the deceased are stated. It is therefore advisable to obtain a copy of the will and keep it safe for future reference.
- When an object is *exchanged*, it is important to keep the correspondence in which the non-financial transfer is arranged. The transfer has to be signed by both parties.

The above-mentioned official documents have to be carefully filed in such a way that they are linked to the object's documentation. Every acquisition will receive a unique registration/accession number that, in future, will relate the object to the information that has already been documented. It is therefore important that this registration number is physically applied to the object by means of a reversible method (see below).

The next step in the acquisition procedure is to add the object to a page-numbered registration book in one of two ways. The first method registers the object in a pre-bound book which documents its registration number. A brief description is given of the transfer details (method, date and name) and the reference number on the form of entry or the donation form. The second, more modern method uses computer printouts (on quality paper: NEN 2728 or DIN 6738 (Lebensdauer-Klasse 24-85), ISO 9706 or ICN quality requirements no.1) of the newly registered objects. These printouts should be carefully filed, the pages numbered and preferably bound annually.

When the object is physically added to the collection, the following steps should be taken:

- *Describe* the object using structured description guidelines;
- Assign a definite *location* to the object;
- *Number* the object;
- Make a *condition report*;
- Take a (digital) *photograph* of the object.

11.5.1 Describing the object

The purpose of describing an object is to gather information about it and other related matters onto a description form, which should be kept up to date. In this way information about the collection – as well as the documentation about acquisition, loan, conservation treatments, condition and exhibition – is always available. An accurate data file about the collection is not only important for the efficient internal functioning of an organisation, but is also a prerequisite for an effective exchange of information between collectors. Each museum will have to set its own policy for recording information about an object but it should be made clear which members of staff are responsible for processing this information. In general, all information about an object – relating to the identification, description, history of an object, or any contextual data – should be collected and recorded on a description form. It is important to agree on data formulation, i.e. the terminology used. Internal guidelines should be set that state the aim and the application of the terminology to be used.

Description form
Information about every object is recorded in the description form (Fig. 103). The description should include the basic registration details, recorded in predefined fields and following well-defined rules. This basic information can be refined and augmented with, for example, physical properties (i.e. colours, styles and shapes). Any trademarks should be recorded together with their position and the method of application. Associated information, for example, about the original use of an object, may be connected to people, places, events and dates. Specific information about the manufacture can be augmented with information about the role of the manufacturer and the place of manufacture. References to literature (i.e. title, author, location and classification code) may be added when information about a specific object is available in books, magazines or reports.

Note that it is not necessary for all information to be registered on the registration card – loan or donation agreements, requirements, condition and treatment reports, insurance data or reproductions can all be cross-referenced (this data can easily be linked in a computerised relational database system).

Terminology
When an object is registered, several different keywords should be used to document this information, for example to indicate the name of the object, the representation, the material, the manufacturing technique, the method of acquisition etc. The reference to proper names, such as the manufacturer or artist, the author of a publication, the name of the donor or lender is equally important. If the information in fields is made accessible using a list of keywords (index), a word check is essential. Computers are a powerful tool in making data accessible but it is a fallacy to think that the search for data in a computerised system is no longer problematic – automatic indexing of all words results in the generation of irrelevant information and slows down data retrieval. This may be caused not only by the use of synonyms and homonyms but also by

Identification	*Description*	*Manufacturing*	*Location*
Name of institution	Representation keyword	Manufacturer	Location
Institution's number	Title	Manufacturing data	
Registration number	Description		
Object keyword	Measurements		
	Material		
	Condition		
Acquisition	*Comments*	*Image*	
Acquisition	Two free fields	Image of the object	
Date of acquisition	Comments		
Acquired from			

Figure 103 Description form

the use of abbreviations and variations in spelling. Word control, for example, by means of a thesaurus, is therefore recommended. The benefit of using a thesaurus is that specific data, rather than irrelevant information, can be retrieved quickly.

Three types of relationship can be defined in a thesaurus: the hierarchical, the synonymous and the associative relationship. For each term, these relationships are recorded. For example, the 'preferred term' *dress* has the following relationships:

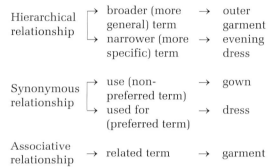

A thesaurus also uses 'guide terms'. These terms should not be used, but instead should help to make long enumerations clearer by grouping them according to certain aspects, for example:

<dresses according to shape>

All 'preferred terms' are provided with a 'scope note', a brief description of its meaning. An example is given below:

Outer clothing:
Clothing worn on top of other clothing as the outermost layer, especially clothing worn to provide insulation or protection against the weather. Use the terminology mentioned under <protective clothing> for those types of clothing that are specifically worn for protection against dirt or danger.

Every term listed in a thesaurus has to be unique. In order to separate homonyms, the so-called 'qualifier' is placed between brackets after the term. For example: *Cocked hat (headgear)*.

Art and Architecture Thesaurus (AAT)

Most museums with a textile collection have neither the desire nor the resources to build a complete thesaurus. A more practical solution would be to join a system which already exists. One of these is the Art and Architecture Thesaurus (AAT). This thesaurus is suitable for describing and accessing cultural historical and art historical collections. The AAT offers museums not only the possibility of using standardised terminology lists, but also the opportunity for international exchange (the US equivalent of every term is available). It not only includes terms to describe objects, such as clothing, but also terminology to describe materials, style and historical period, manufacturing procedures and techniques.

A search for the term 'raincoat' could begin under the category 'Clothing'. In the structure of the thesaurus, the more dots present, the more specific a term is:

Clothing	<clothing by function>	..outer garments
		... overcoats
		....raincoats

The period indication 'late Victorian dress' can be found under Style and Period:

| Style and Period | <modern British styles according to government> | .Victorian |
| | | ..late Victorian |

The weaving technique 'damask' can be retrieved under Materials and Techniques:

| Materials and Techniques | <textile materials according to weaving technique> | .damask |
| | | ..block damask |

Other terminology systems exist such as classification or controlled entry lists. Each individual institution needs to decide which system it will use and adhere to it rigorously.

Vocabulary of basic terms for cataloguing costume

A classification is a division of terminology into groups and subgroups according to specified characteristics. The ICOM International Committee for Museums and Collections of Costume set up a classification of terms used to describe costumes: the *Vocabulary of Basic Terms for Cataloguing Costume* (Buck et al. 1989). This list is available in English, French and German, and is currently being translated into Dutch. In naming costume items and accessories, the terminology is based on the objects themselves and their relationship to the bodies of women, men and children. Every item of costume, or accessory, has a basic sort name, which is also the first catalogue name. This is then followed by a second term that defines the type of object more clearly within its basic form. A third term may be used to define a variant on the second term. Other names, for example, regional names, may be added

Women's Garments

Main Garments

1.1	*Covering body above and below the waist* **Dress** (Types 1–6)	
1.11	**Dress (1)** one piece	
1.12	**Dress (2)** two pieces	
1.13	**Dress (3)** three or more pieces	
1.14	**Dress (4)** as 1 to 3 with additional, optional piece, but complete without it (including dresses with alternative day/evening bodices)	
1.15	**Dress (5)** one piece needing additional garment for completion	
1.16	**Dress (6)** two pieces needing additional garment for completion	

Note: The pieces referred to in this classification are the main parts of the whole, e.g. **Bodice** and **Skirt** in **Dress (2)**; **Gown**, **Petticoat**, **Stomacher** (18th century) (3). A trouser suit will be **Dress (2)** if made up of **Bodice**, **Pullover** and **Trousers**; **Dress (6)** if made up of **Bodice**, **Waistcoat** and **Trousers**. Such accessories as belt and collar are not taken into account; a separate catalogue entry gives this information.

Figure 104 An example of the vocabulary of basic terms for cataloguing costume which includes a drawing of the clothing and accessories of each classification number as it is worn on the body (source: http://www.mda.org.uk/costume/vbt01e.htm).

as second, third or fourth terms if necessary (placed in parentheses). Defining the terms of an object is based on the context of the basic information, i.e. the basic term for a swimsuit or a wedding gown is the same: 'dress'. The terms are applicable to both fashionable and unfashionable clothing within the sphere of European fashion.

The use of the main term for an object (i.e. the most general, comprehensive term) has a number of advantages such as: a non-specialised registrar is able to identify the correct category of an object; a specialist is forced to simplify matters and therefore does not cause confusion by their depth of knowledge. The *Vocabulary of Basic Terms for Cataloguing Costume* includes a drawing of the clothing and accessories of each classification number as it is worn on the body (Fig. 104).

Index of entries
Word control may also be achieved by using an index of entries. This is an alphabetical list of those entries and/or proper names that are frequently used in certain fields on the description form, sometimes referred to as the reference list. An example is the list with terminology which relates to the method of acquisitioning.

Loans: incoming and outgoing
Incoming loans are objects that do not belong to a museum's own collection but may be included for a period of time, such as for the duration of a temporary exhibition. Sometimes they become part of the collection for an indefinite period of time, for example, if an object is required to complete the collection. Most museums will deal with incoming as well as outgoing loans; the latter usually form part of their own collection. These two types of loans require different procedures and it is therefore necessary to archive documentation relating to them separately.

Usually, the museum requesting a loan writes to the lender giving the following details:

- the period of the loan;
- the reason;
- the location;
- the name of the institution and contact person;
- a brief description of the object(s) required;
- a statement that the borrower will arrange the insurance and compensation.

When the lender consents in principle to the loan, further agreements will have to be made dealing with:

- the ownership;
- the dimensions;
- the condition;
- the value of the objects(s).

In addition, requirements regarding the exhibition conditions (light, climatic conditions, showcases, etc.) should be determined. It should also be made clear who is allowed to handle the object(s) and how. It may be useful to add photographs and contextual information about the object(s).

When both parties have agreed upon the loan, the final loan agreement is drawn up in duplicate. Usually, the lender takes the initiative unless, of course, the lender does not have the required documents, for example, in the case of a loan by a private individual to a museum, in which case the museum can then draw up the two copies of the loan agreement (one for the lender and one for the borrower).

Basic information on a loan form
This should include:

- The names of the lender, the borrower and the members of staff dealing on behalf of these organisations;
- A brief description of the object;
- The registration number;
- The insurance value;
- The period of the loan;
- The method of termination of the loan;
- A statement from a professional, preferably a textile conservator, of the condition of the object both upon leaving the borrower's premises and its arrival back at its original location.

In the loan agreement, conditions are incorporated relating to the care of the object(s) during the period of loan. These include not only stipulations for handling, security and positioning of the object(s), but also environmental requirements. It is often the case that the lender arranges the execution, guidance and supervision of the loan, while the borrower is responsible for financing the insurance, packaging materials and transport. The loan agreements may also contain provisions for conservation or restoration. For example, the lender should always be contacted first if the condition of an object changes drastically and treatment by a (textile) conservator is required. If necessary, the loan agreement may include clauses which address if (and how) the owner should be credited when the object is on display; photography of the object;

and the use of images of the object. Long-term, unnumbered loans will receive a loan number that may become the registration number of the object in consultation with the owner. In this respect the loan objects are treated in a similar way to new acquisitions. Be aware that the owner may request the return of a loan without due observance of the period of notice.

11.5.2 Location control and the moving of objects

All objects should be given a specific location which can be retrieved from the collection database by means of the object's registration number. Nonetheless, objects may be removed from their set location (internal or external to the museum) and placed elsewhere either temporarily or permanently. It is therefore important to record all moves so that the whereabouts of an object is known at all times. These changes will have to be recorded in the collection database or on the description form of the object. If the move is temporary, its location should be documented with a beginning and end date. The location registration should always be kept up to date and checked regularly by means of a spot check.

An object's move is often first recorded manually on a form after which it is entered into the system's database. The following data should be gathered:

- the registration number;
- the name of the object;
- the reason for the move;
- the date of the move;
- the return date;
- moved by.

Unfortunately, the procedure described above often leads to mistakes, which is one of the reasons why barcodes, and more recently radio frequency identification (RFID) have found their way into collection registration (see below).

11.5.3 Numbering of textile objects

Every object in the collection should have a registration number linking the object to its associated information. When numbering objects, attention should be paid to the appearance and uniqueness of the number, its position on the objects and the materials used.

Uniqueness
The appearance of the registration number should be made as simple as possible. The underlying principle is that all information relating to an object can be retrieved from the collection database. A system using successive numbers is the most effective: each object, or group of strongly related objects, receives a unique number upon acquisition. When deciding whether a group of objects is strongly related, the uniqueness, the history of origin and the acquisition information should be considered. The objects within a group may receive the same unique registration number with the addition of an extension. For example, when numbering a pair of shoes, one shoe may be given the registration number 347.a and the other shoe 347.b. The composite parts of an original costume (trousers, jacket, waistcoat, shirt and tie) may be allocated the registration numbers 348.a, 348.b, 348.c, 348.d and 348.e. Detached parts, such as a loose button or a piece of a broken fan, should be separately numbered with the same unique registration number of the object to which they belong. This will ensure that they can always be linked back to the object.

Position and appearance
The registration number should be attached to the object and be easily retrievable to ensure handling of the object is minimised. The position of the number should be inconspicuous but not impossible to find. It is useful to agree upon a certain position for similar types of objects, for example: in the collar of coats; at the reverse bottom right-hand corner of curtains; at the reverse two corners on opposite sides of a carpet etc. The numbers should be clear, but be aware that some numbers can be read upside-down (606 and 909 or 801 and 108). Confusion can be avoided by placing a dot at the end of the number. The size of the label bearing the number depends upon the object – in most cases a small label of a few square millimetres is all that is needed but for large objects (such as tapestries and carpets), a label of several square centimetres would be more suitable.

Apart from numbering the object itself, the registration number should also be recorded on the outside of any packaging material (e.g. when objects are packed away for storage). To help with the identification of objects in storage it is recommended that a small photograph of the object be placed on the outside of packaging. Modern RFID technology simplifies the identification of objects inside packaging (see below).

Material
The number can be written or typed onto a suitable carrier such as pieces of cotton tape, Japanese paper and certain types of polyester, polyethylene or polypropylene non-woven fabrics (see section 9.2.7) using waterproof ink to create a label. The carrier should be thin and flexible, but firm. To check the ink for fastness to water, wet a sample and leave it to dry on top of a layer of absorbent paper; the ink should not bleed into or stain the paper. After the label has been prepared it can be attached to the textile object by stitching. An extremely fine needle (such as a surgical needle) and fine thread should be used. Silk filament is suitable as it is very thin but strong. Another option is a thin polyester-cotton thread pulled out of a yarn. In principle, the tensile strength of the thread should not be greater than that of the textile object, i.e. if a sudden force is applied to the label, the thread used to stitch it in place should break without damaging the object.

In order to minimise the number of stitches in the object, it is best to fasten and finish the thread in the label. Finally, stitch one of the shorter ends of the label with a few loose stitches into the object – do not pull the thread too tightly or it will cut into the textile. It should be noted that some textile objects are so weak that any stitching could cause irreversible damage (e.g. archaeological textiles) in which case the label will have to remain detached from the object and attached either to the support or the packaging.

Those objects that belong to a textile collection, but are not made of a textile material – shoes, fans, dolls – are usually numbered using a varnish-ink-varnish system (always use materials that have been tested). In some cases it may be better to use a loose label, for example, when the object is too small to be numbered or when the number may be too conspicuous. The label can be made from durable paper (as mentioned above for computer printouts) or inert plastic (soft and flexible) onto which the number is written with a tested pen.

Computerised (location) registration
In addition to the numbering of objects, other computerised systems are used to identify objects and their location such as the barcode system. Data are stored by means of a sequence of broad and narrow black and white stripes. This information can be read by a special portable scanner using infrared radiation. The scanner can be attached to the main computer system to exchange information with the database. The information stored in the barcode cannot be changed so in order to document the location of an object, which might change, it is best to label cupboards, shelves and boxes with their own barcode. The barcode system is an administrative aid to identifying objects quickly and efficiently. The barcode label is usually placed next to the object or is attached to its packaging – the label is fairly large and it is not possible to apply the label directly to the object safely and reversibly. Another disadvantage is that barcode labels have to remain visible in order to scan them. This may result in unnecessary handling of the object thereby increasing the risk of damage.

Radio frequency identification (RFID)
Objects have to be lifted, taken out of their packaging, turned, twisted, etc. in order to retrieve the registration/accession number, which can result in damage. Modern RFID technology, adapted for use in a museum environment (Stuart 2002), makes use of harmless high frequency radio waves that are capable of travelling through almost all materials. A chip or tag – in which digital information including both permanent and temporary data can be stored, managed and retrieved – is attached to or placed near the object. A selection of applicable data generated by an existing database is then transferred to and from the tag by means of radio signals emitted by an antenna. Because radio waves can travel through a material, the tag does not have to be visible and can be accessed without touching the object.

The clear advantage of this technology is that the risk of damage caused by the handling of objects is minimised – objects can be identified without having to physically touch them even when they are concealed inside packaging. Thus, the transportation of single objects and entire collections can be registered automatically, avoiding human error. Apart from the minimisation of risk situations, there are other advantages. Unlike barcodes or other labels, it is possible to store information inside the tag, for example, specific condition requirements for the preservation of an object. This information is always available without the need to consult the database. The system can also be used to simplify inspections or to establish integration in disaster planning, it allows integration with audio-visual information systems and reduces the time it takes to identify objects.

11.5.4 Condition reports

The inspection of a collection not only aims to determine the general condition of the objects, but it also investigates the shortcomings in the preservation conditions and, in turn, suggests improvements. There are many arguments in favour of regular inspections of textile collections. First, the ever-present risk of an infestation of fungi, or insects, e.g. moths, carpet beetles and silverfish. Secondly, the degradation of objects can be monitored by inspections. It should be clear who is responsible for the inspections within an institution, to what extent the objects are inspected and how often an inspection should take place. There are several different ways to inspect the condition of an object:

- *Condition check*: controls the condition of an object by means of observation; as a result recommendations are made for use, handling, treatment and environmental factors.
- *Condition survey*: a succession of inspections that determine whether the condition of an object is stable or if it is deteriorating. In general, it can be stated that each object should be checked at least every five years, at which point its present condition should be compared to the findings of the previous inspection.
- *Condition audit*: an assessment of the condition of many objects together by means of random checks. It is necessary to set up a systematic two-yearly random sample inspection of the collection so that the potential damage from a calamity can be minimised. It should be carefully recorded which objects were inspected, when and by whom (Keene 1996).
- *Technical assessment*: a thorough scientific study of the condition of an object that results in a detailed report with recommendations for use, handling, treatment and environmental factors.

The subject of condition reports is further discussed in section 12.2.1.

11.5.5 Photography

It is important to document objects with photographs as these can be used for a catalogue or research. If proper photo-documentation of an object exists, it is not always necessary to take an object from storage. As stated above, a photograph of the object on the outside of its packaging will help to identify packed objects. If an object is partly damaged or perhaps even completely destroyed in an accident, the photograph may be all that remains. A photograph taken of an object prior to any damage is of great value to a conservator.

It is recommended that photographic material of the collection be renewed at least every 25 years, as not only does the photographic material itself degrade, but the objects also are subject to degradation. Old photographs should never be discarded, as they are incredibly important records of the degradation processes of objects. Photographic documentation is only useful when it is of good quality. Out-of-focus or badly exposed photographs are of no use. Therefore the member of staff responsible for the photography should be aware of the technical aspects involved. Some institutions use in-house professional photographers, in which case the photographer should be instructed in the handling of textiles. It is advisable for a textile conservator or knowledgeable collection keeper to assist the photographer – most textile objects cannot be safely handled unassisted. If possible, dedicate a specific space for photography so that a studio setting of photographic equipment is always available.

The camera
Ideally use a camera on which the lens opening (aperture), the shutter speed, and the focus can be controlled either manually, semi-automatically (either shutter speed or aperture priority) or can be set on fully automatic. The most suitable camera for this type of work is the single-lens reflex (SLR) – 35mm and medium format. Its unique feature is that it permits viewing and focusing of the image directly through the lens. These types of cameras have the option of overriding automatic settings, so that the photographer can select shutter speed and aperture. In this way, he can take control of the end result, influencing, for example, the depth of field of the image.

The lens
On SLR cameras, the lens can be replaced with other lenses. Called interchangeable lenses, these allow for the selection of precisely the right lens for each shot and are therefore highly recommended for conservation photography. For example, for the photographing of large items such as tapestries, a wide-angle lens (focal length of 20 to 35 mm) is useful, whereas for general photography work (samplers, fans, etc.) a normal lens (50 mm) will suffice; a macro lens is important for photographing small objects or details. Zoom lenses allow the focal length to be changed without the need to change lenses. For example, a 28–70 mm zoom lens can be adjusted – usually by turning the barrel – to shoot at any focal length from 28 mm to

70 mm. Because of the complex optics required to create this versatility, however, zoom lenses suffer from two basic disadvantages: they are bulky and heavy and they are generally not as sharp at any given focal length as the best conventional lenses of that specific focal length.

Film

There are many different types of film, for example, ISO 100, 200, 400 etc. This number represents the sensitivity or 'speed' of the film. The higher the rating, the faster the film, i.e., the more sensitive it is to light. A film rated at ISO 100 is twice as fast as a film rated at ISO 50, i.e. twice as sensitive to light. This is a vital point. It means that if a scene is shot using an ISO 200 film and an exposure of 1/250 second at f8, then the same scene shot with ISO 100 film will require twice the exposure. The light meter should be set to the ISO rating of the film otherwise an incorrect reading for exposure is obtained.

Some films display more graininess than others – as a general rule, the faster the film, the grainier the image. The more the graininess of the image, the rougher, less sharp and less detailed the image. For all-round balance between speed and grain, films in the ISO 200 to 400 ranges are recommended.

Traditionally, photography has been in an analogue format, i.e. on film. Today, digital imaging has become popular. There are many advantages in taking digital images of a textile collection: they can be incorporated into the computerised database and made accessible to the public via the Internet. Digital images can be obtained either by using a digital camera or by digitising analogue images by means of scanning. Scanners are available that can scan negatives, slides and prints to high resolutions. Digital images can also be printed. Professional photographic laboratories use colour laser printers that give a good quality picture.

Digital photography

Unlike traditional cameras that use film to capture and store an image, digital cameras use a solid-state device called an image sensor. These fingernail-sized silicon chips contain millions of photosensitive diodes called photosites. Just as in a traditional camera, light enters a digital camera through a lens controlled by the shutter. Each photosite records the intensity or brightness of the light that falls on it. The data are stored as a set of numbers that can be used to set the colour and brightness of dots on the screen or ink on the printed page to reconstruct the image.

Camera resolutions

Image sensors contain a grid of photosites – each representing one pixel in the final image. The sensor's resolution is determined by how many photosites there are on its surface. For example, a camera may specify its resolution as 1800 × 1600 pixels. This means that the image has 1800 pixels horizontally and 1600 pixels vertically, 2.8 million pixels in total. Low-end cameras have resolutions around 1 million pixels, although this number is constantly improving. Better cameras, those with 6 million or more pixels, are called mega-pixel cameras.

The larger the image size in pixels, the larger the image file size needed to store it. For example, a photo that is taken on a 6 million pixel camera at its highest setting creates a file size of approximately 35 Mb.

Images can be captured and saved in different ways. Most cameras have two options to take and store images: the camera's own format and JPEG format. When the images are uploaded onto the computer, they can be manipulated using photographic software. Files can get very large very quickly but the file sizes of the stored images can be reduced in several ways:

- by reducing the resolution (not appropriate if the image is to be printed);
- by reducing the number of colours in the image pallet;
- by using a format that compresses the file, e.g. JPEG.

Artificial lighting

Artificial lighting plays a key role in indoor photography. There are two basic artificial light sources: flood or flash. The term 'flood' refers to continuous incandescent lighting that divides into two categories: floodlights and spotlights. 'Flash' refers to instantaneous lighting that divides into two categories: flash bulbs and electronic flash. The use of flash is recommended for conservation photography. It should be noted that this type of lighting generates heat and should therefore be aimed at the objects for as short a period of time as possible.

Measuring light

It is recommended that an incident-light meter is used for balanced studio lighting. This is aimed from the subject towards the camera and measures the light that falls on the subject. The meter is designed to indicate the correct exposure for that amount of light assuming the subject includes an average range of tones from light to dark. This setting is then used on the camera.

Tripods
Whenever possible, use a tripod – the greatest single failing of all shots is camera shake. As a general rule of thumb, if a shot is to be taken below a shutter speed of 1/60, a tripod should be used to avoid camera shake. The ideal tripod should be light enough to carry easily from place to place, yet not so light that it provides insufficient support for the camera.

Aids/tools in the photographing of textiles
These can include:

- A rigid board (see sections 8.5 and 9.2.1) on which small, two-dimensional textiles can be displayed. The board should be covered with a soft material such as brushed cotton; this creates a certain amount of friction and keeps the objects in place. It should be washable for practical purposes. Small, two-dimensional textiles, such as samplers, are best photographed by placing them on the board at a slight angle of 45 degrees or less. The camera should be held at the same angle in order to prevent a trapezium-shaped deformation of the image. In cases where it is necessary to hold the object in place, use thin entomological pins (nos. 00, 0 or 1).
- A beam on a pulley system covered with the hard, hooked side of hook and loop fastener. The corresponding soft, loop side of the fastener should be machine stitched onto cotton twill tape. This can then be pinned to the reverse top edge of large two-dimensional textiles in good condition, such as tapestries and carpets, which can then be fixed to the beam. Flags and banners that still have their original pole may be hung underneath this beam by means of tapes.
- Backgrounds: several colours of background paper or fabric should be available but in general, a neutral grey background colour is the most useful.
- Numbers: it is sometimes necessary to document the object's registration number in the photograph. Use a standard type numbering so that the same number type is used throughout. There are different types of numbering systems in use, one of which makes use of magnetic numbers that can be arranged on a metal strip in any order. If the photographs are to be used for publication, the registration number might not be required. Place the number some distance away from the object so that it can be cut out of the image if necessary.
- Scales: it is advisable to photograph a colour or grey scale together with the object. Such a scale can be used to give an indication of the size of the object and is useful in establishing whether or not the photograph represents the correct colour of the object. If photographs are to be used for publication, the scale might not be required. Place the scale some distance away from the object so that it can be cut out of the image if necessary.
- Stuffings and fillings: if the condition of three-dimensional objects is sufficiently sound, they should be filled in order to give the correct impression of their shape. Soft, springy material should be used to stuff and fill objects (see section 9.2.7).

Practical tips
When using analogue cameras it is useful to have two cameras available, each one loaded with a different film type, usually one black and white and the other transparency. Black and white has the best archival quality and suffices for basic registration but an image in colour is often required. Transparency films are preferred to colour negative films as they give a higher quality image and can be used in different ways such as mounted into slides for presentations. Transparency films require precise exposure – these films can handle a range of about 1½ stops of underexposure and one stop of overexposure – making it much more difficult to obtain the correct exposure. Therefore, if in doubt, bracket the shots, i.e. take three shots instead of one. In addition to the basic exposure, shoot one stop over and one stop under. For example, when the light meter indicates f8 (aperture 8), take one photograph at f8 (the basic exposure); one at f11 and one at f5.6. Of course, the shutter speed should remain the same for all three shots. The cost of a few 'wasted' frames of film is a lot less than the cost of setting up the shot again.

Photographic documentation should be maintained: a record should be kept of who took the photographs and when, which negative frame shows which object and what shutter speed, aperture and lighting were used.

11.6 Appendix

11.6.1 Form of entry

Institution _____	Sequence number 2006/ _____

Received from/Purchased from: _____	Owner (when different):
Address _____	Address _____
_____	_____
Postal code _____	Postal code _____
City _____	City _____
Telephone _____	Telephone _____

Description of object	Condition	Collection
		Yes/no (pto)
		Yes/no (pto)
		Yes/no (pto)

Reason for delivery to institution

☐ Donation   (I hereby donate the above-mentioned object(s))

☐ Sale   (I hereby offer for sale the above-mentioned object(s))

☐ Loan   (I hereby offer the above-mentioned object(s) on loan (refer to loan agreement L 2006/ _____))

☐ Identification (I hereby leave the above-mentioned object(s) until date: _____)

I confirm that the information on this form is correct.

Signature owner/delegate: _____   Date: _____

Additional agreement (FOR DONATIONS / SALES)

☐ I, the owner, hereby declare that I have exclusive rights to the above-mentioned object(s); and that I agree to part with these on behalf of the Institution _____

OR

☐ I, the owner's delegate, hereby declare that the owner has exclusive rights to the above-mentioned object(s); and that the owner parts with these on behalf of the Institution_____

_____

and that I have been authorised by the owner to act on his/her behalf.

The right of ownership of the above-mentioned object(s) has been transferred under agreed terms
to the Institution _____

- The agreement is independent of any financial transaction.
- Described object(s) are transferred to the Institution _____
  in its/their present condition, recorded at (date)_ _____
- The donor declares that he/she distances him/herself completely from the above-mentioned object(s).
- The Institution _____
  is empowered to decide freely the future of the above-mentioned object(s).

Signature owner/delegate: _____ Date: _____

Signature Institution's delegate _____ Date: _____

Document as much information as possible for each object: *(object name, maker, when it was made, provenance, user/consumer, when, where and how it was used, completeness, originality, any documentation material available, i.e. photograph, receipt, etc.*

11.6.2 Form of return

RETURN TO OWNER/DELEGATE

I, the owner/delegate, hereby declare that I have received the object(s) described in this form in good condition.

Signature owner/delegate: _____   Date: _____

The Institution _____

has **DONATED/LOANED/SOLD** the object(s) described in this form to:

Name: _____

Address: _____

_____

Postal code: _____

City: _____

Telephone: _____

Signature receiver: _____   Date: _____

Signature Institution's delegate _____   Date: _____

Please note: it is advisable to seek legal advice in the country concerned for the correct terminology to be used in this form.

12
Collection management

'Collection management' is the collective term used to describe the implementation of a collection plan, a maintenance plan and a disaster plan. It is an essential part of a policy plan for a museum or any other institution involved in preserving cultural heritage. The policy plan of an institution outlines its policy over the forthcoming period, which is usually a period of four to five years. It is in a museum's own interest to have a policy plan; governments and funding bodies may well ask for this plan when considering subsidies for the institution. It is not appropriate within the scope of this book to discuss the policy plan fully but some of its composite parts are described.

12.1 Collection plan

A collection plan is indispensable when preserving a collection. It provides the means to gain an insight into the composition and importance of a collection (Luger 1998: 4). A collection plan can:

- Establish the aim/objective of an institution including an outline of the collection and the institution's activities;
- Establish the scope of the collection;
- Indicate how important the collection is compared to other related collections;
- Simplify loans; the exchange of collection plans from different organisations provides a better insight into who is collecting what;
- Determine how objects are to be used: in exhibition, in storage, for study purposes, etc.;
- Indicate the level of registration, documentation and research required;
- Help with setting priorities in preventive conservation, active conservation and restoration.

The collection plan should describe the history of the collection: how, by whom and why the collection has been brought together. A description of the collection should be given. It is often useful to divide a collection into well-organised and manageable subcollections. The core of the collection needs to be established, i.e. that part of the collection that characterises the essence of the institution. It is important to establish the cultural-historic value of each subcollection as objectively as possible. What is the significance of the collection for the region or the nation? In the 1990s, the Dutch government established the so-called 'Delta plan for the preservation of cultural heritage', aimed at addressing the backlog in registration and preventive conservation. In this plan, four categories were described in which collections could be classified according to their cultural historic value (*Deltaplan* 1990). Category A includes objects that belong to the higher echelons of Dutch cultural heritage, i.e. objects that are irreplaceable and indispensable. Category B consists of objects that have a high attraction or presentation value, but are not of the greatest cultural-historic importance. Collections that have a special 'ensemble' value, i.e. they are important due to their completeness, also belong to this group. Category C includes objects that match the requirements of an institution's collection policy, but are not as important as the objects from the first two categories. These objects are often found in storage. Category D contains objects that no longer match the collecting policy of an institution – it may well be the case that some of these objects would belong to a higher category if placed in a different collection. Museums are therefore encouraged to try to allocate these objects to more appropriate collections following a strict protocol. In those instances where objects are clearly superfluous, an institution can decide whether or not to discard them or to use them for educational purposes. These objects need to be de-accessioned.

It may be stating the obvious to say that the borders between these categories are sometimes vague. For example, a simple dress categorised in group C may have warranted a group A category had the owner been famous. Also, a fairly ordinary tapestry may become a B category object if it has been made to fit a certain historic interior and is still exhibited there.

It is important to know the level of registration of each subcollection. This level is a percentage of the total number of objects registered according to the minimum requirements of collection registration (see section 11.3.1). As such, the backlog in registration can be established. The physical and environmental conditions should be described for each subcollection. This information can be used to establish a maintenance plan which will help to prioritise preventive conservation, active conservation and restoration.

An important part of the collection plan is the policy for collecting, selecting and de-accessioning. This policy is critical as every newly collected object needs care (storage space, registration, conservation), which, of course, costs money. As the financial means of many institutions are often limited, well-considered choices will have to be made. In the case of donations, the situation can be sensitive; if a regional museum refuses a donation, other donors might be dissuaded from donating interesting items in the future. Therefore, it is important to explain to the donors why a certain object has not been accepted and to help them in finding a more suitable recipient. If, for whatever reason, an institution has to accept a donation, it is best to include a special clause in the 'transfer of ownership' document that establishes full authority over the donation.

12.2 Maintenance plan

The maintenance plan is an important part of the collection plan. The previous chapters in this book have explained that responsible storage and exhibition of objects does not guarantee the 'eternal' existence of the collection. Textile collections in particular are vulnerable because almost all the materials present are, to some extent, ephemeral. Appropriate preservation conditions will, of course, delay natural degradation. It is therefore important to check the condition of the objects regularly, both in storage and on display, so that any new damage can be spotted immediately and appropriate measures can be taken. A maintenance plan sets out a structured approach to preserving a collection; it deserves active implementation.

The current situation should be described in the maintenance plan: the location of the collection (in storage, on display, on loan) and the prevailing environmental conditions in these locations (light, relative humidity, temperature, environmental pollution, etc). What is the level of preventive conservation, i.e. are there adequate supports and proper storage facilities? What about conservation: is there a backlog and how can this be dealt with? This information should help to establish the budgets required so that funding can be sought.

The maintenance plan should describe any necessary actions. If, for example, it is found that the subcollection of hats and shoes does not have appropriate supports in storage, a plan can be drawn up to make up the deficiency over the next five years. If the RH in one of the exhibition rooms is found to be unsuitable on several occasions, a plan can be made to measure and log the climate in this room over the coming year in order to establish the cause of this. If daylight is allowed to enter the exhibition room, immediate action might be taken by fitting UV filters on the window and, at the same time, putting up a curtain.

The maintenance plan should set out a timetable for inspections of objects (both in storage and in exhibition) for evidence of the presence of insects, fungi or new damage and outline the action that should be taken if any are found. The frequency of the inspections will differ: textiles on open display require more frequent inspection than those in storage. It should be clear who is responsible for the inspections and what they should be looking for.

The maintenance plan should also describe the level and frequency of dust removal from objects on exhibition. It should state who is responsible and who should carry out the task. Another vital part of the plan is the replacement of yellowed and embrittled packaging material (acidified) with conservation-grade material. As the replacement of packaging materials has financial consequences, it would be practical to set aside a certain percentage of the budget for this purpose every year.

To summarise; the maintenance plan should include the following:

- A description of the condition of the collection and the level of conservation needed;
- A description of the physical condition of the building (and how often maintenance and inspections are carried out);
- Preventive conservation: the indoor climate, the use of materials, lighting, integrated pest management, etc.;
- A plan and projected budget for the forthcoming period (four to five years);
- Appendices (collected data, maps of the building, equipment).

12.2.1 The condition report

Condition reports form an important part of the maintenance plan. The condition of the objects should preferably be established in a dedicated space, for example, in the quarantine area. A condition report should be made at specific points in time:

- Inspect an object when it enters the collection (new acquisition, donation, returned loan, outside loan) in the presence of the provider in order to establish its condition. This protocol also protects the collection from infestations from the outside.
- When an object is acquisitioned, the condition report gives advice on the preferred environmental factors or necessary conservation treatments required.
- Before an object is moved – either internally or externally – it should be established whether its condition is sound enough to withstand handling.
- When an object is requested for an exhibition, the condition report should indicate under what circumstances this is possible.

The condition check should always be made by a textile conservator or an experienced conservation assistant/collection management assistant and should include a detailed report. Attention should be paid to the ownership of the objects, for example, if the object is not the property of the institution, formal permission should first be requested from the owner before checking the object.

The following details should always be registered in a condition report: the date of the check; the name of the executor; the methodology used; the registration number of the object; the reason for the check and the findings. Recommendations for handling the object and guidelines for (preventive) conservation may also be given. The information can be recorded on special condition forms – either hard copy or computerised – which are usually available in a museum. Make sure that all information about an object is retrievable via its registration number.

The condition report describes the condition of the object at the time it was examined. Information should never be copied from a previous condition check without first inspecting the object. It is nonetheless important to retrieve and compare information from previous condition checks so that a survey of the condition of an object can be obtained. It is strongly recommended that objects that degrade rapidly, e.g. objects made from weighted silk or chintzes with iron-gall mordants are monitored with greater regularity. It is also advisable to photograph them at every inspection as it can be difficult to describe damage or degradation clearly in words. A series of photographs of the same area of the object is a valuable aid in registering its decline. If conservation treatment is required, the level of urgency and an indication of the time necessary should be documented. Many museums now use a priority of need numerical system which gives an indication of urgency on a scale of 1–4: 1 indicating poor condition/in immediate need and 4 indicating good condition/no immediate treatment required.

12.3 Disaster plan

More often than not, it seems that a disaster is only discussed after the event – no one was prepared for the consequences. It is therefore the responsibility of every institution to identify potential risks to a collection by means of risk analysis and determine the actions to be taken in the event of a problem. If potential problems have been properly identified and anticipated, the consequences of a disaster may be limited and manageable. Most disasters are not restricted to a specific institution but affect a wider area. In the event of natural disasters – such as floods, heavy storms, earthquakes and volcanic eruptions – and other catastrophes such as wars, (inter)national aid will first and foremost be aimed at rescuing people from the disaster area. Salvaging cultural treasures is a lesser priority. When dealing with localised damage such as a burst water pipe, fire or vandalism (termed a calamity in this book), it is often possible to focus directly on salvaging the collections.

In its risk assessment, the institution should differentiate between disasters and calamities; in most cases, the chance of a calamity is greater than that of a disaster. The disaster plan has to be drawn up with the fire brigade, the police and specialised salvage companies. An important part of this plan should be dedicated to the prevention of possible calamities. Preventive measures include thorough and regular maintenance checks of the building to include cleaning drains and gutters, sealing cracks and checking electrical wiring. Burglar and fire alarms are also considered preventive measures. The plan should describe the actions that have to be taken if a calamity or a disaster occurs. It is therefore important to discuss with local authorities which space (such as a school or gymnasium) might be available to store collections temporarily in the event of a calamity.

Staff should be aware of the disaster plan, the different tasks they have been allocated, and who has overall responsibility for its execution. The plan has to be checked and updated regularly and staff drills carried out.

12.3.1 Textile calamities and first aid

Most calamities result in water damage: a burst water pipe, a faulty sprinkler, a leaking roof, blocked drains and even water damage from fire extinguishers. Water damage requires swift and immediate action as it is extremely harmful to textiles; most fibres swell when absorbing water, and, as a result, objects can lose their shape. Colours can bleed in dyed or printed textiles and paint layers can become detached. Objects made from a combination of materials suffer badly as the materials respond differently to water. There is a high risk of fungal explosion or even an attack from bacteria, which can multiply quickly in damp textiles especially when the water is contaminated (rainwater or fire-extinguishing water from a nearby water source, etc).

12.3.2 Water damage

The help of one or more textile conservators should be requested when dealing with water damage to textiles. The choice of salvaging methods depends upon the nature of the damaged textiles. Handling wet textiles is risky and using the wrong methods may result in further damage as the tensile strength of most fibres is reduced when wet. Wet textiles can tear easily because of their increased weight; they should never be piled on top of each other. The objects will have to be moved one by one, fully supported on boards or plastic sheets; folds and creases should be avoided as much as possible. A rolled-up towel, a tube or something similar should be used to support folds.

Textile dyes are not always fast to water – they can bleed in contact with water but this is often not noticed until the textile dries. At this point, the dyes migrate with the water from wetter to drier areas in the textile. This is why dyes from an embroidery, which remains wetter for a longer period because of its thickness, migrate into the surrounding area which has dried more quickly because it is thinner. So, when moving wet coloured textiles it is best to place a barrier layer in between textile layers to help to prevent dyes from migrating from one layer into another.

It is difficult to determine which salvage method will result in the least amount of damage – a textile conservator can assist in this decision-making process. When an object is partially wet and its dyes begin to bleed it should be dried as quickly as possible. This can be achieved to some extent by absorbing the water with towels or filter or tissue paper, after which the drying process can be accelerated by increasing air movement with the use of fans or hairdryers. These should be set on the cold setting – the use of warm or hot air should be avoided as it induces a greater risk of shrinkage that will cause tension between the more quickly drying areas and the surrounding wetter areas. If the entire object is wet and its colours are bleeding, however, damage may be limited by keeping the object wet until a textile conservator is available to carry out the salvage treatment (ideally within 48 hours). It is more dangerous to keep an object wet when part of it is made from other materials, such as paper, as some materials will slowly lose their structure completely. In cases where textiles have been completely soaked by dirty water, they should be rinsed with clean, preferably purified, water before drying. During rinsing, the textile should be fully supported by, for example, a sheet of Melinex, plastic gauze or something similar. After rinsing, the superfluous water should be absorbed and the textile then left to dry. Again, increasing air movement may accelerate the drying process.

Hanging wet textiles on a washing line or placing on a drying frame should be avoided.

During drying, attention should be paid to bleeding colours, tension differences etc. If insufficient staff are available to monitor the drying process, those objects most at risk may be deep frozen until a textile conservator can be found. Although this will prevent the development of fungi and bacteria, ice crystals are larger in volume than water and may damage the textile fibres when they are formed during the freezing process: the quicker the freezing process, the smaller the ice crystals. Deep freezing may also be the best option when there is no clean water available for rinsing dirty, wet textiles. This may also be a temporary solution for objects that cannot be rinsed because they are too fragile or have been severely damaged.

Wet textiles can also be dried by freeze-drying, a technique that is frequently used in the salvage of wet paper (archives). In this process, wet textiles are dried in a special vacuum chamber at temperatures below freezing. Under these conditions, frozen water sublimates, i.e. transfers from a solid to a gaseous phase without passing through the liquid phase. In this way, damage caused by swelling or potential deformation of the fibres is avoided. The bleeding of colours is also avoided as the textile dries without the water present becoming liquid.

It is nearly impossible to completely remove the soot resulting from a fire from textile objects. Apart from the visual damage, soot also causes a penetrating smell that lingers for a long time. The smell of soot can be minimised by wrapping the textile in active carbon cloth that is capable of absorbing the smell. Always use a permeable barrier layer between the active carbon cloth and the textile, to avoid direct contact and possible staining from the black carbon.

As already stated, prevention is better than cure. It is obvious that simply making a disaster plan is not enough – the annual evaluation and adjustment of the plan is just as important. People are the most important element in the success of a plan. Regular training and staff drills are crucial to the preparation for potential calamities or disasters.

Glossary

Acid A compound that generates hydrogen ions (H⁺) in an aqueous solution.

Acidic An aqueous solution is acidic when it contains more hydrogen ions (H⁺) than hydroxyl ions (OH⁻). Examples are vinegar (acetic acid CH₃COOH), hydrogen chloride (HCl) and formic acid (HCOOH).

Alkali A substance that contains hydroxyl ions (OH⁻) in an aqueous solution.

Alkaline An aqueous solution is alkaline when it contains more hydroxyl ions (OH⁻) than hydrogen ions (H⁺). Examples are solutions of old-fashioned soap, soda (sodium carbonate Na₂CO₃), lye (sodium hydroxide NaOH) and ammonia (NH₃).

Amino acid The building unit of proteins. In nature, there are 24 amino acids but only 21 are constituents of proteins.

Amorphous Area in a polymer in which the molecule chains are disoriented. Not crystalline.

Anion A negatively charged ion; for example, OH⁻.

Candela *Candela* is the Latin word for candle. Originally, it represented the intensity of an actual candle, assumed to be burning whale tallow at a specified rate in grains per hour. Later this definition was replaced and it is now defined to be the luminous intensity of a light source producing single-frequency light over a complete sphere centred at the light source.

Cation A positively charged ion; for example, H⁺.

Cellulose The building material of all vegetable fibres.

Colour rendering index Expresses the quality of the light in rendering all colours correctly. Sunlight contains a complete and continuous spectrum as a result of which all colours present in objects will be rendered correctly when illuminated by the sun. The index is represented by a number from 0 to 100: 90–100 is good; 50–80 moderate; 0–50 is poor.

Colour temperature Is expressed in degrees Kelvin (0 °K = −273.15 °C, absolute zero). It represents the colour and the intensity of the light emitted by a light source.

Condensation The transition of a substance from the gas or vapour state to the liquid state.

Covalent bond is a chemical bond between atoms which is formed by the sharing of electrons.

Cross-linking The formation of chemical bonds between polymer chains, as a result of which the polymer forms a less flexible, three-dimensional polymer structure.

Crystalline Area in a polymer in which the molecule chains are aligned. Not amorphous.

Crystallinity The percentage of the crystalline areas (as opposed to amorphous areas) within a polymer.

Cysteine One of the natural amino acids. It contains sulphur.

Degree of polymerisation (DP) The average number of monomer units linked together in a polymer.

Dewpoint The exact temperature of a surface upon which water vapour starts to condense from the surrounding warmer atmosphere. It depends upon the absolute moisture content of the atmosphere.

Disulphide cross-links Chemical linkages comprising two sulphur atoms that form between adjacent polymer chains.

Dipole-dipole interactions Electrostatic forces created in molecules containing electronegative heteroatoms (e.g. oxygen, nitrogen). These atoms attract the bonding electrons, causing a partially negatively charged pole in the molecule. As a result, the other side of the molecule becomes partially positively charged. The negatively charged sites of a polymer chain attract the positively charged sites of the adjacent one.

Elasticity The ability of a material to resume its original form, size or shape after removing the forces that caused its deformation.

Elongation at break The elongation of a fibre at the moment it breaks, represented as a percentage of the original fibre length.

EMC The equilibrium moisture content which represents a material's (hygroscopic) moisture content when in equilibrium with the surrounding atmosphere. 'Equilibrium' means that after an arbitrarily long period, no further net weight gain or weight loss occurs.

Ester A substance formed by the chemical reaction between an alcohol and an (organic) acid.

Ether A substance formed by the dehydration reaction between two alcohols.

Fibroin A liquid protein extruded by the silkworm. In the air it becomes hard, forming a continuous silk thread.

Glass transition temperature (Tg) Temperature range at which a thermoplastic polymer transforms from a glass-like to a rubber-like condition.

Hydrogen bond Special type of dipole-dipole interaction, between partially positively charged, bound hydrogen atoms and other partially negatively charged bound atoms (usually oxygen).

Hydrolysis The chemical decomposition of a substance by the action of water.

Hydrophilic Having a strong affinity for water and the ability to absorb water or moisture.

Hydrophobic Having an aversion for water (water-repellent). Not able to absorb water or moisture.

Hydroxyl group The functional group in a molecule consisting of an oxygen and a hydrogen atom (–OH).

Hygroscopic The ability to absorb water or moisture from the atmosphere.

Inorganic Substance of non-living or mineral origin.

Iso-electric point The pH at which a protein molecule will have no overall ionic charge and so will have its minimum solubility in water. Different proteins have different isoelectric points. Small changes in pH can add or remove hydrogen ions (H^+) ions from side chain groups on the surface of a protein, without causing any permanent damage to the conformation.

Keratin The protein from which wool and hair are made.

Light intensity A measure of the quantity of light on a surface expressed in lux. 1 lux equals 1 lumen per m^2.

Lignin A woody substance that is, besides cellulose, a building material in plants. It is a hydrophobic substance that rapidly turns brown and acid under the influence of light.

Lumen The Latin word for light, it is a unit for measuring the flux of light being produced by a light source or received by a surface. The intensity of a light source is measured in candelas.

Lux Unit for measuring the illumination (illuminance) of a surface. One lux is defined as an illumination of one lumen per square metre (1 lux = 1 lumen/square metre).

Microclimate The condition in which a small area within a larger space has different environmental conditions compared to the rest of that space.

Moisture content The amount of water contained in a material, expressed as a percentage of its oven dry weight. The value depends upon the temperature and relative humidity.

Moisture regain The capacity of a fibre to absorb moisture from the surrounding atmosphere. It is the amount of moisture or water contained in the fibre and expressed as a percentage of its oven dry weight. The value depends upon the temperature and relative humidity.

Monomer A building unit of a polymer.

Morphology The study of the shape and structure of organisms.

Organic Substance from living origin, composed essentially of carbon and hydrogen, often with oxygen and nitrogen.

Peptide bond The chemical bond between two amino acids.

pH The pH is a measure of the acidity of an aqueous solution. A solution with an excess of hydrogen ions (H^+) is acidic; an excess of hydroxyl ions (OH^-) is alkaline. In water, H^+ and OH^- are in relation to each other: $H_2O <=> H^+ + OH^-$. In a neutral solution, the concentration of both ions is equal (10^{-7} mole per litre). The equilibrium in water requires the product of the concentrations of both ions to be constant (at a certain temperature). At 20 °C, this product is 10^{-14}. The pH of a solution is defined as the negative value of the exponential of the hydrogen ion's concentration. The pH of neutral water is 7. In a solution where the pH is 1, the hydrogen ion concentration [H^+] is 10^{-1} mole/l. The solution is acidic and has very few hydroxyl ions. Note: the stronger the acid, the lower the pH value; the stronger the alkali, the higher the pH value.

Polymer A large, long molecule built from many smaller units, the monomers.

Protein The building blocks of all animal fibres.

Psychrometric chart Graph with the temperature plotted along the horizontal axis and the absolute humidity (in grams of water vapour per m^3) along the vertical axis. It displays curves which connect points of equal relative humidity (at 10, 20, …, 100%).

Relative humidity (RH) The relationship between the quantity of moisture present in the atmosphere (expressed in grams per m^3) and the maximum quantity of moisture that the atmosphere can contain at the same temperature.

Semi-synthetic Manufactured artificially from natural raw materials.

Sericin An adhesive that is extruded by the silkworm at the same time as fibroin.

Starch A substance built up from α-glucose units. It forms a gel in water and is used for stiffening textiles.

Sublimation The transition of a substance from the solid state directly to the gas or vapour state without passing through its liquid state.

Tenacity Records the specific stress at break related to the fineness of a fibre or yarn (expressed in centinewtons per tex (cN/tex) or grams per denier (g/den)). Its specific value for a material depends upon temperature and relative humidity.

Tensile strength The breaking strength of a fibre expressed as a force per unit of cross-sectional area. Its specific value for a material depends upon temperature and relative humidity.

Thesaurus A thesaurus is a collection of terms selected from the natural use of words and from which basic relationships are recorded.

Van der Waals' forces Weak electrostatic forces between adjacent polymer chains named after the Dutch scientist Johannes Diederik van der Waals.

Bibliography

Adrosko, R.J. (1971) *Natural Dyes and Home Dyeing: A Practical Guide with over 150 Recipes*. New York: Dover.

Aghemo, C. and M. Fillipi (1997) 'Lighting to show: designing experiments for some temporary exhibitions', in *LUX, Europa Conference*. Amsterdam: Nederlandse Stichting voor Verlichtingskunde, pp. 336–47.

Ashley-Smith, J. and L. Hillyer (1997) 'Can high productivity be productive?' in *Fabric of an Exhibition: An Interdisciplinary Approach Preprints*. Ottawa: Government of Canada, pp. 3–8.

Ashley-Smith *et al.* (2002) 'The continuing development of a practical lighting policy for works of art on paper and other object types at the Victoria and Albert Museum', in *ICOM-CC 13th Triennial Meeting, Rio de Janeiro 2002. Preprints Volume I*. London: James and James, pp. 3–8.

Ayres, J.M. *et al.* (1988) *Energy Conservation and Climate Control in Museums*. Los Angeles: Getty Conservation Institute.

Bachmann, K. (1992) *Conservation Concerns: A Guide to Collectors and Curators*. Washington DC: Smithsonian Institution Press.

Ballard, M.W. (1984) 'Mothproofing museum textiles', in *ICOM-CC 7th Triennial Meeting, Copenhagen 1984. Preprints Volume I*. Copenhagen: ICOM, pp. 84.9.1–84.9.6.

Bamberger, J.A. *et al.* (1999) 'A variant Oddy test procedure for evaluating materials used in storage and display cases', *Studies in Conservation* 44: 86–90.

Berg, S. van den *et al.* (1998) *Syllabus bij de basiscursus Registratie en Documentatie*, 2nd edn. Tilburg: Stichting Landelijk Contact van Museumconsulenten.

Bilson, T. *et al.* (1997) 'Mechanical aspects of lining "loose hung" textiles', in *Fabric of an Exhibition: An Interdisciplinary Approach Preprints*. Ottawa: Government of Canada, pp. 63–9.

Blank, S. (1990) 'An introduction to plastics and rubbers in collections', *Studies in Conservation* 35: 53–63.

Boeijink, N. (1999) 'De conservering van beschilderde delen van vaandels, problemen en multidisciplinaire aanpak', in *Vlaggen en Vaandels, textieldag gehouden op 25 april 1996*. Amsterdam: Stichting Textielcommissie Nederland, pp. 61–8.

Boekhorst, G. *et al.* *Een klein musée imaginaire: voorbeeldenboek bij het registreren van museumobjecten*. Amsterdam: Nederlandse Museumvereniging.

Boersma, F. (1992) *Na restauratie onbeperkt houdbaar*. Amsterdam: Centraal Laboratorium voor Onderzoek naar Voorwerpen van Kunst en Wetenschap (unpublished report).

Boersma, F. (1993) *The Conservation of a USTC Flag*. Washington DC: National Museum of American History (unpublished conservation report).

Boersma, F. (1996) 'Literatuurstudie voor de conservering van een vlag uit de Amerikaanse Burgeroorlog, Casestudy: een stage in Amerika', in *Bronnenonderzoek voor textiel, textieldag gehouden op 14 november 1991*. Amsterdam: Textielcommissie Musea, pp. 57–64.

Boersma, F. (1997) *Tapestry Conservation, Support Methods and Fabrics for Tapestries. Part I Tapestries: General Background Information. Part II: Chemistry and Physics of Flax (Linen) and Cotton*. Amsterdam: Instituut Collectie Nederland (unpublished report).

Boersma, F. (1998) 'The conservation of an Indonesian flag', in *International Perspectives on Textile Conservation*, Papers from the ICOM-CC Textiles Working Group Meetings, Amsterdam 13–14 October 1994 and Budapest 11–15 September 1995, A. Timar-Balazsy and D. Eastop (eds). London: Archetype Publications, pp. 23–5.

Boersma, F. *et al.* (2000) *Op de keper beschouwd. Hand-*

boek voor het behoud van textielcollecties. Amsterdam: Stichting Textielcommissie Nederland.

Boetzelaer-Korotkova, O. Van (2000) *Brandpreventie voor wandtapijten.* Unpublished final year project of the Textile Conservation Course. Amsterdam: Insituut Collectie Nederland, pp. 37–44.

Bois, W.F. du (1971) *Textielvezels.* Groningen: Wolters-Noordhoff.

Brill, T.B. (1980) *Light: Its Interaction with Art and Antiquities.* New York: Plenum Publishing Corporation.

Brokerhof, A.W. (1998) 'Het duistere bestaan van de houtboorders', in *Derde Nederlandse Symposium Hout- en Meubelrestauratie,* P. van Duin and D. van Loosdrecht (eds). Amsterdam: VeRes/ICN, pp. 1–4.

Brokerhof, A.W. (1999) 'Insectenbestrijding', in *Conserveren Natuurhistorische Collecties.* Amsterdam: Werkgroep Behoud Natuurhistorische Collecties/Instituut Collectie Nederland, pp. F1–F16.

Brokerhof, A.W. (2003) 'The solar tent: cheap and effective pest control in museums', *AICCM Bulletin* 28: 93–7.

Brokerhof, A.W. et al. (1999) *Pluis in huis; geïntegreerde bestrijding van schimmels in archieven.* Amsterdam: Instituut Collectie Nederland.

Brokerhof, A.W. et al. (2004) 'Wie de handschoen past ... Handschoenen getest voor het hanteren van collecties', *Cr Interdisciplininair tijdschrift voor conservering en restauratie* 5(1): 50–57.

Brommer, B. (1990) 'Kunstzijde en synthetische vezels', in *Van kimono tot ruimtepak., zijde – kunstzijde – kunstvezel.* Helmond: Gemeentemuseum Helmond, pp. 95–101.

Brum, M. and J. White (eds) (2002) *Museum Mannequins: A Guide for Creating the Perfect Fit.* Alberta: Alberta Regional Group of Conservators (ARG).

Buck, A. et al. (1989) *Vocabulary of Basic Terms for Cataloguing Costume.* ICOM International Committee for the Museums and Collections of Costume.

Bullock, L. and D. Saunders (1999) 'Measurement of cumulative exposure using blue wool standards', in *ICOM-CC 12th Triennial Meeting, Lyon 1999. Preprints Volume I.* London: James and James, pp. 21–6.

Burg, J. van der (2003) 'Te huur: depotruimte per m2', in *CR interdisciplinair vakblad voor conservering en restauratie* 4: 45–51.

Burnham, D.K. (1980) *A Textile Terminology: Warp & Weft.* London: Routledge & Kegan Paul.

Burnham, E. (1999) 'Some recent successes in displaying costume', *Textile Conservation Newsletter* supplement.

Cackett, S. (1992) 'Disaster planning', in *Manual of Curatorship: A Guide to Museum Practice,* J.M.A. Thompson (ed.). London: Butterworth-Heinemann, pp. 487–90.

Calmes, A. (1985) 'Charters of Freedom of the United States', *Museum* 37(2): 99–101.

Caminada, J.F. and D. Parker (1994) 'Museums and art galleries: a brief review of some important considerations', *International Lighting Review* 2: 42–4.

Cassar, M. (1984) 'Proposal for a typology of display case construction designs and museum climate control systems', in *ICOM-CC 7th Triennial Meeting, Copenhagen 1984. Preprints Volume II.* Paris: ICOM, pp. 84/17/11–84/1/15.

Cassar, M. (1989) 'Relative humidity and temperature control, the ideal and the possible: the use of microclimates', in *Where to Start, Where to Stop? Papers from the British Museum/MEG Ethnographic Conservation Colloquium, London, 9–10 November 1989.* Hull: Museum Ethnographers Group, pp. 73–84.

Cassar, M. (1994a) 'Lighting design and energy efficiency in museums and galleries', in *Museums Environment Energy,* M. Cassar (ed.). London: HMSO.

Cassar, M. (ed.) (1994b) *Museums Environment Energy.* London: HMSO.

Cassar, M. (1994c) 'Preventive conservation and building maintenance', in *Museum Management and Curatorship.* London: Butterworth-Heinemann, pp. 39–47.

Cassar, M. (1995) *Environmental Management: Guidelines for Museums and Galleries.* London: Routledge.

Cassar, M. and G. Martin (1994) 'The environmental performance of museum display cases', in *Preventive Conservation: Practice, Theory and Research. Preprints of the Contributions to the Ottawa Congress, 12–16 September 1994.* London: International Institute for the Conservation of Historic and Artistic Works, pp. 171–6.

Cassee, N. (1999) 'Het project "Vlaggen en Vaandels" in de provincie Noord-Holland', in *Vlaggen en Vaandels, textieldag gehouden op 25 april 1996.* Amsterdam: Stichting Textielcommissie Nederland, pp. 27–38.

Chaplin, R.E. (1994) 'The development of a modern museum showcase system', in *Scottish Society of Conservation and Restoration Conference, 21–22 April 1994.* Edinburgh: Scottish Society for Conservation and Restoration, pp. 63–71.

Child, B. (1993) *Electronic Environmental Monitoring.* Denbigh: Archetype.

CIE (2004) *Control of Damage to Museum Objects by Optical Radiation.* Technical Report 157. Vienna: CIE.

Colby, K.M. (1998) *A Suggested Exhibition/Exposure Policy for Works of Art on Paper.* Montreal: Internet.

Cooke, B. (1988) 'Creasing in ancient textiles', *Conservation News* 35: 27–30.

Cooke, B. (1990) 'Fibre damage in archaeological textiles', in *Archaeological Textiles, Proceedings of the Conference on Textiles for the Archaeological Conservator.* London: United Kingdom Institute for Conservation (UKIC), pp. 5–14.

Covitti, A. and A. Regginai (1997) 'Approach to the method to find the spectrum of a lighting source to illuminate a painting with a definite chromatic content', in *LUX, Europa Conference.* Amsterdam: Nederlandse Stichting voor Verlichtingskunde, pp. 1130–5.

Cowton, J. (ed.) (1997) *SPECTRUM: The UK Museum Documentation Standard,* 2nd edn. Cambridge: Museum Documentation Association.

Craddock, A.B. (1994) 'Construction materials for storage and exhibition', in *Care of Collections,* S. Knell (ed.). London: Routledge, pp. 129–34.

Cuttle, C. (1996) 'Damage to museum objects due to light exposure', *Lighting Research and Technology* 28(1): 1–9.

Daalen, F. van and N. Lingbeek (1999) 'Conservering en berging van een waaiercollectie', *CARE* 5: 21–33.

Daniels, V. and R. Kibrya (1998) 'Effects of freezing on museum objects', *Conservation News* 66: 20–21.

Dawson, J.E. and T.J.K. Strang (1992) *Solving Museum Insect Problems: Chemical Control*, CCI Technical Bulletin 15. Ottawa: Canadian Conservation Institute.

Debruyne, M. (1988) *Handboek voor de organisatie van kunsttentoonstellingen*. Deventer: Van Lochem Slaterus.

Deltaplan voor het cultuurbehoud. Onderdeel: Plan van aanpak achterstanden musea, archieven, monumentenzorg en archeologie (1990) Rijswijk: Ministerie van Welzijn, Volksgezondheid en Cultuur.

Derbyshire, A.and J. Ashley-Smith (1999) 'A proposed practical lighting policy for works of art on paper at the V&A', in *ICOM-CC 12th Triennial Meeting, Lyon 1999. Preprints Volume II*. London: James and James, pp. 38–42

Diderot, D. (1959) *L'Encyclopédie, ou Dictionnaire Raisonné des Sciences, des Arts et des Métiers*, C.C. Gillespie (ed.). New York: Dover Publications.

Diehl, J.M. et al. (1991) *Textiellexicon, verklarende weeftechnisch woordenboek*. Amsterdam: Textielcommissie Musea.

Disano, G. and A. Rogora (1997) 'The art of illuminating art', *Right Light* 4(1): 175–8.

Druesedow, J.L. (1991) 'Development of mannequins at the Costume Institute', in *New Forms of Presentation in Museum Costume Collections, textieldag gehouden op 31 augustus 1989*. Amsterdam: Textielcommissie Musea, pp. 5–10.

Elementen voor een beleidsplan van een museum (1999) Amsterdam/Tilburg: Instituut Collectie Nederland, Stichting Landelijk Contact van Museumconsulenten, Nederlandse Museumvereniging.

Eremin, K. and P. Wilthew (1998) 'Monitoring concentrations of organic gases within the National Museums of Scotland', *SSCR Journal* 1: 15–19.

Erhardt, D. and M. Mecklenburg (1994) 'Relative humidity re-examined', *Preventive Conservation: Practice, Theory and Research*. Paris: International Institute for Conservation (IIC), pp. 32–8.

Feller, R.L. (1968) 'Control of deteriorating effects of light on museum objects: heating effects of illumination by incandescent lamps', *Museum News* May: 39–47.

Feller, R.L. and R. Johnston-Feller (1981) 'Continued investigations involving the ISO blue-wool standards of exposure', in *ICOM-CC 6th Triennial Meeting, Ottawa 1981. Preprints Volume III*. Ottawa: ICOM, pp. 81/18/1-1–81/18/1-7.

Finch, K. and G. Putnam (1977) *Caring for Textiles*. London: Barrie & Jenkins.

Fraia, L. di (1997) 'Lighting of photosensitive works of art: a proposal of standards', in *LUX, Europa Conference*. Amsterdam: Nederlandse Stichting voor Verlichtingskunde, pp. 1137–43.

Fukai, A. (1991) 'Research on period mannequins and their use', in *New Forms of Presentation in Museum Costume Collections, textieldag gehouden op 31 augustus 1989*. Amsterdam: Textielcommissie Musea, pp. 11–20.

Ganiaris, H. and D. Sully (1998) 'Showcase construction: materials and methods used at the Museum of London', *The Conservator* 22: 57–67.

Geijer, A. (1982) *A History of Textile Art*. London: Pasold Research Fund.

Gill, K. and D. Eastop (2001) *Upholstery Conservation, Principles and Practice*. Oxford: Butterworth-Heinemann.

Glover, J.M. (1992) 'Conservation and storage: textiles', in *Manual of Curatorship: A Guide to Museum Practice*, J.M.A. Thompson (ed.). London: Butterworth, pp. 302–39.

Gohl, E.P.G. and L.D. Vilensky (1987) *Textile Science: An Explanation of Fibre Properties*. Melbourne: Longman Cheshire.

Graaf, A.J. de (1974) 'Het oprollen van vlakke textielprodukten', in *Verslag van de Textieldag met de onderwerpen 'Kleurstoffen in textiel' en "Opbergsystemen in depot*. Amsterdam: Textielcommissie Musea, pp. 23–4.

Graaf, A.J. de (1980) 'Tensile properties and flexibility of textiles', in *Conservation and Restoration of Textiles. International Conference, Como*, F. Pertegato (ed.). Milan: CISST Lombardy Section, pp. 54–61.

Green, L.R. and D. Thickett (1995) 'Testing materials for use in the storage and display of antiquities: a revised methodology', *Studies in Conservation* 40(3): 145–52.

Grijzenhout, F. (1996) *Handreiking bij het afstoten van museale collecties*. Den Haag: Rijksdienst Beeldende Kunst.

Groeneweg, I. (1987) *Technieken in de kunstnijverheid 4, textiel (1)*. Leiden: Rijksuniversiteit, Kunsthistorisch Instituut.

Groff, J.R. and P.N. Weinberg (1999) *SQL: The Complete Reference*. Berkeley: Osborne/McGraw-Hill.

Grzywacz, C. and B. Metro (1992) 'A showcase for preventive conservation', *Colloque international de l'ARAAFU*. Paris, 1992, pp. 207–10.

Grzywacz, C. and N.H. Tennent (1994) 'Pollution monitoring in storage and display cabinets: carbonyl pollutant levels in relation to artifact deterioration', in *Preventive Conservation: Practice, Theory and Research*. Ottawa: International Institute for Conservation (IIC), pp. 164–70.

Guichen, G. de (1972) 'Why curators do not use silica gels or the three uses of silica gel', in *ICOM, Rome*. Rome: ICCROM, pp. 4–19.

Guichen, G. de and V. Gai (1984) 'Controle du Climat autour de 197 instruments de musique', in *ICOM-CC 7th Triennial Meeting, Copenhagen 1984. Preprints Volume II*. Paris: ICOM, pp. 84.17.19–25.

Guichen, G. de et al. (1998) *Climate Control in Museums: Criterion-referenced Instruction*. Vols 1–3. Rome: ICCROM.

Hallebeek, P.B. (1987) 'Verkeerd gebruik van materialen in depots', in *CL Themadag 11 'Het inrichten van depots uit conservatorisch oogpunt' (20-05-1987)*. Amsterdam: Centraal Laboratorium, pp. 58–68.

Hallebeek, P.B. (1993) 'Verkeerd gebruik van materialen in depots', in *Depot-inrichting en archiefconservering. Passieve conservering* (herdruk verslagen CL-Themadagen 10/11). Amsterdam: Centraal Laboratorium voor Onderzoek van Voorwerpen van Kunst en Wetenschap, pp. 139–49.

Hammick, S. (1989) *Warning: Dichlorvos Resin Strip Fumigation*. Edmonton: University of Alberta.

Handreiking beoordeling restauratieoffertes (1998) Amsterdam: Instituut Collectie Nederland.

Handreiking voor het schrijven van een collectieplan (1998) Tilburg/Amsterdam: Stichting Landelijk Contact van Museumconsulenten, Instituut Collectie Nederland.

Hanzawa, S. (1990) 'Design of display case for cultural properties', in *International Symposium on the Conservation and Restoration of Cultural Property: Cultural Property and its Environment, 11–13 October 1990*. Tokyo: Bunka-cho Tokyo Kokuritsu Bunkazai Kenkyujo Hozon Kagakubu, pp. 131–43.

Hedley, G. (1993) *Measured Opinions: Collected Papers on the Conservation of Paintings*. London: UKIC.

Hefford, W. (1971) 'The restoration of the tapestries', in *The Devonshire Hunting Tapestries*, G. Wingfield Digby (ed.). London: Victoria and Albert Museum, pp. 57–82.

Henderson, A. et al. (1991) 'Lighting dyed materials requires a balance between fading and visibility', *Lighting Design and Application* (May): 16–25.

Hilberry, J.D. and S.K. Weinberg (1994) 'Museum collections storage', in *Care of Collections*, S. Knell (ed.). London: Routledge, pp. 155–75.

Hilbert, G.S. (1996) *Sammlungsgut in Sicherkeit: Beleuchtung und Lichtschutz, Klimatisierung, Sicherungstechnik, Brandschutz*. Berlin: Gebr. Mann, p. 426.

Hilbert, G.S. (1997) 'Die Erfindung der 50 lux', *Licht* 2–3: 190–92.

Hilbert, G.S. and S. Aydlini (1991) 'Museumsbeleuchtung zur Beleuchtung musealer Exponate unter Beachtung neuerer konservatorischer Erkenntnisse', *Licht* 7–8: 566–77.

Hildering, B. (1990) *Lesmateriaal van de Opleiding Restauratoren*. Amsterdam [not published].

Hofenk de Graaff, J.H. (1984) *Informatie, samenstelling bobbeltjesplastic voor verpakking van textiel en samenstelling van vers-houd-folie*. Amsterdam: Centraal Laboratorium voor Onderzoek naar Voorwerpen van Kunst en Wetenschap.

Hofenk de Graaff, J.H. (1993) *Onderzoek naar verbruining van papier in passepartouts (projectnummer 90/126)*. Amsterdam: Centraal Laboratorium voor Onderzoek naar Voorwerpen van Kunst en Wetenschap.

Hofstede, E. Ter (1990) *Versleten en verschoten, tips en adviezen om vroegtijdig verval van historisch textiel en kostuums te voorkomen*. Assen: Drents Museum.

Hogenboom, J. (1988) *Basisregistratie voor collecties voorwerpen en beeldmateriaal*. Rotterdam: Stichting IMC.

Hogenboom, J. and G.J. Koot (1995) 'Automatisering', in *Bedrijfsvoering in Musea*. Den Haag: VUGA.

Hollen, N. (1988) *Textiles*. New York: MacMillan.

Holm, S.A. (1991) *Facts and Artefacts: How to Document a Museum Collection*. Cambridge: Museum Documentation Association.

Hunter, J.E. (1994) 'Museum disaster preparedness planning', in *Care of Collections*, S. Knell (ed.). London: Routledge, pp. 246–61.

Hutchison, B. (1990) 'From restoration to conservation: parallels between the traditions of tapestry conservation and carpet conservation', *The Textile Museum Journal* 29: 9–12.

Institute of Measurement and Control (1996) *A Guide to the Measurement of Humidity*. London: Institute of Measurement and Control.

Instituut Collectie Nederland (2000) *Nummeren van museumvoorwerpen met schrijfstifen*. Amsterdam: Instituut Collectie Nederland.

Instituut Collectie Nederland (2003a) *Nummeren van museumvoorwerpen met schrijfstifen. Nieuwe materialen getest – update 2003* Amsterdam: Instituut Collectie Nederland.

Instituut Collectie Nederland (2003b) *Spreken is zilver... Een aantal aspecten van zilverconservering*. Amsterdam: Instituut Collectie Nederland.

Instituut Collectie Nederland (2005) *Het beperken van lichtschade aan museale objecten: lichtlijnen*. Amsterdam: Instituut Collectie Nederland.

Keene, S. (1994) 'Audits of care: a framework for collections condition surveys', in *Care of Collections*, S. Knell (ed.). London: Routledge, pp. 60–82.

Keene, S. (1996) *Managing Conservation in Museums*. London. Butterworth-Heinemann.

Keune, P. (1997) 'De groene sieraden oftewel het gebruik van de Oddy-test', *kM (Kunstenaars Materialen)* 22: 13.

Kipp, A. (1987) 'Inrichting van depots van textiele verzamelingen van de Rotterdamse musea', in *CL Themadag 'Het inrichten van depots uit conservatorisch oogpunt' (20-05- 1987)*. Amsterdam: Centraal Laboratorium, pp. 4–13.

Kipp, A. (1991) 'The costume display in the City Museum of Rotterdam', in *New Forms of Presentation in Museum Costume Collections, textieldag gehouden op 31 augustus 1989*. Amsterdam: Textielcommissie Musea, pp. 65–70.

Kleinert, T.N. (1968) 'Schädigungen von Zellulosetextilien durch Altern und Licht', *Lenzinger Berichte* 25: 33–40.

Klimatologische gegevens van Nederlandse Meetstations, normale en extreme waarden van 15 hoofdstations voor het tijdvak 1961–1990 (1992). de Bilt: KNMI.

Knell, S. (1994) *Care of Collections*. London: Routledge.

Knight, B. (1994) 'Passive monitoring for museum showcase pollutants', in *Preventive Conservation: Practice, Theory and Research*. Ottawa: International Institute for Conservation (IIC), pp. 174–6.

Kort, J.H.G.M. de (1999) 'De consequenties van belichting van kunstvoorwerpen', in *Studiedag over nieuwbouw in musea*. Amsterdam [not published].

Kostuumcollecties. Richtlijnen voor beheer en behoud (1999). Amsterdam: Instituut Collectie Nederland/ Textielcommissie Nederland.

Kouwenberg, R. (1991) 'How to use light in the museum', in *New Forms of Presentation in Museum Costume Collections, textieldag gehouden op 31 augustus 1989*. Amsterdam: Textielcommissie Musea, pp. 71–80.

Kumaran, M.K. (1994) 'Fundaments in transport and storage of moisture in building materials', in *Moisture Control in Buildings*, Heinz Trechsel (ed.). ASTM Manual Series, MNL 18. Philadelphia: ASTM.

Lafontaine, R.H. (1984) *Silica Gel*, CCI, Technical Bulletin 10. Ottawa: Canadian Conservation Institute, pp. 1–44.

Lamers-Nieuwenhuis, F. (1990) 'De kleding van Spitsbergen in relatie tot Nederlandse klederdrachten uit de 19ᵉ en 20ᵉ eeuw', in *Textielvondsten op Spitsbergen, textieldag gehouden op 3 oktober 1988*. Amsterdam: Textielcommissie Musea, pp. 29–34.

Landi, S. (1992) *The Textile Conservator's Manual*. Oxford: Butterworth-Heinemann.

Lanting, R.W. (1989) *Luchtzuivering in musea, archieven en bibliotheken*. Delft: TNO.

Larkin, N.R. *et al.* (1998) 'Plastic storage containers: a comparison', *The Conservator* 22: 81–7.

Larouche, D. (1997) 'Intersecting silhouette mannequins', in *Fabric of an Exhibition: An Interdisciplinary Approach. Preprints*. Ottawa: Government of Canada, p. 171.

Lawson-Smith, P. (1998) 'Environmental control in historic buildings', *Journal of Architectural Conservation* 1: 42–55.

Leath, K. and M.M. Brooks (1998) 'Velcro and other hook and loop fasteners: a preliminary study of their stability and ageing characteristics', *Textile Conservation Newsletter* 34: 5–11.

Lehrgang für die berufliche Bildung, Beurteilungsmerkmale textiler Faserstoffe (1986). Berlin: Bundesinstitut für Berufsbildung.

Ligterink, F. and G. di Pietro (1999) 'Prediction of the relative humidity response of backboard-protecting canvas paintings', *Studies in Conservation* 44: 269–77.

Linnie, M.J. (1994) 'Pest control in museums: the use of chemicals and associated health problems', *Care of Collections*, S. Knell (ed.). London: Routledge, pp. 234–9.

Lloyd, H. (2002) 'The effects of visitor activity on dust in historic collections', *The Conservator* 26: 72–84.

Luger, T. (1998) *Handreiking voor het schrijven van een collectieplan*. Tilburg/Amsterdam: Stichting Landelijk Contact van Museumconsulenten/Instituut Collectie Nederland.

Lugtigheid, R. (1988) 'Katoen in vele kleuren: de vezel van de kust', in *3000 jaar weven in de Andes, textiel uit Peru en Bolivia*. Helmond: Gemeentemuseum

Lyons, J.W. (1970) *The Chemistry and Uses of Fire Retardants*. New York: Wiley-Interscience.

Matsumura, Mamiko *et al.* (2002) 'Monitoring emissions from cellulose nitrate and cellulose acetate accessories: an evaluation of pH indicator dyes on paper, cotton tape and cotton threads', *The Conservator* 26: 57–69.

McGregor, C. (1994) *The Effects of Storage and Display Materials on Museum Objects*. Cirencester: Committee of Area Museum Councils/Scottish Museum Council.

McIntyre, J.E. and P.N. Daniels (eds) (1995) *Textile Terms and Definitions*. Manchester: The Textile Institute.

McNeill, I.C. (n.d.) 'Fundamental aspects of polymer degradation', in *Polymers in Conservation*, N.S. Allen (ed.). Manchester: Centre for Archival Polymeric Materials, pp. 14–31.

Maekawa, S. (ed.) (1998) *Oxygen-free Museum Cases: Research in Conservation*. Los Angeles: J. Paul Getty Trust.

Martin, D. (1997) 'Lighting', *Museum Practice* 2(3): 38–98.

Martin, G. (1992) 'Development of a preventive conservation strategy and its implementation', in *La Conservation Préventive*. Paris: ARAAFU, pp. 41–6.

Massari, G. (1993) *Damp Buildings, Old and New*. Rome: ICCROM.

Matsumura, M. *et al.* (2002) 'Monitoring emissions from cellulose nitrate and cellulose acetate accessories: an evaluation of pH indicator dyes on paper, cotton tape and cotton threads', *The Conservator* 26: 57–69.

Mecklenburg, M. and M. Frost (991) 'Planning for preventive conservation', in *The Manual of Museum Planning*. London: HMSO, pp. 127–60.

Meetresultaten 1992, regio 6-9 (1992) RIVM, Landelijk Meetnet Luchtkwaliteit.

Michalski, S. (1984) 'The control of relative humidity – recent developments', in *ICOM-CC 7th Triennial Meeting, Copenhagen 1984. Preprints Volume II*. Copenhagen: ICOM, pp. 84/17/33–37.

Michalski, S. (1990) 'Towards specific lighting guidelines', in *ICOM-CC 9th Triennial Meeting, Dresden 1990. Preprints Volume II*. Dresden: ICOM, pp. 583–8.

Michalski, S. (1992a) 'Damage to museum objects by visible radiation (light) and ultraviolet radiation (UV)', in *Lighting in Museums, Galleries and Historic Houses*. London: Museums Association, pp. 3–16.

Michalski, S. (1992b) *A Systematic Approach to the Conservation (Care) of Museum Collections*. Ottawa: Canadian Conservation Institute.

Michalski, S. (1997) 'The lighting decision', in *Fabric of an Exhibition: An Interdisciplinary Approach. Preprints*. Ottawa: Government of Canada, pp. 97–104.

Miller, J.E. and B.M. Reagan (1989) 'Degradation in weighted and unweighted historic silks', *Journal of American Institute of Conservation* 28: 97–115.

Mitchell, D.M. (1997) 'The linen damask trade in Haarlem', in *Textiel aan het Spaarne, Haarlem: van linnen damast tot zijden linte, textieldag gehouden op 8 juni 1995*. Amsterdam: Stichting Textielcommissie Nederland, pp. 5–33.

Miura, S. (1981) 'Studies on the behavior of RH within an exhibition case. Part II: The static and dynamic characteristics of sorbents to control the RH of a showcase', in *ICOM-CC 6th Triennial Meeting, Ottawa 1981. Preprints Volume III*. Paris: ICOM, pp. 81/18/5-1–81/18/5-10.

Miura, S. (1990) 'Temperature and humidity in a large glass showcase for a temple hall (part 2)', in *ICOM-CC 9th Triennial Meeting, Dresden 1990. Preprints Volume II*. Paris: ICOM, pp. 592–5.

Moffatt, E.A. (1984) *Conservation Material Report Summary, Artcor*. Canadian Conservation Institute.

Morton, W.E. *et al.* (1997) *Physical Properties of Textile Fibres*. Manchester: The Textile Institute.

Mosk-Stoets, L.H. (1992) *Voor het kalf verdronken is, Handleiding voor het maken van een museaal calamiteitenplan*. Amsterdam: Centraal Laboratorium voor Onderzoek van Voorwerpen van Kunst en Wetenschap.

Mourier, H. and O. Winding (1975) *Elseviers gids van nuttige en schadelijke dieren*. Amsterdam: Elsevier.

Muller, F. and E.H. Renkema (1982) *Beknopt Latijns-Nederlands woordenboek*. Groningen: Wolters-Noordhoff.

Museum and Art Gallery Lighting: A Recommended Practice (1996) New York: IESNA.

National Trust Manual of Housekeeping: The Care of Collections in Historic Houses Open to the Public (2005). Amsterdam: Elsevier.

Nes, C.J. van (1991) 'Comments on the use of mannequins', in *New Forms of Presentation in Museum Costume Collections, textieldag gehouden op 31 augustus 1989*. Amsterdam: Stichting Textielcommissie Musea, pp. 21–38.

Nicholson, J.W. (1991) *The Chemistry of Polymers*. Cambridge: Royal Society of Chemistry.

Oosten, Th.B. van (1991) *De degradatie van fibroïne onder invloed van de verzwaring, 'state of the art'*. Amsterdam: Centraal Laboratorium voor Onderzoek van Voorwerpen van Kunst en Wetenschap.

Oosten, Th.B. van (1998) 'The degradation of early synthetic materials incorporated in the accessories of a textile collection: cellulose nitrate, cellulose acetate, Galalith, Bakelith', in *International Perspectives on Textile Conservation*, Papers from the ICOM-CC Textiles Working Group Meetings, Amsterdam 13–14 October 1994 and Budapest 11–15 September 1995, A. Timar-Balazsy and D. Eastop (eds). London: Archetype Publications, pp. 4–7.

Otte, M. (1999) 'Het vlaggen- en vaandelproject in Gelderland en Overijssel', in *Vlaggen en Vaandels, textieldag gehouden op 25 april 1996*. Amsterdam: Stichting Textielcommissie Nederland, pp. 39–48.

Paassen, W.J.C. van et al. (1977) *Eenvoudige warenkennis*. Groningen: Wolters-Noordhoff.

Padfield, T. and P. Jensen (1990) 'Low energy climate control in museum stores', in *ICOM-CC 9th Triennial Meeting, Dresden 1990. Preprints Volume II*. Paris: ICOM, pp. 596–601.

Padfield, T. and S. Landi (1966) 'The light fastness of the natural dyes', in *Studies in Conservation* 11(4): 181–96.

Padfield, T. et al. (1984) 'A cooled display case for George Washington's commission', in *ICOM-CC 7th Triennial Meeting, Copenhagen 1984. Preprints Volume II*. Paris: ICOM, pp. 84/17/38–42.

Paine, C. (ed.) (1998) *Standards in the Museum Care of Costumes and Textiles*. London: Museums & Galleries Commissions.

Park, S.C. (1994) 'Moisture in historic buildings and preservation guidance', in *Moisture Control in Buildings*, H. Trechsel (ed.). ASTM Manual Series, MNL 18. Philadelphia: ASTM.

Peacock, E. and E. Griffin (1998) 'Rehousing a collection of archaeological textiles', *The Conservator* 22: 68–80.

Pedley, M. (ed.) (1998) *Standards in Action: A Guide to Using SPECTRUM, Book 1*. Cambridge: Museum Documentation Association.

Piening, H. (1993) *Die Bekämpfung holzzerstorender Insekten mit Kohlendioxid sowie Verträglichkeit des Gases an gefassten Objekten, Diplomarbeit*. Koln, Fachhochschule.

Pinniger, D. (2001) *Pest Management in Museums, Archives and Historic Houses*. London: Archetype Publications.

Pool, M.J.B. (1999) 'De Nederlandse legervlaggen en vaandels', in *Vlaggen en Vaandels, textieldag gehouden op 25 april 1996*. Amsterdam: Stichting Textielcommissie Nederland, pp. 11–14.

Restaurator: een profiel van het beroep (1998). Amsterdam: VeRes/Instituut Collectie Nederland.

Richard, M. (1994) 'The transport of paintings in microclimate display cases', in *Preventive Conservation: Practice, Theory and Research. Preprints of the Contributions to the Ottawa Congress, 12–16 September 1994*. London: International Institute for the Conservation of Historic and Artistic Works, pp. 185–9.

Rijksgebouwendienst (1996) *Adviesrichtlijn luchtkwaliteit museumdepots*. Den Haag: Ministerie Ruimtelijke Ordening en Volkshuisvesting.

Robinet, L. And D. Thickett (2003) 'A new methodology for accelerated corrosion testing', *Studies in Conservation* 48(4): 263–8.

Rose, C.L. and A.R. de Torres (1992) *Storage of Natural History Collections: Ideas and Practical Solutions*. Pittsburgh PA: Society for the Preservation of Natural History Collections.

Rose, W. (1994) 'Effects of climate control on the museum building envelope', *Journal of the American Institute for Conservation* 33(2): 199–210.

Samson, R.A. and E. Hoekstra (eds) (1994) *Schimmels in musea en archieven; Handleiding van een driedaagse cursus georganiseerd in samenwerking met het Algemeen Rijksarchief, 's-Gravenhage en het Scheepvaartmuseum, Amsterdam*. Baarn: Centraalbureau voor Schimmelcultures.

Saunders, D. (1990) 'Protecting works of art from the damaging effects of light', in *International Symposium on the Conservation and Restoration of Cultural Property: Cultural Property and its Environment, 11–13 October 1990*. Tokyo: Bunka-cho Tokyo Kokuritsu Bunkazai Kenkyujo Hozon Kagakubu, pp. 167–78.

Schellen, H.L. (1999) 'Klimaatbeheersing in Monumentale Gebouwen', in *Studiedag: Klimaatbeheersing*. Zeist: Rijksdienst voor de Monumentenzorg.

Schlichting, C. (1987) 'Coroplast box construction using hot-melt rivets', *Textile Conservation Newsletter* Fall: 7–11.

Schlichting, C. (1991) 'Constructing oversized textile storage trays and boxes', *Textile Conservation Newsletter* Spring: 21–6.

Schlichting, C. (1994) *Working with Polyethylene Foam and Fluted Plastic Sheet*, CCI Technical Bulletin 14. Ottawa: Canadian Conservation Institute.

Schouten, R. et al. 'Insecten in musea', in *Conserveren van Natuurhistorische Collecties*, A.W. Brokerhof et al. (eds). Amsterdam: Werkgroep Behoud Natuurhistorische Collecties/Instituut Collectie Nederland, pp. E0–E49.

Scott Williams, R. (1997) 'Concerns about plastics during exhibition and transport of textile objects', in *Fabric of an Exhibition: An Interdisciplinary Approach. Preprints*. Ottawa: Government of Canada, pp. 91–6.

Scottish Society for Conservation and Restoration (1989) *Environmental Monitoring and Control*. Dundee: Scottish Society for Conservation and Restoration.

Selzer, W. (1985) 'A new flexible display system', *Museum* 37(2): 108–11.

Sieders, R. et al. (1955) *Het restaureren en conserveren van oude weefsels en weefselfragmenten, een nieuwe methode van montage op een starre ondergrond*. Delft: TH Delft.
Standards in the Museum Care of Photographic Collections (1996). London: Museums and Galleries Commission.
Staniforth, S. (1990) 'The logging of light levels in National Trust houses', in *ICOM-CC 9th Triennial Meeting, Dresden 1990. Preprints Volume II*. Paris: ICOM, pp. 602–7.
Staniforth, S. (1994) 'Appropriate technologies for relative humidity control for museum collections housed in historic buildings', in *Preventive Conservation: Practice, Theory and Research. Preprints of the Contributions to the Ottawa Congress, 12–16 September 1994*. London: International Institute for the Conservation of Historic and Artistic Works pp. 123–8.
Stappers, M. and W. Kragt (2003) *Dataloggers. Vergelijkend onderzoek naar temperatuur- en vochtigheidsmeters*. Amsterdam: Rijksdienst voor de Monumentenzorg en Instituut Collectie Nederland.
Starre, J. van der (1999) Lijst met beoordelingscriteria voor museale registratieprogrammatuur. Opgesteld t.b.v. de NMV cursus 'Kiezen van registratieprogrammatuur', november 1999.
Stuart, M. (2002) 'Objecten identificeren zonder hanteren., inperking van risico momenten met Talking-Tag®' in *CR interdisciplinair vakblad voor conservering en restauratie* 3: 14–19.
Sutter, H. (1986) *Holzschädlinge an Kulturgütern erkennen und bekämpfen*. Stuttgart: Verlag Paul Haupt.
Syllabus bij de basiscursus Behoud en Beheer. Passieve Conservering, deel 1: Condities (1996). Tilburg: Stichting Landelijk Contact Museumconsulenten.
Syllabus bij de basiscursus Behoud en Beheer. Passieve Conservering, deel 2: Materialen (1996) Tilburg: Stichting Landelijk Contact Museumconsulenten.
Syllabus bij de basiscursus Preventieve Conservering (2002) Tilburg: Stichting Landelijk Contact Museumconsulenten.
Syllabus praktijkdag museumdepot inrichting en opberging (2002) Amsterdam: Stichting Landelijk Contact van Museumconsulenten.
Tammes, E. and B.H. Vos (1966) *Vocht in bouwconstructies*. Rotterdam: Bouwcentrum.
Tegelaers, J.M. (1995) 'Verslag van een onderzoek naar zuurvrij kartonnen dozen', in *Deltaplan en textiel, uitwerking van het 'Deltaplan' op textielcollecties, textieldag gehouden op 10 december 1993*. Amsterdam: Stichting Textielcommissie Nederland, pp. 35–8.
Tennent, N.H. and J. Townsend (1994) 'Light dosimeters for msueums, galleries and historic houses', in *Lighting: A Conference on Lighting in Museums, Galleries and Historic Houses*. Bristol: The Museums Association and UKIC, pp. 31–6.
Tetreault, J. and R.S. Williams (1992) *Materials for Exhibit, Storage and Packing* (version 4.1). Ottawa: Canadian Conservation Institute.
Textiel grondstoffen (1987) Tilburg: Nederlands Textielmuseum.
Thickett, D. (1998) 'Sealing of MDF to prevent corrosive emission', *The Conservator* 22: 49–56.
Thomson, G. (1978) *The Museum Environment*. London: Butterworths in association with the International Institute for the Conservation of Historic and Artistic Works.
Thomson, G. (1985) 'Lighting for conservation', in *Light in Museums and Galleries*. London: Concord Lighting, pp. 20–58.
Thomson, G. (1986) *The Museum Environment*, 2nd edition. London: Butterworths in association with the International Institute for the Conservation of Historic and Artistic Works.
Thomson, G. (1994) *The Museum Environment*, 2nd edn. London: Butterworths in association with the International Institute for the Conservation of Historic and Artistic Works.
Timar-Balazsy, A. and D. Eastop (1998) *Chemical Principles of Textile Conservation*. Oxford: Butterworth-Heinemann.
Turner, J. (1994) *Lighting: An Introduction to Light, Lighting and Light Use*. London: Batsford.
US Department of the Interior (1997) *Standards for Managing Museum Property*, Departmental Manual 411. Washington DC: US Department of the Interior.
VeRes Ethische Code (1992). Amsterdam: VeRes.
Verkerd, C. (1994) 'Conserverkerd; Het mysterie van de zwarte madonna', *Nieuwsbrief Conservering en Restauratie* 9: 6.
Vingelsgaard, V. and A.L. Schmidt (1986) 'Removal of insecticides from furs and skins: registration of conservation condition', in *Symposium on Ethnographic and Waterlogged Leather*. Amsterdam: ICOM, pp. 51–9.
Visser, R. (1996) 'Museumcollecties gebaat bij aangepaste verlichting', *Licht* 10: 12–17.
Vosteen, R. (1995) *Adviesrichtlijn luchtkwaliteit archieven*. Den Haag: Ministerie Volkshuisvesting.
Vuistregels voor textielconservering (1985). Amsterdam: Textielcommissie Musea.
Vuistregels voor textielconservering aan de praktijk getoetst, textieldag gehouden op 6 april 1989 (1990). Amsterdam: Textielcommissie Musea.
Wadum, J. (1998) 'Microclimate boxes for panel paintings: the structural conservation of panel paintings', in *Proceedings of a Symposium at the J. Paul Getty Museum, 24–28 April 1995*. Los Angeles: GCI, pp. 497–522.
Walker, S. (1989) 'Using Tyvek in protective covers for artifacts', *Museum Quarterly* 16(4): 23–32.
Waterschadewiel (1999). Amsterdam: Instituut Collectie Nederland.
Weintraub, S. (1981) 'Studies on the behavior of RH within an exhibition case. Part 1: Measuring the effectiveness of sorbents for use in an enclosed showcase', in *ICOM-CC 6th Triennial Meeting, Ottawa 1981. Preprints Volume III*. Paris: ICOM, pp. 81/18/4-1–81/18/4-11.
Weintraub, S. and S.J. Wolff (1995) 'Macro- and microclimates', in *Storage of Natural History Collections: A Preventive Conservation*. Washington DC: Society for the Preservation of Natural History Collections, pp. 123–34.
Wellheiser, J.G. (1992) *Nonchemical Treatment Processes for Disinfestation of Insects and Fungi in Library Col-*

lections. München: IFLA Publications 60, K.G. Saur Verlag.

Willman, P. (1997) 'Fabricating Ethafoam disc mannequins', in *Fabric of an Exhibition: An Interdisciplinary Approach Preprints*. Ottawa: Government of Canada, p. 175.

Windsor, D. (2002) 'The role of pressure mounting in textile conservation: recent applications of U.S. techniques', in *ICOM-CC 13th Triennial Meeting Rio de Janeiro 2002. Preprints Volume II*. Rio de Janeiro: ICOM, pp. 755–9.

Zanen, B. van (1999) 'Insectenvallen', in *Conservering Natuurhistorische Collecties*, A.W. Brokerhof *et al.* (eds). Amsterdam: Werkgroep Behoud Natuurhistorische Collecties/Instituut Collectie Nederland, pp. K1–K8.

Zycherman, L.A. and J.R. Schrock (1988) *A Guide to Museum Pest Control*. Washington DC: Association of Systematics Collections.

Index

AAT *see* Art and Architecture Thesaurus
abrasion, problems in historic interiors 109
absolute humidity (AH) 33, 43–4, *43*
accession numbers *see* numbering
acetate *1*, *3*, 10–11, 24
acetic acid 85
acid-free card/cardboard 87, 120, 124
acid-free tissue paper 126
acidity, indicating degradation 29
acquisition of objects
 documentation 139–48
 see also collection plans
acrylic *1*, *3*, 11–12, 24
 adhesives 125
active carbon 99, 128, 157
active conservation 133
adhesives
 for conservation 3, 85–6, 125–6
 effects of low relative humidity 34
 see also tapes, adhesive
Aerolam *see* Hexlite
Ageless 99, 111, 128–9
Ageless Eye 74, 128
AH *see* absolute humidity
air-conditioning systems 38, 41–2, 81, 109, 110
 in showcases 111
air pollution *see* pollution
air transportation 104–5
alpaca wool *1*, 7
American cockroaches 65, *65*
ammonia, materials emitting 85

angissas, storage 95, *96*
angora *1*, 7
animal fibres 1, *1*, 3–4, 7–10, *8*
 see also proteins; silk; wool/hair
Aplix *see* hook and loop fasteners
appliqué 14, 16
Araldite 125
archaeological textile fragments
 cleaning 136
 display 114, 114
 documentation 145
 fungi in 76
 history of conservation 132
 storage 91–3, 92
arsenic compounds 77
Art and Architecture Thesaurus (AAT) 141
Art Sorb 128, 129
art transporters 104
artfoam *see* Kapaline
asbestos 1, *1*

bags
 display 118, 120
 storage 96, 97
 transportation 106
 zip-lock bags (for storage) 129
banners
 degradation 31, 31, 50
 display 115, 116
 history of conservation 132, 133
 painted 16, 16
 photography 148
 storage 93
 see also flags
barcode system, for registration 145

barrier foils 126
beds and bedding, in historic interiors 108, 110, 111
beetles *see* carpet beetles; woodborers
biological degradation 23, 24
 see also fungi; insects
blue wool standard 49, *49*, 59
boards
 padded, for display 114, 115, 120–22, 121–2
 padded, for photography 148
 for storage 92, 92, 93, 97
bonnets, storage 95
boxes, for storage 91–3
 see also cardboard storage boxes
brazilwood 17
bristletails 65–6, *65–6*
bubble wrap 126–7
buckram *see* Etamine
buffering *see* passive buffers

cabinet beetles 64, *64*
calamities 28, 156
 see also disasters
calendering 18
camel hair *1*, 7
cameras *see* photography
camphor 76, 77
caps, storage 95
carbon, active *see* active carbon
carbon dioxide, high concentration, as fumigation method 73–4, 78
carbon fibres *1*, 12
card/cardboard, acid-free 87, 120, 124

cardboard, honeycomb 124
cardboard storage boxes 84, 87, 92–3, *92*
  for three-dimensional textiles 95, 96, 97, 98
carpet beetles 61, 63–4, *64*, 72, 76, 78
carpets
  cleaning 136
  disinfestation methods 73, 77
  display 108, 109, 110, 112, 115
  knotted carpets 14, 93, 115
  moth-proofing agents 19
  photography 148
  storage 89–91, 93
  weaving technique 14, 15
case-bearing clothes moths 63, *63*
cashmere 7
  shawls 89, 113
castles *see* interiors, historic
Cellite *see* Hexlite
cellulose 3, 4, 10
  fire hazard 20
  natural decay 21–3, *22*
  see also vegetable fibres
cellulose nitrate, storage problems 28, 99
Centerfoam 120, 124
central heating 34–5, 38, 39
chairs
  display 111
  history of conservation 131–2
  storage and protection 98, 99, 110
  transportation 102
  see also upholstered furniture
chintzes 18, 26–7, *27*
chipboard 85
cigarette beetles 61
cleaning
  mechanical cleaning of textiles 108, 110, 135–6
  of storage facilities 82
  see also dry cleaning; dust
climate
  climate-controlled trucks 104
  climatic zones in museums 38, 42
  in historic interiors 109, 110, 111–12
  stable indoor climate in storage facilities 81
  see also microclimates
clingfilm 126
clothing *see* costumes; protective clothing
coat hangers *see* hanging storage
coatings, used on storage materials 86
cochineal 17, *17*
cockroaches 61, 64–5, *65*, 71, 78
collection management 153–7
collection plans 153–4

common furniture beetle ('woodworm') 66–7, *67*, 74, 76
compact storage 83
computerisation
  data loggers 37, 48, 106
  documentation 137–8, 145
condensation 32–3
  see also relative humidity
condition reports 107, 145–6, 155
conservation and restoration
  defining tasks 135–6
  history of 131–3
  materials for conservation 123–9
  terminology 133
  textile conservator, role of 133–5
containers, for transportation by ship 105
contracting out conservation work 134–5
control of environmental conditions 37–42
cooling systems 39
Correx 120, 124
costumes
  degradation 25, 26, 28, 28
  disinfestation methods 77
  display 116–18, *116*, 118–19
  documentation 141–3, *142*, 144
  storage 83, 93–5, 95
  transportation 105–6
cotton *1*, *3*, 5–7, *6*
  degradation 21, 51
  equilibrium moisture content 44, 45
  textile finishes 18, 19, 20
couriering 106
cow hair 7
crates, for transportation 104, 105–6
crease-resisting agents *18*, 20
crochet 14
cross-linking, polymer chains 22, *22*, 24
crystallinity 2
cupboards, for storage 83, 93
Cupro (rayon) *1*, 10
curtains, display 108, 109–10, 113

damask 14
data loggers 37, 48, 106
DDT 77–8
deathwatch beetle 66, 67, *67*
decay
  intrinsic 26–7, 28
  natural 21–4
  see also degradation of textiles
decorative techniques 14–16
degradation of textiles 21–9
dehumidifiers 39–41
Delta traps 71–2, *71*
description forms 140–43, *140*
Desi Pak 128
digital photography 147

dirt *see* cleaning; dust; soiling and stains
disasters 28
  disaster plans 155–7
discharge lamps *54*, 55–6
  see also fluorescent lighting; neon lights
display cases *see* showcases
display of textiles 107–22
documentation 137–51
dolls
  display 119–20
  documentation 145
  storage 98, 98, 99
donations, documentation 139, 150–51
dosimeters, light 49
drawers, for storage 83, *84*, 92, *92*, 93
  for three-dimensional textiles 95, 98, 98
drugstore beetles 61
dry cleaning, to control insects and fungi 76
dummies, for costume display 116–18, *116*, *118–19*
durable press agents *18*, 20
dust 28, 35, 111, 135–6
  removal 110, 135, 136
dustcovers 84, 93, 95, 98, *99*, 110
dyes
  degradation caused by dyeing 26–7, 27, 28
  direct dyes 17, 18
  dyeing techniques 16, 17
  light sensitivity 28–9, 28, 34, 50, 60, 60
  mordant dyes 17, 26–7, *27*
  natural dyes 16–17, 50
  synthetic dyes 17–18
  vat dyes 16–17, *17*

Ebicel *see* Ibicel
ecclesiastical garments 93, 94–5
elastic fibres 12
electromagnetic spectrum 47, *48*
elongation of textiles 25–6, *26*
embroidery
  rolling embroidered textiles 90–91
  techniques 14, 16, 16
EMC *see* equilibrium moisture content
energy efficiency, lighting 53, 56, 57, *57*
environment
  environmental effects of lighting methods 57
  in historic interiors 108, 109, 110
  influence of environmental circumstances on decay 22–3, 24

museum environment 31–45
epoxy glue 125
equilibrium moisture content (EMC)
    44–5, *44–5*
Etamine 125
Ethafoam 125
ethical code of conservation 134
ethnographic collections
    chemical treatments 77
    display 116–17, 118
    soiling 28
    storage 89, 93, 94–5, 96
    see also traditional costume
ethylene oxide 69, 75
Eulan 78
exhibitions
    (semi-)permanent 107–8
    temporary 107
    see also display of textiles

fabric samples 60, 91–2, 96, 114
    see also blue wool standard
fading 28–9, *28*, 34, 50, *50*, 59–60,
    59–60
    see also blue wool standard
fans
    cleaning 136
    degradation 35
    display 118, 119–20
    documentation 144, 145
    storage 97–8, *98*
feathers, degradation 23
felting 8
fibre optics 56, *57*
Fibrefill *see* polyester, wadding
fibres 1–12, *1*, *3*
    see also animal fibres; semi-
        synthetic fibres; synthetic
        fibres; vegetable fibres
Filmoplast 120, 125
filters, for UV radiation 52
finishes *see* textile finishes
fire damage 157
fire prevention 28, 82
    flame-retarding agents 18, 20
firebrats 61, 65–6, *66*, 78
fishermen's clothing, waterproof
    19–20, 102
fishing line, nylon 128
flags
    degradation 27
    display 115, *115*
    history of conservation 132, *133*
    photography 148
    storage 89, 91, 93
    see also banners
flame-retarding agents *18*, 20
flax *1*, *3*, 4–5, *5*
    see also linen
fluorescent lighting 53, *53–54*,
    55–6, 57, *57*
    energy-saving lamps 53, 54, 56,
        57, *57*

foamboard *see* Kapaline
form of entry 138, 149–50
form of return 151
formaldehyde
    finishes 20
    materials emitting 35, 85
formic acid, materials emitting 85
'foxing' 68
fragility, assessment for
    transportation 101–3
framed textiles
    degradation 35
    display 115–16
    microclimates 38, 110
    storage 84, 93
    see also samplers
freeze-drying 72, 157
freezing
    to control insects and fungi
        72–3, 75, 78
    textiles with water damage 157
FreshPax 128, 129
fumigation methods 73–4, 78
fungi 34, *34*, 67–72, *68*, 74–9, 82,
    88
fungicides 77–8
fur, degradation 23
fur beetles 61, 64, *64*
furniture *see* chairs; upholstered
    furniture
furniture beetle *see* common
    furniture beetle

gamma radiation, to control fungi
    75
gas sprinkler installations 82
German cockroaches 65, *65*
glass fibres *1*, 12
glass transition temperature 2–3,
    73, 78
gloves
    display and storage 96, 97, 120
    as protective clothing 76, 127
glues *see* adhesives
Gluton 126
goat fur *1*, 7, 8
    see also cashmere; mohair
gold thread 14–16
Gudy 120, 125
gummed paper tape 125–6

hair *see* wool/hair
hair hygrometers 36
halogen lamps 53, *53–54*, 54–5,
    56, *57*
handbags *see* bags
handling, as cause of degradation
    28
hanging storage 93, 94–5, *95*
hardboard 85
hat boxes (original) 97, *97*
headgear
    display 118–19, *119*

storage 95, 96–7, *97*
transportation 106
health hazards
    from fungi 68, 76
    from humidifiers 40
    from insect repellents,
        insecticides and fungicides
        76, 77
    see also protective clothing
heat treatment, as disinfestation
    method 73, 78
heating systems *see* central heating
Hexlite 120, 124
high carbon dioxide concentration,
    as fumigation method 73–4, 78
high-density storage systems 83
historic interiors *see* interiors,
    historic
honeycomb cardboard 124
hook and loop fasteners 84, 112–13,
    113, 127–8
horsehair 7
house longhorn 66
humidifiers 39–40, *40*, 41
humidity *see* absolute humidity;
    relative humidity
hydrogen sulphide 36, 85
hydrolysis 22, *22*, 24
hysteresis 25, *25*

Ibicel 125, 127
ikat technique 16, *16*
illuminance (light intensity) 47–8,
    51
incandescent light bulbs 53–4,
    53–54, 57, *57*
indexing, description forms
    140–41, 143
indigo 16, *17*
information plans 137
infrared radiation *see* IR (infrared)
    radiation
insects 61–7, *61–7*, 69–74, 76–9,
    82, 88
    insect repellents 76–7
    insect traps 71–2, *71*
    insecticides 76, 77–8
inspections
    textiles in historic interiors 109
    see also condition reports
insurance, for loan transportation
    101, 106
integrated pest management (IPM)
    69–72, 82
    logbooks 70, *70*, 72
interiors, historic, textiles in 34–5,
    39, 108–12
intrinsic decay *see* decay
ionisation detectors 82
IPM *see* integrated pest management
IR (infrared) radiation 47, *48*, 50, 52
ironing 28
Itef *see* Ethafoam

Japanese paper 128

Kapaline 120, 124–5
kermes 17
kimonos 93, 94–5, 118
knitting 14
knotting 14, *15*
   knotted carpets 14, 93, 115
Kubicel *see* Plastazote

laboratory coats 76
lace 14
lampas 14
lamps, types *54*
   see also discharge lamps;
      fluorescent lighting; halogen
      lamps; incandescent light
      bulbs; LEDs
leather
   equilibrium moisture content
      44, *44*
   relative humidity 34
LEDs (light emitting diodes) 56
legacies, documentation 139
Legionnaires' disease 40
light 47–60
   as cause of degradation/
      damage 48, 50, 51, 52,
      59–60, *59–60*; *see also* fading;
      photodegradation
   lighting in historic interiors
      108–9, 112
   lighting for photography 147–8
   lighting in showcases 112
   lighting in storage facilities 81–2
   sunlight 50–52, 53, 73, 108
light bulbs, incandescent 53–4,
   53–54, 57, *57*
light emitting diodes (LEDs) 56
LightCheck strips 49
linen 4–5
   degradation 21, 25, 27
   equilibrium moisture content 44
   textile finishes 18, 19, 20
   see also flax
loans
   documentation 143–4, 151
   transportation 101
location control 144
logwood 17
low oxygen atmosphere, in storage
   facilities 83
low oxygen concentration, as
   fumigation method 74, 78
luminance 47–8
lux-hours, controlling and recording
   59–60, *59–60*
lux meters 48, *49*
lyocell *1*, 10

madder 17
magnetic strips, for hanging display
   113, 115

maintenance plans 108, 154–5
   see also condition reports
man-made fibres *see* semi-synthetic
   fibres; synthetic fibres
management *see* collection
   management
mangling 18
Marvelseal 120, 126
masking tape 126
masks *see* respirator masks
materials 1–20
   for conservation 123–9
   for storage 85–7
   see also dyes; fibres; textile
      finishes; textile techniques
MDF *see* medium density
   fibreboard
measuring and recording museum
   environment 36–7
mechanical cleaning *see* cleaning
mechanical forces, causing
   degradation 25–6
medium density fibreboard (MDF)
   85
Melinex (Mylar) 120, 126
mercerising 18
metal
   metal thread 14–16, *16*
   as part of composite objects 34
   as storage material 86–7
methyl bromide fumigation 74, 78
microclimates 35, 38, 41, 45,
   111–12
mildew *see* fungi
mineral fibres *1*, *1*
modal *1*, 10
mohair *1*, 7
moiré *16*, 18–19
Moistop 120, 126
moisture
   as cause of degradation 25, *25*,
      27
   see also equilibrium moisture
      content; hydrolysis; relative
      humidity; water damage
mold *see* fungi
mordants 17, 26–7, *27*
moth-proofing agents *18*, 19, 78
mothballs 76
moths 61, 62–3, *63*, 72, 76–7, 78
mould *see* fungi
Multifoam *see* Ibicel
museum beetles 63
   see also carpet beetles
Museum Centerfoam *see*
   Centerfoam
'museum dust' 28
museum environment 31–45
Mylar *see* Melinex

naphthalene 76
neon lights 53
Nexa-Lotte strips 76, 77

nitrogen dioxide 35, 36
nitrogen fumigation 74
nitrogen oxides, materials emitting
   85
non-woven fabrics 13
   for use in conservation 127–8
Nopafoam *see* Ethafoam
numbering, registration/accession
   numbers 88–9, 139, 144–5,
   148
nylon *1*, *3*, 11, *12*, 24
   fishing line, use in storage and
      display 128
   net, use in conservation 128

Oddy test 111, 123–4
open display 110–11
Oriental cockroaches 65, *65*
oxidation 21–2, *22*
oxygen, low *see* low oxygen
   atmosphere; low oxygen
   concentration
oxygen absorbers/scavengers 74,
   99, 111, 128–9
oxygen-free environment 99, 111

packaging
   materials for conservation 126–7
   for transportation 105–6
padded boards *see* boards
painted textiles
   banners 16, *16*
   rolling 90–91
paints, used on storage materials
   86
palaces *see* interiors, historic
'paperfish' (grey silverfish) 65–6,
   78
para-dichlorobenzene 76–7
parasols 98
   see also umbrellas
passive buffers 41, 128, 129
passive conservation 133
permanent exhibitions 107–8
Perspex
   as display material 114, *114*,
      115, 119, 120, 125
   as radiation filter 52
pest management *see* integrated
   pest management
pesticides 69, 76–8
PH pens 129
pheromones, in insect traps 72
photocells 51
photodegradation 23–4, *23*
   see also light, as cause of
      degradation/damage
photography, for documentation
   146–8
physical-mechanical processes,
   leading to degradation 24–6
plaiting 14
planes *see* air transportation

plant fibres *see* vegetable fibres
Plastazote   125
plastics
    objects made from or with, storage   98–9
    safe to use in textile conservation   129
Plexiglass *see* Perspex
plywood   85
pollution   23, 42
    air pollution   23, 28, 35–6, 42
polyamide   *1*, 11, 24
    see also nylon
polycarbonate   125
polyester   *1*, *3*, 11, 24
    glues   126
    wadding   120, 125
polyethylene   *1*, 12
    corrugated sheets *see* Correx
    tape *see* Tyvek
polymers   1–4, *2–3*
    cross-linking, polymer chains   22, *22*, 24
polyolefins   12
polypropylene   *1*, 12
    non-woven fabric (PP fabric)   128
polysulphide glues   126
polyurethane   *1*, 12
    foam   125
    glues   126
polyvinyl acetate (PVAc) adhesives   120, 121, 126
polyvinyl chloride tape (PVC)   126
powderpost beetles   66, 67, *67*
PP *see* polypropylene
pressure mounts, for archaeological textile fragments   114, *114*
preventive conservation   133, 135
printing textiles   16
Pro Sorb   129
protective clothing   *75*, 76, 106, 127
proteins   3–4, *4*
    natural decay   23–4
    see also animal fibres
psychrometric charts   33, 43–4, *43*
purple dyes   17
PVAc *see* polyvinyl acetate
PVC *see* polyvinyl chloride
pyrethroids   69, 76, 78

quarantine rooms   70, 83

rabbit fur   *1*, 7, *8*
racks
    for storage   83–4
    for transportation   103–4
radiation *see* gamma radiation; IR (infrared) radiation; UV (ultraviolet) radiation
radio frequency identification (RFID)   145
rayon   *1*, *3*, 10, 24
    see also viscose
recording, museum environment   36–7
reflection of light   47–8
registration   137, 145
    objects entering collection   138–9
    registration/accession numbers   88–9, 139, 144–5, 148
relational databases   137–8
relative humidity (RH)   25, 27, 32–5, *32–4*
    control   37–42
    and equilibrium moisture content   44–5
    measuring and recording   36–7
    psychrometric charts   33, 43–4, *43*
    in storage facilities   81
replicas, in historic interiors   109–10
resins, used with storage materials   86
respirator masks   76, 127
restoration
    definition   133
    see also conservation and restoration
'restorer', profession of   131–2, 133–4
reversibility principle   134
RFID *see* radio frequency identification
RH *see* relative humidity
ribbons, storage   89, 90
risk analysis, for transportation   103–5
rolling textiles   *84*, 89–91, *90–92*
RP System   128, 129
rubber
    fibres   1, 11
    storage of rubber objects   99
    for waterproofing   20, 99
rubber cement glue   126

safety glasses, for handling infected objects   76
safety measures *see* health hazards; protective clothing
salvaging methods   156–7
samplers   14, 38, 84, 91–2, *93*, 148
    see also framed textiles
saris   89, 113
satin weave   13, *13*
seasonal closure, historic interiors   110
Sellotape   126
semi-synthetic fibres   1–2, *1*, 10–11, 21, 24
shawls, cashmere   89, 113
ships, for external transportation   105
shock, during transportation   102–5
shoes
    display   120
    documentation   144, 145
    storage   87, 96, 97, 99
    transportation   106
showcases   110–12, 120
    microclimates   35, 41, 45
silica gel
    as dessicant   41
    as passive buffer   128, 129
silk   *1*, *3*, 8–10, *8–9*
    degradation   23, *23*, 24, 26, 27
    silk crepeline, use in conservation   128
    weighted   19, *19*
silver thread   14–16
silverfish   61, 65–6, *65–6*, 78
smoke detectors   82
soiling and stains   28, 135
    see also dust
solarisation   73
spinning   13, *13*
sprang   14
sprinkler systems   82
Stabiltex *see* Tetex
stains *see* soiling and stains
starching   19
    storage of starched objects   95, 96
storage   81–99
stretching, and degradation   25–6, *26*
sulphur dioxide   35, 36, 85
sunlight
    in disinfestation treatment   73
    problems caused by direct sunlight   50–52, 53, 108
superglue   125
supports
    materials for making   124–5
    for three-dimensional objects   96–7, *97*
synthetic corrugated sheet material   87
    see also Correx
synthetic dyes   17–18
synthetic fibres   1–2, *1*, 11–12, 24

tablet weaving   14
tapes
    adhesive   121–2, 125–6
    fabric   127–8
tapestries
    degradation   25, 26, 29, 50, 63
    disinfestation methods   73, 77
    display   108, 109, 113, 114
    history of conservation   19, 131, 132, 132
    photography   146, 148
    storage   89–91
    weaving technique   14, *15*
tapestry moths   63, *63*
teddy bears   98, 120

temperature 25, 27–8, 32, *33*, 35
  control 37–42
  and equilibrium moisture content 45
  measuring and recording 36–7
  psychrometric charts 33, 43–4, *43*
  see also climate
temporary exhibitions 107
tension, and degradation 25–6, *26*
Tetex 128
textile conservator, role of 133–5
textile finishes 18–20, *18*
textile techniques 12–16
thermo lignum method 73
thermohygrographs 36–7, *36*
thermohygrometers 37, *49*
thesauri 141
thymol 77
traditional costume
  display 117, 118, 119
  storage 93, 95
transportation 101–6
trolleys, racks and carts, for transportation 103–4
trousers, storage 94
trucks, for transportation 104, 105
tubes, for rolling textiles 90–91
tubular bandage 128
twill weave 13, *13*
Tyvek 86, 128

tape 121, 122, 126

ultraviolet radiation *see* UV (ultraviolet) radiation
umbrellas 98, 118, 119–20
uniforms 77, 93, 94
upholstered furniture
  display 108, 109, 110, 111, 120
  history of conservation 131–2
  storage 98, 99
UV (ultraviolet) radiation 47, *48*, 50, 51–2
  and insect control 72
  UV meters 49, *49*

vacuum cleaners, use of 75, 136
Vapona cassettes 76, 77
varnishes, used on storage materials 86
vegetable fibres 1, *1*, 3, 4–7
  see also cellulose; cotton; flax; linen
Velcro *see* hook and loop fasteners
velvet 14, 93, 115
vibration, during transportation 103–5
vicuña wool *1*, 7
viscose *1*, 10, 23
visitors to historic interiors, protection of textiles from 108, 109

Vocabulary of Basic Terms for Cataloguing Costume 141–3, *142*

washing, to control insects and fungi 76
water damage 28, 156–7
  see also hydrolysis; moisture
watered effect *see* moiré
waterproofing agents *18*, 19–20, 99, 102
weaving 13–14, *13*, *15*
webbing clothes moths 62–3, *63*, 72
weighted silk 19, *19*
weld 17
woad 17
wood, as storage material 85–6
woodborers 62, 66–7, *67*
  common furniture beetle ('woodworm') 66–7, *67*, 74, 76
wool/hair *1*, 3, 7–8, *8*
  degradation 23–4, *23*, 25
  flame-retarding agents 20

yellowing, indicating degradation 29

zip-lock bags 129
zones, critical and non-critical, in museums 38, 42